BRITISH RAILWAYS OPERATING HISTORY No.1

MANCHESTER to DERBY (AMBERGATE)

C.BENTLEY

Britannia 70017 'Arrow' passes Great Rocks with the 16.25 St Pancras to Manchester Central in the summer of 1959

'All vitality is concentrated through those throbbing arteries into the central cities' (Ruskin)

Entitled an Operating History, this book - and the series of which it is a part - is primarily intended to complement the many railway histories already available by addressing an area normally beyond the reach of the general writer and thus add a colourful, if not valuable, dimension to those works which recall dates and personalities but not - at least in any great depth - trains and services. This additional layer of detail is made possible by the fact that the publishing team consists almost entirely of retired railwaymen who in the course of their workings lives had access to aspects of the railway denied to outsiders. Although convention histories record - often in the greatest of detail - dates of construction, openings, closures, little attention has been paid to the trains which ran over the system, how they were organised and where they went from and to and in this connection it is sobering to recall that goods trains - which outnumbered passenger services by a ratio of about 10:1 - have never until now received the descriptive attention which is their due. This imbalance has, we hope, been corrected in this volume with similar attention being given to the locations which despatched and received freight services together with details of the organisation that regulated their operation.

Whilst operational matters form the backbone of the book, motive power matters have not by any means been neglected and included are novel examples of the power outputs demanded of express passenger engines on some of the principal services between Manchester and Derby. This allows, for the first time, an exact comparison to be drawn between the relative performances of the various types of express locomotives which plied the route during the days of steam.

In this book the trains which worked between Manchester and Ambergate are listed in detail and it is hoped it will not only provide the reader with an idea of how busy the line was, but may allow him to relive the atmosphere of the route as it existed when 5XP 4-6-0's were the principal express engine and Rowsley and Gowhole were names to be reckoned with. The date of all operations, unless otherwise stated, is for the period 1953/4; a time when little change had taken place for many years past or was to occur for some time to come.

Whilst the name of the author is that of the principal contributor, this book and those that follow, are the product of a publishing organisation set up by former railwaymen all of whom worked under steam and whose collective railway experience in both the operating and motive power departments amounts to several hundred years. Indeed it is our boast that one of our number both knew and worked under no less a personality than Gresley himself.

Where steam and traditional railway operations are concerned, we are proud of our claim.....

WE WERE THERE!

37 Rhydfadog
Carnarvon
(01286 870817)

ACKNOWLEDGEMENTS
Photographs : H. Townley, L.M.Hobdey, J.Wooliscroft, N.K. Harrop.
Text and Maps : P. Webb, A J. Somers, G. Waite, L. Stagg.

Printed by
Birkenhead Press Ltd
1&3 Grove Road
Rock Ferry, Birkenhead
L42 3XS

MANCHESTER CENTRAL

MANCHESTER : NEW MILLS SOUTH JUNCTION

The similarity between St Pancras and Manchester Central is made apparent in this view of 5XP 4-6-0 45560 'Prince Edward Island' as it rests in Manchester after having brought in the 09.06 Nottingham (Midland) - Liverpool (Central) on an unrecorded date in 1954.

DINING CAR CIRCUITS : MANCHESTER : ST PANCRAS (1935)

IiNWARD	OUTWARD	BALANCE
07.23 Leicester : Buxton	10.12 Buxton : St Pancras	02.25 St Pancras : Leicester (Empty)
08.25 St Pancras : Manchester	13.45 Manchester : St Pancras	
10.25 St Pancras : Manchester	16.35 Manchester : St Pancras	
12.25 St Pancras : Manchester	17.50 Manchester : St Pancras	
	07.20 Manchester : St Pancras	14.25 St Pancras : Manchester
	09.45 Manchester : St Pancras	16.25 St Pancras : Manchester
	08.55 Manchester : St Pancras	16.25 St Pancras : Manchester
	12.20 Manchester : St Pancras	18.25 St Pancras : Manchester

Although Manchester and the Midland Railway were closely identified with each other, it is a curious fact that the Midland never possessed its own route into the city - it owned an isolated section of line in the north east of the city - but started - looking north to south - in a green field a short distance south of Chorlton-cum-Hardy station, three and a half miles out of Manchester; the last few miles into the city itself being achieved through an alliance with a competitor.

The Midland had not found its entry to Manchester an easy matter. The LNWR controlled the easy terrain to the south and west of the city whilst the Manchester, Sheffield & Lincoln (later to become the Great Central and, for the sake of simplicity, referred to as such) had access from the east; both united in their resolve that no other railway, other than the Lancashire & Yorkshire in the north of the city, should gain a foothold in the area.

The Midland therefore had to approach from the south which meant building over and through the great Derbyshire Peaks, the summit of which rose to no less than 982 feet above sea level. Initially the company had intended to build from Derby as far as Buxton from which point it was hoped an accommodation could be reached with the LNWR concerning access into Manchester. The London & North Western, however, were less than sympathetic and as a result the Midland was compelled to bypass the spa town - thus forever condemning Buxton to a secondary role - and to extend forward to New Mills where an agreement was reached with the Great Central (who, fortuitously, were in a dispute with the LNWR) for running powers into Manchester, London Road.

Thus in 1867 the Midland commenced its London - Manchester services, deriving advantage from its recently opened London extension from Bedford to St Pancras and running into Manchester under the protection of the Great Central but disgorging its passengers under the very nose of the London & North Western whose trains also arrived in London Road station.

The arrangement with the Great Central had far wider implications than simply being a means by which the Midland could run the last few miles into Manchester and on 15th August 1867 the two companies, together with the Great Northern, formed the Cheshire Lines Committee whose purpose was to take control of a

From the mid-1930's until the arrival of diesels the Jubilee 5XP 4-6-0's were the usual power for most Midland expresses and were diagrammed for all the London services from Manchester Central until the LMR motive power revision of 1957 when the line received an allocation of Britannia Pacifics and Royal Scot 4-6-0's. The view above was repeated many times daily for nearly thirty years as 45568 'Western Australia' prepares to leave for the south. Although the Jubilee's monopolised the St Pancras services, this particular example, coming from Leeds (Holbeck), was something of a rarity.

number of small railways in the Manchester and Liverpool areas and to expand them in order to allow each of the three partners to have access to a region which had hitherto been under the dominion of the LNWR.

Having gained a substantial foothold in West Lancashire, it was necessary to consolidate matters by bringing together as much of the system as possible into a single Manchester terminus, something that was not possible so long as London Road remained the city's station for the south. In any event the Great Central possessed only a small part of London Road - three platforms as against the six owned by the LNWR - and this was barely sufficient for their needs let alone those of the Midland. Thus from 1872 various parliamentary powers were granted to the committee with the object of constructing a new station in Manchester which would not only act as a focal point for the lines of the three partners - the Great Northern had running powers over the Great Central and, to a more limited extent, the Midland - but would make available the space needed for the expansion of services.

Following five years of construction the new station - Manchester Central - was opened on a temporary site on 9th July 1877, the permanent building being ready for use on 1st July 1880.

In attempting to compete with the LNWR for the lucrative London passenger traffic the Midland suffered a number of disadvantages. Its mainline whilst relatively level (and fast) between London and Derby then to climb through the Derbyshire Peak district with double figure gradients to an altitude at Peak Forest summit which was greater than that of Shap. On top of this Midland trains then had to make a lengthy detour through the Stockport area - the joint GC/MR line - was both circuitous and heavily graded and not suited for the high speed running that was essential if timings from St Pancras were to stand comparison with those from Euston and the largely level route of the LNWR.

There was little the company could do with regard to the gradients over the Peaks except to limit the weight of trains so far as was practicable and to ensure that the rolling stock used was at the very least equal to with the best the LNWR could provide. It did, however, eliminate much of the frustrations caused by the pedestrian rates demanded over the GC in the Manchester suburbs by opening, in 1902, a cut-off route from New Mills to Heaton Mersey which reduced the mileage between Manchester and Derby by a mile and a half and eliminated the slow running required through Stockport. (It did, however, prevent London trains from calling at Stockport, as the LNWR did, and Midland services serving the area called either at Didsbury or Cheadle Heath as an alternative. The only fast train to continue using the old route through Stockport was the night London passenger train on Mondays which took 39 minutes to pass New Mills as opposed to 26 by the other London trains).

Passenger trains at Manchester Central were frequent and varied although most departures came under the aegis of the Great Central - whose motive power held dominion until the LMR took over the CLC during the 1950's - who operated a brisk service of trains to Liverpool (Central), Warrington, Chester (Northgate) and Wigan (Central) plus a number of workings eastwards to Guide Bridge and beyond. The Midland was something of a junior partner in the terminus, its trains being limited to the London expresses - which ran at roughly two-hourly intervals - the occasional Derby stopping trains plus a miscellany of local trains to Chinley, Sheffield, Stockport and Buxton. Motive power, in the tradition of the Midland, was on the small side with the longer distance trains being handled by 4-4-0's (invariably a Compound with, if the load was more than about eight vehicles, a 2P as pilot) whilst the locals tended to be worked by 'Flatiron' 0-6-4 tanks. With the arrival of the Stanier regime in the mid-1930's most of the longer distance 4-4-0 workings were gradually taken over by 5MT or 5XP 4-6-0's whilst the reliable 0-6-4T's were replaced by 3MT 2-6-2T's; a change that was not universally regarded as progressive.

Although the London trains were invariably strengthened south of Derby in deference to the gradients over the Peak District, the hills did not prevent the Midland from including dining facilities from their Manchester trains and all the principal workings included restaurant cars throughout the journey. Eight sets were provided for the service, four being allocated to

The 4-4-0's which had worked out of Manchester for as long as anyone could remember remained in evidence almost until dieselisation although an attempt was made to reduce their numbers in the late-1950's by allocating two new BR standard 4MT 2-6-0's (76088/9) to Trafford Park as replacements. 76089 stands ready to depart with the 13.35 stopping train to Chinley via Stockport (Tiviot Dale) during the summer of 1962. The service, which was the return working of the 08.00 Buxton - Manchester, ran through to Sheffield (Midland) after recessing for half an hour at Chinley. (J.M.Bentley)

Manchester with three at St Pancras and one (nominally) at Leicester. The last mentioned was something of a curiosity and was attached to the 04.25 St Pancras - Manchester between Leicester and Millers Dale, to be tripped to Buxton where it reversed to form part of the 10.12 stopping train to London, not reaching St Pancras until 15.26. The dining car returned to Leicester empty on the 02.25 Derby newspaper service.

The remaining vehicles all worked daily out and home duties, each making one return trip of 380 miles per day, the only anomaly concerning the 08.55 and 09.45 services ex Manchester the single car of the former combining with the two vehicles of the latter in London to work the 16.25 business express from St Pancras.

For the most part motive power for the express services was concentrated at Trafford Park, the chief exceptions being the services which were the return workings of foreign diagrams. During the days of the 4-4-0's the majority of services were shared between Trafford Park and Derby although the LMS, once Stanier had revitalised the locomotive fleet, brought widesweeping changes through the introduction of complex cyclic engine diagrams which saw Trafford Park and Kentish Town engines working through from London to Manchester. One express even had a Bristol 5XP working between Derby and Manchester whilst the evening business train from Manchester Central to Buxton was for years diagrammed to the Kentish Town Jubilee 4-6-0 which had come down from St Pancras with the 10.25 express. Local trains were shared between Trafford Park and Buxton, the latter possessing three 2P 4-4-0's and nine 4MT 2-6-4 tanks for its share of the workings. (Most of Buxton's remaining 50-odd allocation was for freight work whilst the greater part of Trafford Park's work was directed to the CLC services between Manchester and Liverpool).

One particularly anomalous feature of Midland motive power affairs was that it did not possess a passenger engine shed of its own in or near Manchester, finding it more convenient to allocate its engines to the CLC shed at Trafford Park. The nearest Midland depot had been at Buxton until a reorganisation in 1935 which merged the Midland facilities with those of the LNWR, after which the closest shed to Manchester was at Rowsley, forty miles towards Derby.

The only Midland MPD in Manchester was at Belle Vue, located near the boundary with the Lancashire & Yorkshire system and used to re-engine freight services which came to the Midland from North Manchester and to provide power for the marshalling yards at Gowhole, near Chinley.

In the years prior to 1914 the shed had enjoyed a limited measure of passenger work with the local service which operated between Manchester Victoria and Chinley, a service that suffered badly during the economies of the great war - in LMS days the workings consisted in the main of through London coaches from the L&Y to the Midland - and ceased altogether during the last war.

In this connection it has to be pointed out that from the time of the last war services between the north and south of Manchester were as bad as those between the north and south of London whilst Manchester, of course, had no underground system. The LNW ran a sparse service - 07.55 and nothing afterwards until 17.34 - from Stockport to Manchester Victoria during the 1950's whilst the MR Derby - Manchester timetable dropped all reference to Manchester Victoria. Passengers from, say, Chinley to Preston invariably had to resign themselves to crossing Manchester under their own steam.

Goods traffic was as varied as the passenger traffic although its motive power saw less change, the 0-6-0 tender engine remaining pretty well universal until the arrival of diesels in the mid-1960's. 2-8-0's were also common but tended to be used on the longer distance services such as the limestone workings between Peak Forest and Northwich and the heavy flow of coal from Kirkby, Nottinghamshire.

The principal Midland goods station was at Ancoats, adjacent to London Road station, and access was via the joint line from New Mills through Reddish, Belle Vue and Ashburys. Other regular flows were to Trafford Park via the direct line and Cornbrook Junction, and to Merseyside via Stockport and Heaton Mersey.

To the enthusiast of the 1950's, the first few miles out of Manchester Central were both interesting and dramatic. There were nine platforms of which the first four tended to be used by CLC services to Liverpool whilst Midland trains ran from the remainder. (There was no hard and fast rule about this but it tended to keep the risk of conflict to a minimum if trains kept to their respective sides of the station). One of the Midland platforms - No.9 - had been built outside the great overall roof and was constructed of wooden planks; a feature it retained until the station closed.

Although the Midland, GC and GN were, in a sense, all one in Manchester Central, the name CLC was about the only common de-

At a time when most season ticket holders were being turned away from the railway by unpalatable diesel multiple-units, those from Buxton were fortunate in that some of their workings remained steam-hauled almost until the end of steam. Stanier 5MT 4-6-0 44851 stands on the loco release line between platforms 8 and 9 after bringing in the 08.50 ex Buxton, a service which covered the 32 miles in only 50 minutes in spite of stops at Peak Forest, Chapel-en-le-Frith, Chinley and Cheadle Heath. The next turn of duty for the Black Five is a train of empty coaching stock to Cornbrook Sidings after which it will run light to Trafford Park MPD where the crew will exchange it for BR 2-6-0 76089 to work the 13.35 service to Chinley. Standing in platform 6 is the station pilot, Fairburn 4MT 2-6-4T 42697, itself a casualty of dieselisation having been moved to Manchester from Glasgow (Corkerhill) following the introduction of multiple-units between Glasgow (St Enoch) and Ayr.

Manchester Central provided an astonishing variety of motive power during the early 1950's with ER engines working in from Guide Bridge and across to Liverpool Central. At that time the Manchester - Liverpool service was worked by a virtually unpredictable array of engines and included Great Eastern D16 and Great Central D11 4-4-0's in addition to the Stanier 5MT 4-6-0's and 2-6-4 tanks which were starting to oust the LNER locomotives. In the loco sidings from the end of Manchester's platform 9 in 1954 Darnall B1 4-6-0 61181 creates some atmospheric conditions between GC duties that have brought it in from Sheffield (Victoria) via Wilbraham Road and Chorlton Junction.

TRAIN WORKING : WITHINGTON (1953)

Train	Down	Up	Destination	Train	Down	Up	Destination
19.35 Derby (Chaddesden)	*00/07*		*Warrington*	13.55 Cheadle Heath	14.05		Manchester
00.00 MANCHESTER		00/09	ST PANCRAS	10.15 ST PANCRAS	14/24		MANCHESTER
22.55 Walton		*00/52*	*Sheffield*	14.50 Manchester		15.03	Derby (via T. Dale)
23.55 Brunswick		*01/34*	*Derby (Spondon)*	*14.50 Gowhole*		*15/33*	*Trafford Park*
01.30 Traford Park		*01/48*	*Gowhole*	15.35 Manchester		15.46	Cheadle Heath
23.25 Brunswick		*02/18*	*Whitemoor*	13.05 Derby (via T. Dale)	15.53		Manchester
23.30 Beeston (TThSO)	*04/00*		*Trafford Park*	16.00 MANCHESTER		16/09	ST PANCRAS
03.20 Gowhole	*04/10*		*Trafford Park*	16.03 Manchester		16.15	Sheffield (via T. Dale)
06.05 Manchester		06.18	Millers Dale (via T.Dale)	15.30 LIVERPOOL		16/41	NOTTINGHAM (via T. Dale)
06.20 Cheadle Heath	*06/33*		*Trafford Park*	16.32 Cheadle Heath	16.42		Manchester
06.55 Manchester		07.06	Cheadle Heath	16.36 Manchester		16.47	Stockport (T. Dale)
07.00 Cheadle Heath	07.09		Manchester	*14.30 Rowsley*	*16/52*		*Trafford Park*
07.15 MANCHESTER		07/24	ST PANCRAS	17.00 Manchester		17.11	Cheadle Heath
07.24 Manchester		07.37	Derby	17.10 Manchester		17.21	Stockport (T. Dale)
07.30 Cheadle Heath	07.39		Manchester	17.22 Manchester		17/31	Buxton
07.05 Buxton	07/59		Manchester	17.31 Cheadle Heath		17.40	Manchester
07.50 Manchester		08.01	Cheadle Heath	17.30 Manchester		17.42	Cheadle Heath
07.58 Cheadle Heath	08.07		Manchester	17.42 Stockport (T.Dale)	17.53		Manchester
08.14 Cheadle Heath	08.23		Manchester	17.50 MANCHESTER		17/59	ST PANCRAS
08.15 Manchester		08.26	Cheadle Heath	17.55 Manchester		18.07	Cheadle Heath
08.21 Stockport (T. Dale)	08.33		Manchester	18.05 Manchester		18.17	Cheadle Heath
08.25 Manchester		08.37	Chinley (via T. Dale)	14.15 ST PANCRAS	18/32		MANCHESTER
08.31 Cheadle Heath	08.40		Manchester	18.30 Manchester		18.42	Cheadle Heath
08.00 Buxton	08/51		Manchester	16.10 Derby (via T. Dale)	18.45		Manchester
07.02 Sheffield (via T. D)	09.05		Manchester	18.45 Cheadle Heath	18.55		Manchester
09.00 MANCHESTER		09/09	ST PANCRAS	18.45 Manchester		18.58	Chinley (via T. Dale)
08.05 Sheffield	09/15		Manchester	*19.00 Trafford Park*		*19/19*	*Rowsley*
09.15 Trafford Park		*09.33*	*Gowhole*	17.32 Sheffield (via T. D)	19.36		Manchester
04.15 ST PANCRAS	09/43		MANCHESTER	19.35 Manchester		19/44	Derby
07.10 Derby (via T. Dale)	09.52		Manchester	*15.50 Toton*	*20/21*		*Trafford Park*
09.15 Buxton	10/00		Manchester	16.15 ST PANCRAS	20/44		MANCHESTER
03.35 Carlton	*10/48*		*Trafford Park*	20.26 Chinley (via T. Dale)	21.07		Manchester
10.50 Manchester		11.03	Chinley (via T. Dale)	*15.40 Rowsley*	*21/22*		*Trafford Park*
09.06 NOTTINGHAM	11/23		LIVERPOOL	21.30 Manchester		21/40	Sheffield (via T. Dale)
11.35 MANCHESTER		11/44	NOTTINGHAM	*19.25 Huskisson*		*21/49*	*York*
12.06 Manchester		12.17	Stockport (T.Dale)	19.16 Derby (via T. Dale)	21.53		Manchester
12.30 Manchester		12.41	Cheadle Heath	21.40 Trafford Park		21/58	Rowsley
08.15 ST PANCRAS	12/59		MANCHESTER	22.10 Manchester		22.21	Cheadle Heath
13.02 Cheadle Heath	13.11		Manchester	18.40 ST PANCRAS	23/02		MANCHESTER
13.04 Manchester		13.16	Chinley (via T. Dale)	22.46 Chinley (via T. Dale)	23/25		Manchester
12.50 Chinley	13.36		Manchester	*23.20 Trafford Park*		*23/38*	*Gowhole*
13.37 Stockport (T. Dale)	13.48		Manchester				
13.45 MANCHESTER		13/54	ST PANCRAS				

Goods trains in italics. Oblique : Passing time

nominator between them. The Great Central operated the workings to Liverpool Exchange and branches and did so, not only in isolation of the Midland, but of its parent line which was centred upon London Road. There was, in fact, only a tenuous connection between the GC and the CLC and this consisted of the odd Great Central express between Liverpool and Hull which reversed in the Central and used the Chorlton Junction - Guide Bridge connection, a line which also saw a dwindling service of local trains which ran between Guide Bridge and Manchester Central until July1958.

Ironically the last remnant of the GC Manchester - Marylebone express service continued to use Manchester Central long after the core of the service had been dismantled in 1960; the night train leaving Central at 22.50 for Marylebone, the first part of its journey being behind an LMS 2-6-4 tank as far as Guide Bridge where it gave way to an electric locomotive.

The most invisible part of the Cheshire Lines Committee was the Great Northern whose interests tended to be looked after by the Great Central, the distinction becoming blurred after the grouping, although until 1953 a Great Northern service ran nightly in each direction; the 20.30 Kings Cross (Goods) to Deansgate running via Grantham, Nottingham, Chesterfield and the Hope Valley with the return working leaving at 20.22 and running as far as Colwick yard in Nottingham. The reason for the train's operation - for which a J6 0-6-0 was used - concerned the demonstration of running powers that the GN had over the Midland. The closure of Deansgate as surplus to needs in 1953 raised the question as to why the service had been continued under nationalisation and the traffic was quietly diverted to the Great Central route.

The distinction between the CLC partners continued into the diagrams and links at Trafford Park where the instances of engines working part of the day on the Midland and the remainder on the GC/CLC were all but unknown until the early 1950's when an occasional Sunday Midland working was given a filling-in turn to Liverpool and back. The origins of the arrangement dated back to the formation of the Cheshire Lines Committee when it had been agreed that the Great Central would provide the power for all CLC trains, the Midland taking care of its own services.

On the down side of the terminus, hidden by the station wall, was the CLC goods depot which from 1877 until 1880 had been the temporary passenger terminus, whilst on the up side there was a turntable and a few short locomotive sidings which were used by turn-round engines as an alternative to running back to Trafford Park.

Once the initial maze of tracks outside the terminus had been passed, the lines quickly resolved themselves into two sets of up and down lines - those for Liverpool being referred to as 'route A'; the London lines being 'route B' - plus a carriage line which allowed empty stock to run to and from Cornbrook carriage sidings independently of the running roads.

The Great Northern goods station at Deansgate, which closed in 1953, was passed on the down side before the mainlines found themselves enveloped in the long and impressive girders - the foundations of which can still be seen - which lasted until Cornbrook where, for a short distance, the electrified lines of the Manchester South Junction and Altrincham ran parallel with the Midland. The urban aspect of the Midland did not last for very long upon leaving Manchester but what there was of it evoked memories and more than one enthusiast retains a vignette of rumbling through the girders behind a Jubilee 4-6-0 with steam clinging to the metalwork as ones train thrust forward elbowing its way, so it seemed, through the massed ranks of non-corridor suburban services that arrived thick and fast in the Central at most times of day. A glance to the upside usually gave a glimpse of the South Junction line which, with its overhead electrics, lent a modern touch to the proceedings. (Or so we thought then).

The carriage facilities at Cornbrook were extensive and contained no less than twenty-three sidings for the storage of coaching stock, most of which were accessible only from the spur which left the mainline at Cornbrook West to connect with the South Junction.

After passing Cornbrook the nature of the line changed abruptly with the urban interest being replaced by grass cuttings and suburban

Although a very busy and well-used station, Central always carried an air of neglect although the main section, underneath of the overall roof, was infinitely smarter than platform 9 which was situated outside the station proper and was constructed from timber baulks. Surprisingly it remained in use, without alteration, until the closure of the terminus. The view above shows D11 4-4-0 62669 'Ypres' and a 2-6-2 tank arriving coupled from the loco sidings. The driver is supervising the uncoupling of the engines after which the 4-4-0 will shunt forward to find its Chester (Northgate) service. (Bentley collection)

housing which commenced at Throstle Nest - where a connection from the Liverpool line joined the Derby route - and continued for most of the way to Chorlton-cum-Hardy, the first passenger station on the line. The polarity of the line also changed at this point, trains for Derby and the south being regarded as down services until they reached Throstle Nest East at which point they became up trains. The reason for this was that the cross country routes went up to Manchester and the GC route from Guide Bridge and the Midland itself were required to adopt a common standard. The same complication applied on the LNWR and L&Y lines in the north of the city and their services ran up to Manchester and then down to Bradford or Leeds.

Possessing only an up and a down platform and being served only by local trains, Chorlton did not appear to be a point of significance yet it, or to more accurate - Chorlton Junction, a short distance to the south of the station, marked the start of the Midland railway proper and the end of the GC which veered off to the east to Guide Bridge, Sheffield and, ultimately, Marylebone. This Great Central line which, in pre-grouping times, had had quite a respectable service of local trains between Manchester Central and Guide Bridge had been a focus of false hopes during the early 1950's. Originally included in the GC electrification scheme it had been hoped to revitalise the service but the plans came to nought in the wake of overspending on the civil engineering works on the main-line and the passenger service on the branch was allowed to wither.

In the days when south Manchester was blessed with a good suburban service, Chorlton had enjoyed a frequent service and for much of the day a timetable had hardly been necessary. As time passed and with it the better part of the Guide Bridge and Cheadle Heath trains, the service diminished to the point where people forgot that the railway existed and, apart from the rush hour trade, by the 1950's the trains remaining did very little trade.

After Chorlton Junction the Midland entered the realms of green fields and the smart detached houses of the relatively prosperous dormitory areas of Manchester such as Withington and Didsbury which, in the 1950's, were as close as Manchester came to having a stockbroker belt although at Heaton Mersey, seven miles from Manchester, the line skirted the Stockport area and for a short time was again within sight of heavy industry.

In building its 1902 cut-off the Midland had to pay the price of avoiding Stockport, using instead Cheadle Heath where the CLC route from Liverpool Central trailed in to the north of the station giving the line its only four-line stretch of track (albeit for only the length of the station) between Cornbrook and New Mills South Junction.

Cheadle Heath was the first major station on the route and several London trains made calls there. It possessed extensive carriage sidings for the suburban service and had a number of goods yards including the Exchange sidings where traffic between the Midland and the Cheshire Lines Committee was segregated.

As far as Cheadle Heath the line had been relatively level but this changed abruptly upon leaving the station as south-bound trains were faced with continuous gradients of around 1/100 as far as the two and a quarter mile-long Disley tunnel - the sixth longest in the country - increasing to 1/90 from New Mills South Junction, where the older joint line to Stockport merged.

Apart from the short distance at Cheadle Heath, the route from Manchester had been double-tracked but from New Mills the joint line was extended back as a goods line, allowed quadruple running as far as Chinley North Junction.

Immediately to the south of New Mills South Junction were the marshalling yards at Gowhole into which the heavy flows of traffic from the North Erewash coalfields and the Derby mainline were sorted and tripped to desinations within the Manchester and Liverpool areas.

The emphasis in this part of the line was on goods traffic and the section between New Mills and Chinley North Junction, where the goods lines veered off to Sheffield and Chesterfield, gave the opportunity, to get a glimpse of locomotives, mostly 4F or J11 0-6-0's, from such depots as Belle Vue and Heaton Mersey;

engines that were none too common away from the goods lines of the south Manchester district. At the other end of the scale were the Garratt 2-6-6-2 locomotives from Hasland MPD which were in constant use on the coal trains from Avenue sidings near Clay Cross and it was unusual to pass Gowhole without seeing at least one of these locomotives working in on a train from Avenue sidings, Chesterfield. There was no passenger station at Gowhole although Buxworth, which closed in September 1958, had platforms on the fast lines only a short distance south of the marshalling yard.

A mile or so later freight gave way to passenger activity as Chinley station came into sight. Once a point at which Manchester - London trains attached their Liverpool and Blackburn portions, the station in the 1950's was the starting point of the Manchester outer-suburban workings, most of which ran via Stockport, and the stopping trains to Sheffield via Dore and Totley.

In spite of its status Chinley had no motive power depot and its services had to rely on engines from a varied assortment of sheds such as Heaton Mersey, Trafford Park and Buxton. This naturally gave rise to an interesting variety of locomotives, especially on the Sheffield line which remained a stronghold of 2P and Compound 4-4-0's almost until the end of steam

At Chinley North Junction the four track section narrowed to two as the Sheffield line branched off to the east, leaving the mainline to climb, still at 1/90, through the small station of Chapel-en-le-Frith where, on the down side of the line, occasional glimpses of the LNWR Buxton branch - which the Midland had once hoped to use - could be seen.

Two tunnels heralded the approaching end of the climbing, the first - a rather short affair of just over a hundred yards in length - being appropriately if unimaginatively named simply 'LNWR tunnel' from the fact that the Buxton branch crossed the Midland over the bore whilst the second, Dove Holes, was almost two miles in length, wet in places and solid with smoke from the procession of trains extending themselves on the final miles of the climb.

Emerging from the tunnel a short distance north of the summit at Peak Forest, fears that operating interest would evaporate so high and remote in the hills vanished with the realisation that Peak Forest and the surrounding area was the centre of the Derbyshire quarrying business, an activity which involved the railway on a grand scale in the movement of lime and limestone which was transported in large quantities to a variety of destinations. As with Gowhole, the area seemed littered with 4F 0-6-0 engines, some of which were in the process of working trains whilst others waited for a path back to Rowsley after having banked freight trains from the south to the summit at Peak Forest. Larger engines were also frequent visitors with Stanier 8F 2-8-0's appearing at regular intervals on the vacuum-braked high capacity hopper trains which worked between Peak Forest and Northwich several times a day.

Altogether the Peak Forest complex stretched for about two miles after which one came to the triangular junction for Buxton which allowed services to run from Derby to Buxton and from Buxton to Manchester. The names of locations in the area gave some potential for confusion since, further north, Peak Forest station was controlled by Peak Forest North and South signalboxes whilst the northernmost junction at the triangle was entitled Peak Forest Junction. High Peak Junction, south of Rowsley, did nothing to help whilst Chinley North Junction was actually south of Chinley.

Whilst the politics of railway history prevented Buxton from being placed on a through mainline - no small matter since it was the most populous town in a rather sparsely populated region - the connection to the Midland mainline allowed the running of through trains, the majority of which ran to and from Manchester for business purposes during the rush hour. The competing LNWR service was the more frequent of the two and it cannot be said that the Midland, especially after the grouping, put up much of a fight for the traffic. There was however a frequent service of local trains in operation between Buxton and Millers Dale which connected with all main line services.

All London trains called at Millers Dale, a feature which lent the normally quiet station an air of activity at times and one

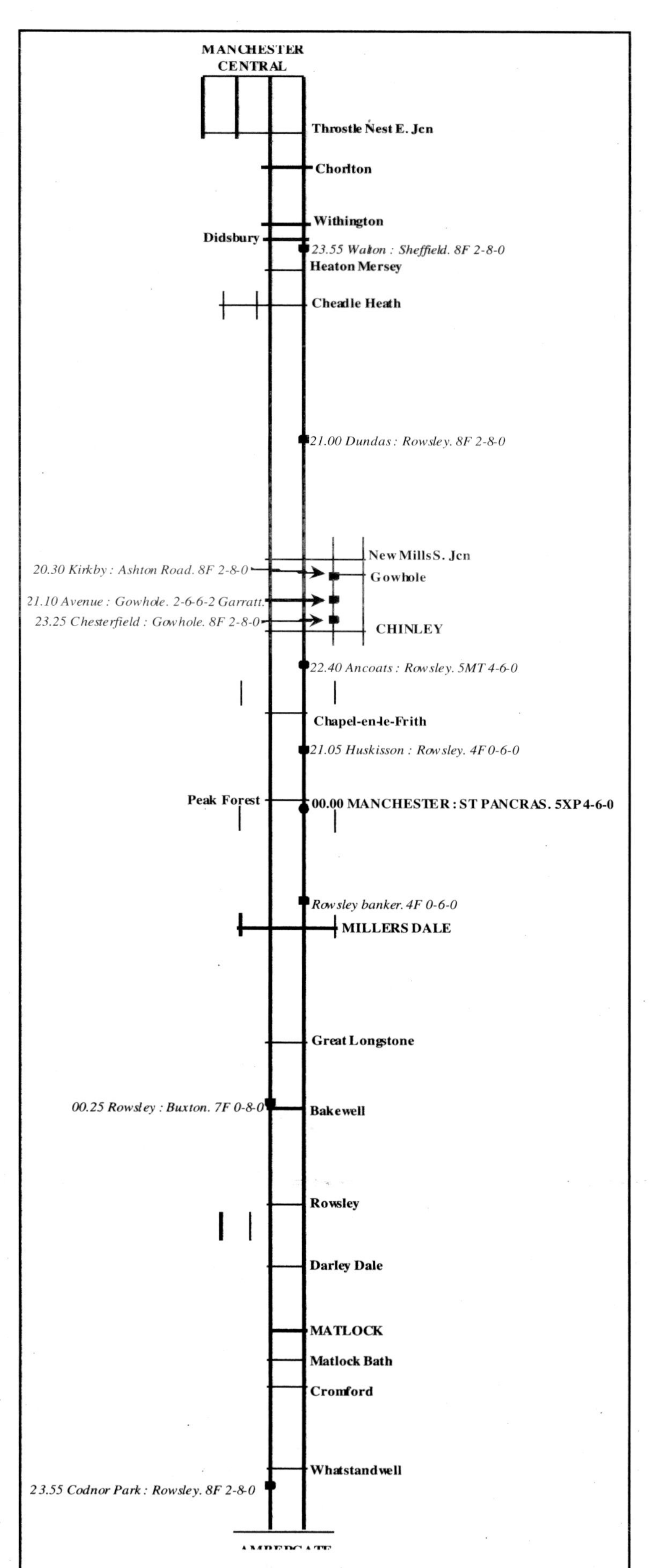

An overall view of the line was maintained by the District Controllers who 'pegged' services on a diagrammatic representation of the area not dissimilar to that shown above, giving a comprehensive view of how trains were running and enabled them to anticipate difficulties, such as congestion, in advance. The diagram above shows the line position at 01.00 on a 1953 weekday, the first wave of night goods trains having passed through the district with the second starting to appear from the south. The up line has been cleared for the passage of the overnight train to London and it will be noted how minimal the facilities for shunting goods trains were in the southern half of the district.

TRAFFORD PARK (9E) : ALLOCATIONS (NOVEMBER 1950) MIDLAND	
Class	Engine
3MT 2-6-2T	40093
	40094
4P 4-4-0 Compound	40900
	40910
	40936
	41052
	41055
	41066
	41076
	41111
	41154
	41181
4F 0-6-0	43896
	43908
	44236
5MT 4-6-0	44938
5XP 4-6-0	45553 Canada
	45618 New Hebrides
	45622 Nyasaland
	45628 Somaliland
	45629 Straits Settlements
	45652 Hawke
8F 2-8-0	48411
	48440
	48680
	48698

recalls the period immediately before dieselisation when the afternoon down Derby stopping train would sit in the down loop for almost twenty minutes, its Black 5 blowing off furiously whilst it was overtaken on the main by the Royal Scot hauled 14.25 ex St Pancras which in turn divested itself of the through coach from London to Buxton; the single brake-compo being worked forward by a Fowler 2-6-4 tank which came out light from Buxton for the purpose. Whilst this was going on the shuttle - a recently introduced multiple unit - would add to the melee by running in to form the 18.02 for Buxton.

South of Millers Dale the line became more rural and there was little sign of operating activity until Rowsley came into sight, a location which, like Gowhole, was a principal centre of operations that laboured under a cloak of anonymity: very few having heard of it. It was also the site of the first engine shed on the line in the entire distance - forty miles - from Manchester.

Rowsley yards were located on the down side of the line and acted in the first stage of preparation for goods trains leaving and entering the area via Ambergate. The limitations of the weight and length of freight trains climbing up to Peak Forest were severe and not only were trains reduced in weight at Rowsley but, more often than not, were banked in rear by a 4F 0-6-0 for the fifteen miles to the summit. Like so many Midland locations it was a home for 0-6-0's and most of its workings being handled by the familiar 4F class, although the shed had on its books a small number of Crab 2-6-0's which tended to be reserved for the night express goods workings to the south.

For northbound services Rowsley represented the beginning of the Peak district and gradients to the south eased considerably whilst the ruggedness of the mountains gave way to greener and more gentle terrain which, if nothing else, demonstrated that Derbyshire was certainly a county of contrasts.

The (relatively) large town of Matlock - population 7,000 - was situated four miles south of Rowsley and was considered of sufficient importance to warrant a stop by almost all London trains - one down train by-passed it - and in fact it was not until the inauguration of the Midland Pullman multiple-unit in 1960 that either Matlock or Millers Dale were ignored on a regular basis.

TRAFFORD PARK (9E) : ALLOCATIONS (NOVEMBER 1950) GREAT CENTRAL (CLC)	
Class	Engine
D16 4-4-0	62532
	62535
	62536
	62568
	62587
	62588
	62599
D10 4-4-0	62651 Purdon Viccars
	62653 Sir Edward Fraser
	62654 Walter Burgh Gair
	62656 Sir Clement Royds
	62657 Sir Berkeley Sheffield
	62658 Prince George
	62659 Worsley-Taylor
D11 4-4-0	62662 Butler-Henderson
	62666 Zeebrugge
	62670 Marne
J39 0-6-0	64723
	64823
	64901
	64954
J10 0-6-0	65137
	65141
	65161
	65168
	65179
	65183
	65184
	65186
	65201
	65204
C12 4-4-2T	67366
	67369
J94 0-6-0T	68064
	68071
J67 0-6-0T	68540
	68583
	68595
J69 0-6-0T	68598
N5 0-6-2T	69252
	69255
	69304
	69326
	69336
	69343
	69347
	69361
	69364
	69370

Looking towards Manchester from Cornbrook West as B1 4-6-0 picks up speed with the 16.05 Manchester (Central) - Sheffield on 6th April 1962. In the extreme right Cornbrook East Junction signalbox and its connection to the South Junction line can just be seen. In the foreground the two lines on the left is route 'B' for Liverpool whilst the B1 is on route 'A' for Chinley, Derby and London. In between is the beginning of the carriage line which extended back to Manchester Central and kept the running lines clear of ECS movements.

12.20 MANCHESTER - ST PANCRAS (1927)							
4P 4-4-0 Compound No. 1049. 9 coaches 246/260 tons (1927)							
m.ch	Station	Gradient	W.T.T.	m.secs	mph	dbhp	pc
0.00	CHEADLE HEATH		0.00	0.00	-	-	-
1.24	MP. 180	168		4.10	30.0	531	1
4.08	Hazel Grove	134		8.40	39.0	870	3
10.69	Buxworth	118		18.54	35.5	850	3
11.65	CHINLEY	105	20.00	20.25	35.0	887	3
					20.0	signals	
13.62	Chapel-en-le-Frith	93		24.10	20.0	594	1
					20.0	Slipping	
17.38	Peak Forest	90	31.00	33.20	20.0	648	1
22.03	MILLERS DALE	-96	36.00	37.50	70.5	195	1
24.58	Monsal Dale	-138		40.05	76.5	-	
26.11	Longstone	-89		41.15	68.0		
29.20	Bakewell	-112		43.25	72.5		
31.68	Rowsley	-144	46.00	46.25	45.0		
34.10	Darley Dale	-360		48.55	62.5	631	3
36.24	MATLOCK	-19140		51.00	66.0	538	3
37.31	Matlock Bath	-359		52.00	60.0		
40.01	High Peak Jcn	-268		54.40	61.0		
41.11	Whatstandwell	-555		55.50	53.5		
43.06	AMBERGATE	-6434	58.00	58.35	25.0		
45.49	Belper	-504		61.45	61.5	1018	5
48.14	Duffield	-478		64.10	69.0	435	3
50.23	Lt Eaton Jcn	-1241		65.55	72.5	622	4
53.34	DERBY	-716	70.00	70.05	-	-	-
MP 180 to Chinley (10.5 miles: 1/121): 858 dbhp at 38.8 mph.							

The focus of interest for enthusiasts beyond Rowsley was the junction near Cromford with the LNWR High Peak branch, a ridiculously graded line serving a number of quarries for which four North London 0-6-0 outside-cylinder tanks - based at Rowsley - had been retained long after any use for them on their parent system had disappeared. The connection with the branch lay on the down side of the mainline at High Peak Junction and included a couple of sidings for any traffic arriving from the Midland section although most of the line's traffic arrived from the LNWR on the daily trip from Buxton.

Ambergate, the point at which the Manchester mainline merged with the Sheffield - Derby route, was not an especially busy station but was of interest in that it lay within a triangle formed by the divergence of an angle which permitted through running from Manchester to Sheffield. The western platforms were used by Manchester - Derby services and those of the east by Sheffield - Derby local

12.20 MANCHESTER - ST PANCRAS (1927)							
Ljungstrom steam turbine. 9 coaches 244/260 tons							
m.ch	Station	Gradient	W.T.T.	m.secs	mph	dbhp	pc
0.00	CHEADLE HEATH		0.00	0.00	-	-	
1.24	MP 180	168		3.30		810	3
4.08	Hazel Grove	134		7.25	45.0	1048	5
9.08	New Mills S. Jcn	135	15.00	13.50	53.5	1099	4
11.65	CHINLEY	94	20.00	17.40	38.0	863	3
13.62	Chapel-en-le-Frith	93		21.00	33.0	878	
15.04	MP 166.25	92		23.28	33.0	859	3
17.38	Peak Forest	109	31.00	27.40	40.0	944	-
22.03	MILLERS DALE	-96	36.00	32.05	70.5		
24.58	Monsal Dale	-138		34.25	71.5	-	-
26.11	Longstone	-89		35.40	71.5		
27.39	Hassop	-475		36.50	72.5		
29.20	Bakewell	-112		37.40	74.0	-	-
31.68	Rowsley	-144	46.00	41.10	25.0	-	-
34.10	Darley Dale	-360		44.10	55.5	775	3
36.24	MATLOCK	-19140		46.45	50.0	-	-
38.14	Cromford	-359		48.50	56.5	91	-
41.11	Whatstandwell	-5400		51.50	53.0	-	-
43.06	AMBERGATE	-527	58.00	54.35	20.0	-	-
45.49	Belper	-504		58.25	53.5	630	3
48.14	Duffield	-478		61.15	60.0	240	1
50.23	Lt Eaton Jcn	-1241		63.15	64.0	371	2
53.34	DERBY	-716	70.00	67.00	-	-	-
MP 180 to Peak Forest (16.2 miles at 1/112) : 969 dbhp at 40.1 mph							

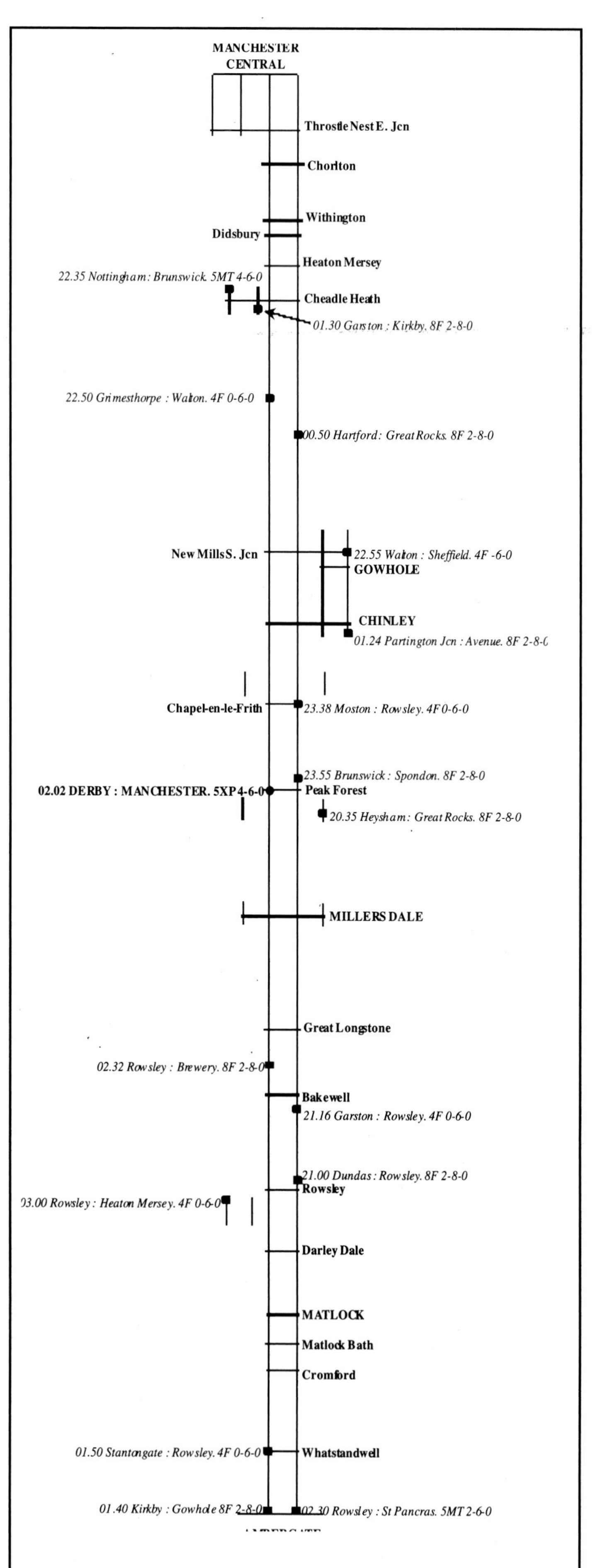

At 03.00 goods traffic is still heavy, especially in the up direction where there are no passenger trains to interfere with the flow of trains. On the down side freight trains have had to be thinned out to clear a path for the express parcels (19.40 ex St Pancras) which ran as a passenger train from Derby to Manchester. Holiday periods when passenger trains ran in large numbers played havoc with the goods working and just a couple of additional expresses could have the operating staff tearing their hair out - especially at night when freight traffic was at its height.

m.ch	Station	Gradient	W.T.T.	m.secs	mph	dbhp	pc
14.25 MANCHESTER - ST PANCRAS (1958)							
BR5 4-6-0 No. 73073. 8:276/295 tons							
0.00	MANCHESTER (C)		0.00	0.00	-	-	-
1.39	Throstle Nest E. Jcn	-111	4.00	3.47	43.0	97	-
3.47	Chorlton Jcn	4821	7.00	6.30	51.0	531	2
5.57	Didsbury	544		8.48	55.5	797	4
		pwc					
7.74	Cheadle Heath	313	12.00	12.42	46.0	224	
17.03	New Mills S. Jcn	139	23.00	24.09	52.0	1153	5
18.64	Buxworth	89		26.30	43.0	1122	5
19.60	CHINLEY	105	28.00	28.15	-	-	

m.ch	Station	Gradient	W.T.T.	m.secs	mph	dbhp	pc
14.25 MANCHESTER - ST PANCRAS (1958)							
5XP 4-6-0 No. 45589 'Gwalior'. 8:272/290 tons							
0.00	MANCHESTER (C)		0.00	0.00	-	-	-
1.39	Throstle Nest E. Jcn	-111	4.00	3.16	48.0	311	1
3.47	Chorlton Jcn	4821	7.00	5.50	50.0	346	2
5.57	Didsbury	544		8.08	58.0	971	5
7.74	Cheadle Heath	313	12.00	10.42	61.0	812	4
17.03	New Mills S. Jcn	139	23.00	22.08	46.0	966	5
18.64	Buxworth	89		24.34	37.0	1087	5
19.60	CHINLEY	105	28.00	26.22	-	-	

trains. The northern side had lost its branch service to Codnor Park on the Erewash Valley in 1947 although it remained heavily used by the mineral services which operated between Kirkby and Manchester. In addition there was an avoiding line which ran to the south of the station for non-stop services between Derby and Sheffield.

A ride on an express between Manchester to Derby therefore was no ordinary trip and even with two alternative routes to London, it was not difficult to justify the choice of the Midland. Motive power played its part in coming to a decision; 6P locomotives were not common on express work generally and it was something of a novelty to run for nearly two hundred miles - and touch some high speeds - on a system that continued the heritage of a small engine policy. (It is true that the Jubilee 4-6-0's were much larger than a Compound or 2P 4-4-0 but most other express routes in the land had long since gone over to class 7 or 8 power; the chief exceptions being the Euston - Birmingham service and the Caledonian mainline north of Glasgow).

For an insight into the actual work done by locomotives over the line a number of logs have been included which depict performances at various stages in the development of motive power.

m.ch	Station	Gradient	W.T.T.	m.secs	mph	dbhp	pc
14.25 MANCHESTER - ST PANCRAS (1958)							
BR7 4-6-2 No. 70014 'Iron Duke'. 8:274/290 tons							
0.00	MANCHESTER (C)		0.00	0.00	-	-	
1.39	Throstle Nest E. Jcn	-111	4.00	4.30	31.0	-	
3.47	Chorlton Jcn	4821	7.00	7.45	40.0	408	2
5.57	Didsbury	544		10.32	50.0	784	4
		pwc : 27 mph					
7.74	Cheadle Heath	313	12.00	14.30	47.0	342	1
17.03	New Mills S. Jcn	139	23.00	25.20	53.0	1254	6
18.64	Buxworth	89		27.22	51.0	1671	9
19.60	CHINLEY	105	28.00	28.53	-	-	

The first two of these runs features the 12.20 Manchester - St Pancras express in 1927, a working which not only made an unadvertised stop at Cheadle Heath to attach a pair of vehicles from Liverpool but included an M&GN section for Great Yarmouth and Lowestoft.

The first run features the standard express locomotive of the day, a compound 4-4-0, and shows the type run at the very limits of its output although throughout the trip the engine only just had sufficient in hand to meet the 70-minute timing and it was mainly by virtue of some fast downhill running that the effects of a pwc at Chapel-en-le-Frith and a bout of slipping in Dove Holes tunnel were overcome.

The best part of the trip came south of Ambergate - outputs of over 1000 drawbar horsepower were unusual at the time and had it not been for a signal check on the approach to Derby the train would probably have arrived with about a minute in hand.

Unable to gain access to Stockport itself, Midland expresses used Cheadle Heath as an alternative where, on 8 July 1950, 5XP 45641 'Sandwich' of Kentish Town pauses briefly with a Manchester (Central) - St Pancras express. Waiting to follow is an unidentified 8F 2-8-0 which has brought a block oil train across from the C.L.C..

Great Central J10 0-6-0 65132 of Heaton Mersey takes the GC route at New Mills South Junction with a trip from Gowhole to Heaton Mersey yard in 1954. The tracks to the right of the picture are the new lines to Cheadle Heath and Manchester (Central) whilst the road in the centre is the extended shunting neck from New Mills goods yard.

Derby-based Black 5 4-6-0 44776 passes New Mills South Junction with an up express on 8th July 1950. The up and down goods lines to the right veer off in the ear of the picture towards Romily Junction for Tiviot Dale and Ancoats whilst those on the left are the new lines to Cheadle Heath and Manchester (Central). An 8F 2-8-0 can be seen approaching in the distance with a goods from Heaton Mersey to Gowhole. The road bridge from which the view was taken obscured the down home signal and repeating arms were affixed to the post to allow drivers to observe the signal both before and after passing the bridge.

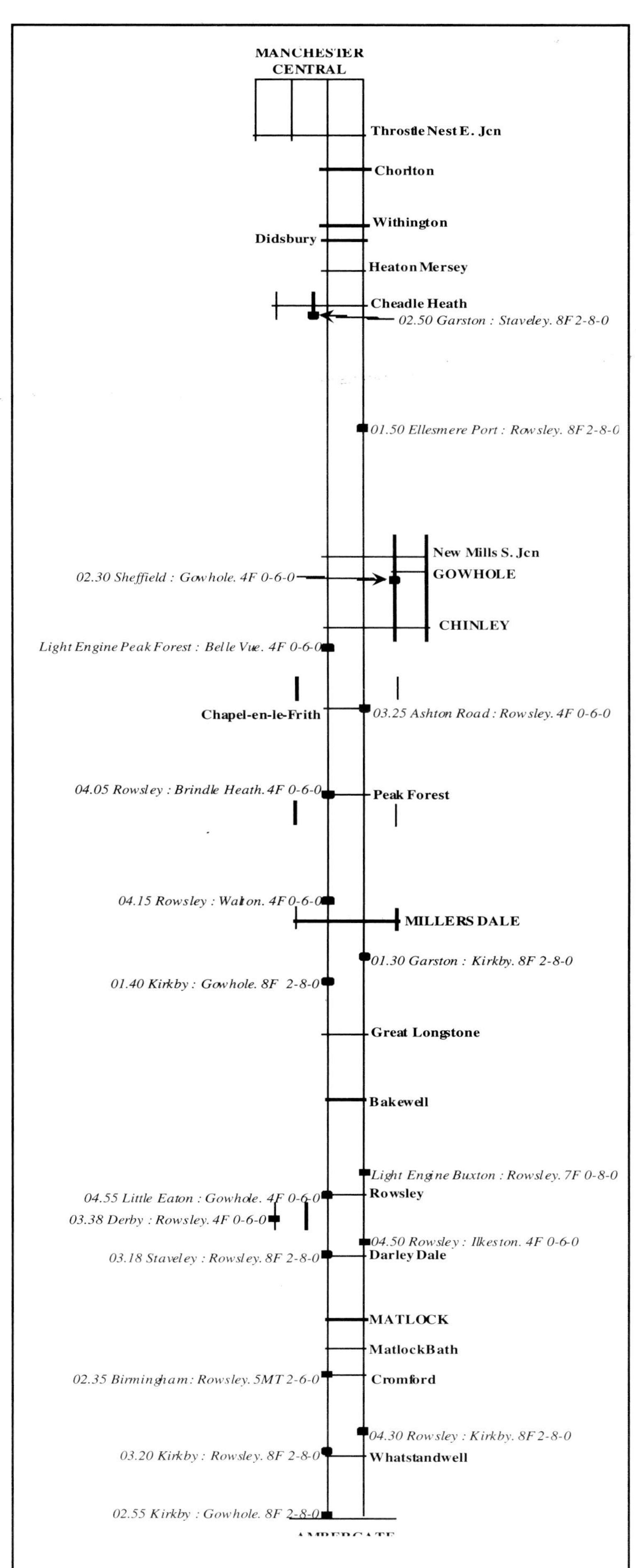

Two hours later, at 05.00, the volume of traffic is still heavy and the controller's workload remains considerable. Two trains on the climb to Peak Forest have 4F loadings and are not therefore banked but a close eye has to be kept on them to ensure that all is well. There are also four through trains on the down line and the relief controller will have been advised of them in order to ensure that any arrangements necessary - engine changes, crew relief, etc. - have been made. On the up road a light 7F 0-8-0 runs downhill to Rowsley to work the 06.15 Rowsley - Buxton.

The second run was made from the same train but with the experimental Ljungstrom steam turbine in charge. Handsome is as handsome does and although the engine was a brute of a thing in terms of appearance its performance was probably superior to anything on British metals at the time. As a yardstick the Gresley Pacifics, in their early form, were just about capable of sustaining 1000 dbhp at very moderate speeds yet the steam turbine equalled this without any apparent difficulty over the eighteen mile climb to Peak Forest. So capable was the locomotive that all but four minutes were shorn from the schedule by Millers Dale after which matters were taken relatively easily for the remainder of the journey to Derby. (In fact the only problems that arose with the engine was at Cheadle Heath when it delayed the train by over three minutes as it tried to attach the through coaches from Liverpool. Shunting, apparently, was not its forte).

The remaining runs depict the variety of motive power that could occasionally be found on the up Palatine - 14.25 from Manchester - and show the demands made on engines over the initial twenty miles to Chinley. The Jubilee 4-6-0 was able to play with the schedule - picking up over a minute and a half - although it is interesting to note that 1000 dbhp was just about the maximum it was able to produce which resulted in a considerable loss of speed on the heavy gradients south of Cheadle Heath. The Standard 4-6-0 had no more trouble with the timing than the 5XP and had it not been for a permanent way slack would have reached Chinley with time in hand. What is interesting is the amount of power that the engine was able to summon on the climb through New Mills and Buxworth, a feature which strengthens suspicions that the class was more of a class 6 than a 5MT. Like all the standard engines they received a mixed reception but those depots that took to them certainly produced work of a higher standard than one would normally expect to get from a class 5.

The Pacific started the journey by making an exceptionally slow start out of Manchester - this may have been due to the excessive slipping that these engines were prone to - and, with the help of a pwc, the train was two and a half minutes to the bad by Cheadle. After that, however, the difference between a class 6 and 7 was more than adequately demonstrated by the production of power that succeeded in all but maintaining the trains' speed on the 1/90 gradients as far as Buxworth

If motive power - Britannia's apart - was on the small side, the stock employed in the London expresses was in every way the equal of anything that might be found on any main line - one has to acknowledge that there had been a time when Midland stock was superior to most but since the grouping the line had tended to become the Cinderella on the LM - consisting of a mixture of latter-day LMS and BR standard vehicles including, on the majority of services, dining or catering stock. To anyone who knew and used the line prior to the days of Beeching it seems unbelievable that it no longer exists.

GOWHOLE

To the outsider a railway was gauged in terms of its passenger service, not unreasonably since the passenger timetable was the only source of information generally available whilst, of course, most people only travelled on passenger trains, with very little regard being paid to its freight operations even though, typically, the latter brought in two-thirds of the revenue and accounted for eighty percent of its activities. This was especially true of the Midland and no description of it can be complete without detailed reference being made to its goods services and the operations which supported them.

The terminal point for goods and mineral traffic in the city of Manchester was the Ancoats branch located near the northernmost extent of the Midland where an end-on junction was made with the Lancashire & Yorkshire which ran from London Road station to the north. Some of the Midland traffic came in over the L & Y - notably a pair of through trains from Carlisle although the majority of workings came in from the south usually after running complete to Rowsley where they were broken up into small loads, usually 4F 0-6-0 worked, to travel via Gowhole and the joint MR/GC line.

LNWR 7F 0-8-0 9166 of Buxton wheels a train of empties from Cheadle Exchange to Buxton on the main line past Gowhole yard on the 6th April 1946. Although the use of an eight-coupled engine seems an advance over the usual 0-6-0, the limit for all unfitted trains over Peak Forest was the 4F loading thus whilst the handling of the train may have been made easier, the provision of a large engine was of limited use to the operating department.

Coal traffic, which was heavy in volume, was dealt with at a variety of destinations in the area - coal for central Manchester was dealt with at Ashton Road yard, adjacent to Ancoast - and arrived in the district by train from Avenue and Staveley running via the Hope Valley line and terminating in Gowhole. There was also a heavy service of coal which ran from Kirkby and these trains were either staged at Rowsley, run over the Peak Valley to Gowhole or, run through to their destination as a block load.

Gowhole, which opened in 1903, was situated a short distance south of the point where the 1902 direct line to Manchester Central diverged from the earlier GC/MR joint and was also conveniently located to receive traffic from both the Hope Valley line and the main line via Peak Forest.

As was commonplace, the sidings at Gowhole were divided into two groups - an up and a down yard - the latter being situated between the main and slow lines whilst the former were located on the up side. The down yard comprised twelve through sidings with accommodation for just under 500 wagons whilst the ten dead-end sidings of the up yard could hold a little less than 400.

Given the fact that Gowhole was the focal point of activities at the northern end of the Midland line, it is surprising that so few people had ever heard of it - indeed such was Gowhole's anonymity that at least three 'definitive' railway atlases make no mention of the place yet for all its lack of recognition the yard not only attended to about 150 arrivals and departures a day but did so without the benefit of local resources; a feature that made the yard almost unique as a major operating centre.

TRAFFIC WORKING : GOWHOLE SIDINGS (1953):NIGHTS

Train	UP YARD Arr	UP YARD Dep	DOWN YD Arr	DOWN YD Dep	Destination
19.05 Staveley			22.05		
				22.10	Brindle Heath
20.08 Sheffield (Grimesthorpe)			22.30		
				23.00	Heaton Mersey
				23.20	Ashton Road
				23.20	Blackwell (Alfreton)
21.00 Rowsley			23.35		(Forward at 23.55)
22.40 Ancoats	23.45				(Forward at 00.44)
(21.00 Rowsley)				23.55	Belle Vue
		23.55			Staveley
23.35 Heaton Mersey	00.20				
23.20 Trafford Park	00.33				
22.50 Sheffeld (Grimesthorpe)			00.42		(Forward at 02.30)
(22.40 Ancoats)		00.44			Rowsley
20.30 Kirkby (Mansfield)			00.51		(Forward at 01.45)
		00.55			Sheffield (Wincobank)
21.10 Chesterfield (Avenue)			01.00		
23.25 Chesterfield			01.10		
				01.25	Heaton Mersey
23.38 Moston	01.35				(Forward at 2.15)
(20.30 Kirkby)				01.45	Ashton Road
		01.45			Leeds (Hunslet)
22.55 Liverpool (Walton	01.45				(Forward at 03.00)
(23.38 ex Moston)		02.15			Rowsley
(22.50 Sheffield Grimesthorpe)				02.30	Liverpool (Walton)
		02.30			Chesterfield (Avenue)
00.55 Sheffield (Grimesthorpe)			02.50		
01.30 Trafford Park	02.53				
(22.55 ex Walton)		03.00			Sheffield
				03.20	Trafford Park
				03.30	Ancoats (trip)
01.10 Chesterfield (Avenue)			03.42		
		03.45			Chesterfield
				03.55	Heaton Mersey
02.30 Sheffield (Wincobank)			05.05		
		05.10		05.10	Chesterfield (Avenue)
03.15 Hollinwood (L & Y)	05.17				
03.05 Chesterfield (Avenue)			05.22		
		05.30			Sheffield (Wincobank)
		05.40			Rowsley

To staff operating a marshalling yard there were basically two types of train. There was the 'starting' service worked by an engine and crew from the local depot and there was the 'return' service which was a train worked by an engine and men that had worked in with an foreign train. The difference between the two was fundamental since the engine and men of a starting turn were fresh on duty and could be guaranteed to present themselves in the yard at the time required whilst those of a return service were not booked to arrive in the yard until half their shift was over halfway and any late running or engine problems experienced on the way in could result in the crew refusing to work back because they were on unwanted overtime. Thus one could never be sure of a return train until it was setting out from the yard on its way back.

The problem with Gowhole was that all its trains were return services since - curiously for a yard of its importance - it had no Motive Power Depot and was therefore wholly dependent upon the co-operation of other locations for the running of its trains. In this respect it was probably unique.

The nearest thing that Gowhole had to a starting service were the workings for which Belle Vue and

Heaton Mersey sent engines and men although neither of these sheds were exactly on the doorstep and delays in running light to start a working from Gowhole could put an entire diagram in jeopardy. As a general rule Belle Vue sent engines for wholly Midland services such as workings to Ancoats and to the L&Y whilst Heaton Mersey provided power for trains running to the Cheshire Lines Committee.

The difficulties inherent in working a major yard without having a local motive power depot were legion and must have made Gowhole one of the most frustrating yards in the country to operate. At any conventional marshalling yard something like 70% of the departures would starting turns whose engines and men could be guaranteed. The remainder would be the return workings of foreign engines and men and were liable to cancellation or delays en route and could never be taken for granted. A mineral train from Sheffield, for example, could quite easily take twice as long on its outward journey as it was supposed to do - bad steaming, poor coal, loss of path, congestion by other traffic, etc., etc., - and upon arrival its crew might decline to work back on the grounds that their time had expired. Apart from routine threats and arguments there was little that could prevent foreign crews from returning home by passenger train or light engine and Gowhole would not only have lost a service but a siding that could have been vacated for a subsequent arrival would not be available and thus the threat of congestion - the dread of all Yard Inspectors - could very easily arise.

Although it had no engine allocation a small number of drivers were based in the yard for shunting duties and did not, in the normal course of events, stray out onto the main line except to relieve the Heaton Mersey 3F 0-6-0 on target 94 at midday and work it up to Peak Forest and back.

Shunting at Gowhole was carried out in a variety of ways. On the down side an 04 2-8-0 engine was provided by the GC to shunt at the 'Baltic end' - the name given to the southern end of the down sidings - whilst shunting in the up sidings was done partially by train engines and mostly by gravity. Although the twelve down sidings were through roads, trains arriving from the south would run past the yard on the main line, come to a stand on the head-shunt and then reverse their loads into the yard after which the 2-8-0 would attend to any further shunting that needed to be done whilst the train engine crossed over to the up side for its return working.

The up yard consisted of ten dead-end sidings and arriving trains would run onto the head-shunt at the south end, uncouple and give the wagons a shove, after which all movements depended upon gravity and the skill of the yard chasers.

Curiously the LMS which was a relatively prosperous undertaking displayed no interest in large mechanised marshalling yards of the type that the LNER placed so much faith and investment in, and until the very end of conventional railway goods moving operations, Manchester's LMS traffic was dealt with in a collection of relatively small and old fashioned locations such as Gowhole and Rowsley with contrasted strangely with the modern establishment built by the LNER at Mottram when incoming GC traffic was sorted.

Because of the lack of interest in the modernisation of marshalling facilities, Midland goods traffic continued to be dealt with in two stages; the first being at Rowsley where traffic for Buxton and the LNWR was abstracted and the second Gowhole where trains specific to Manchester destinations were made up prior to being tripped into the City. In addition to ordinary goods traffic considerable quantities of coal from the north Erewash pits and Kirkby in Ashfield.

One of the most complicated parts of any freight yard inspectors responsibilities was to ascertain - with certainty - the maximum load that a service could take since the calculations necessary were, to say the least, complicated and far removed from the popular belief that an engine of a given type had an established limit which was universally applicable. (Nothing could be further from the truth and there were instances on the mainline where, for example, a Garrett and a 4F were equal in terms of what they were allowed to haul).

The first step in the calculation was to establish the type of train to be run and in the case of scheduled services this could be found in the working time table for the route whilst for special trains an examination of the vehicles concerned was needed with the speed or class of the train being determined by the slowest wagon.

For most purposes there were six categories of goods train, the highest being the class C which had to consist of wagons which were either equipped with automatic brakes or had a through brake pipe. At least half the wagons in the train had to be brake fitted whilst the piped-only vehicles could be marshalled at random provided no more than a quarter of the total were not next to the brake-van. Relatively few wagons being brake-fitted, class C trains were few in number and to allow non-fitted wagons to be conveyed at express speeds a class D train could be made up provided the automatic brake was in use on at least one-third of the vehicles (which, naturally, had to be next to the engine).

A further concession to the number of unfitted wagons on BR was given by the Class E express freight which conveyed non-brake-fitted wagons at speeds higher than that normally granted to unfitted services provided at least four fully fitted vehicles could be placed next to the en-

FIRST IMPRESSIONS

I remember the first time I saw - or noticed - Gowhole yard. It was in 1950 and I was working the 09.44 Derby - Manchester (which was a through Nottingham - Liverpool service). Once Doveholes tunnel had been passed the hard work was over and I could relax for a while - a good firebox full it would run us to Manchester Central without much help from me - and take in the spectacular Derbyshire countryside. Soon after Chinley we passed Gowhole, which lay on the right-hand side, and I recall thinking "Why is that place needed? What a windswept dump..."
P. Webb. Locoman (Derby)

TRAFFIC WORKING : GOWHOLE SIDINGS (1953). EARLY

Train	Up Yard Arr	Up Yard Dep	Down Yard Arr	Down Yard Dep	Destination
01.40 Kirkby (Mansfield)			06.28		
03.10 Little Eaton Jcn (Derby)			06.50		
03.55 Blackwell (Alfreton			06.55		
05.45 Philips Park	07.00				
				07.16	Brewery (Manchester L&Y)
03.35 Carlton			07.20		(Forward at 10.05)
05.58 Warrington (Arpley)	07.33				
		07.35			Sheffield
06.00 Moston	07.38				
				07.45	Port Sunlight
04.45 Chesterfield (Avenue)			07.55		
02.55 Kirkby (Mansfield)			08.00		
		08.10			Chesterfield (Avenue)
05.43 Staveley			08.20		
				08.29	Strines (trip)
08.02 Belle Vue	08.43				(Forward at 09.30)
		09.05			Blackwell (Alfreton)
(08.02 Belle Vue)		09.30			Rowsley
				09.30	Collyhurst Street
		09.40			Chesterfield (Avenue)
07.05 Rowsley			09.40		
				09.50	Portwood Sdgs (Tiviot Dale)
09.15 Cheadle (Exchange Sdgs)	09.55				
				10.00	Brindle Heath
07.20 Staveley	10.05		10.05		
(03.35 Carlton)				10.05	Trafford Park
09.15 Trafford Park	10.20				
		10.25			Staveley
09.25 Collyhurst Street	10.27				
08.18 Moston (L&Y)	10.38				
				10.40	Heaton Mersey
08.10 Ancoats (trip)	10.48				
		10.50			Rowsley
08.00 Alfreton			11.08		
				11.10	Halewood
		11.25			Staveley
09.25 Sheffield (Grimesthorpe)			11.35		
07.25 Kirkby (Mansfield)			11.45		
09.00 Port Sunlight	11.53				
				12.10	Brindle Heath
		12.15			Blackwell (Alfreton)
06.45 Ancoats (trip)	12.20				
		12.30			Chapel-en-le-Frith (trip)
09.55 Sheffield (Grimesthorpe)			12.30		
				12.35	Ashton Road (trip)
11.30 New Mills Junction (trip)	12.38				
10.05 Staveley			13.05		
		13.08			Rowsley
		13.28			Sheffield
				13.45	Brewery (Manchester L&Y)
11.36 Partington Jcn	13.45				
10.02 Carlton			13.48		
10.25 Liverpool (Walton)	13.58				

gine. As an additional precaution the tender handbrake had to be applied in conjunction with the vacuum brake until it was certain that the automatic brake was operating correctly and the train was under control. If the four fitted wagons could not be provided then the train had to be down-graded to a class F.

The loadings that were permitted on each of these services for a Stanier 5MT 4-6-0 were 45 wagons (class C), 50 wagons (class D) and 55 wagons for a class E. Whilst the figures for the two faster services were absolutes (which varied only with the type of engine: a compound 4-4-0, for example, could only take 39 and 43 vehicles respectively) those for the class E were given in equivalents where the standard unit was a wagon of goods and other types of vehicles had to be equated with this standard.

Given the very wide range of wagons at the time, calculating equivalents could be difficult but as a general principal a wagon of coal, assuming that it met the criteria for inclusion in a class E, was equal to 1.75 wagons of goods whilst an empty goods wagon was the equivalent of 1.4 standard units. Thus a class E train consisting only of empty wagons could be made up to 78 vehicles and a brake-van and still be within the limit laid down for a Black 5. (In point of fact a class E train of empty wagons was classified as a Class F train which allowed the load to be increased to 63 = 88 wagons). The loadings for Class C and D trains were more or less universal (they applied anywhere on the LM system) whilst those for Class E services varied according to the route. Trains over Peak Forest with a 5MT 4-6-0,for example, were limited to 49 goods wagons which was 6 less than the regional standard.

Generally speaking, the vehicles which could be included in trains worked as classes C to F were wagons designed for express running and normally had to be fitted with oil axle boxes; a provision that excluded many wagons used for lower class traffic and which were dealt with in class H services.

For class H trains the standard loading was a limit of 76 vehicles for a 5MT 4-6-0 subject to any variations applicable to given stretches of the line where the presence of gradients or other factors imposed a further restriction as was the case with the Peak District which restricted trains to 55 wagons (for a Stanier 5MT) as far as Peak Forest (in the up direction) and 67 beyond. (Through trains had of course to be restricted to the lowest figure applicable to any section on a route).

Class J loaded mineral trains had no standard loading and the calculations were based on tabulations which divided the region into short sections of line each of which had its own characteristics. The unit of measurement was one loaded 13-ton mineral wagon or two and a half empties which meant a significant difference in a length of trains and this could also be a limiting factor. On the main line between Kettering and Wellingborough, for example, a Stanier 8F 2-8-0 was permitted to haul 82 loaded wagons southbound whilst in the down (empty) direction the maximum was a theoretical 170 vehicles; the equivalent of the 68 vehicles permitted northbound. This maximum, however, was well beyond the length of block sections on the route and an arbitrary limit of 90 wagons was imposed as the actual maximum that was allowed in any one train. (The 100 wagon limit that one came across from time to time applied only to goods or empty trains. Loaded mineral services were restricted to a total of 90 vehicles).

Because of its mountainous profile the Peak Forest main line precluded anything like full loads on trains in either direction; the governing factor being not simply the uphill sections but the ability of engines to control trains when descending from the summit at Peak Forest. Most trains from Gowhole to Rowsley ran under class H regulations which allowed from

TRAFFIC WORKING : GOWHOLE SIDINGS (1953): LATE

Train	Up Yard Arr	Up Yard Dep	Down Yard Arr	Down Yard Dep	Destination
		14.10			Buxworth Jcn (Sands Sdg trip)
				14.20	Collyhurst Street
10.30 Kirkby (Mansfield)			14.38		(Forward at 15.27)
11.05 Ellesmere Port	14.47				
				14.50	Trafford Park
14.50 Buxworth Jcn (Sands Sdg)			14.57		
14.22 Cheadle Heath (trip)	15.00				
				15.12	Heaton Mersey
		15.15			Staveley
12.08 Chesterfield (Avenue)			15.15		
		15.25			Sheffeld (Wincobank
(10.30 Kirkby)				15.27	Ashton Road
13.10 Chesterfield (Avenue)			15.30		
13.05 Blackwell (Alfreton)			15.52		
13.40 Brindle Heath	16.05				
14.18 Hartford Sidings	16.14				
				16.20	Heaton Mersey
14.10 Wincobank (Sheffield)			16.27		
				16.35	Cheadle Heath (trip)
14.45 Rowsley			16.43		
14.15 Chesterfield (Avenue)			16.50		
16.10 Cheadle Exchange Sidings	16.50				
		17.10			Chesterfield (Avenue)
13.17 Kirkby (Mansfield)			17.25		(Forward at 19.40)
14.45 Blackwell (Alfreton)			17.47		
		18.20			Chesterfield (Avenue)
				18.30	Brewery (Manchester L&Y)
13.58 Codnor Park			18.30		
		18.42			Sheffield (Wincobank)
				18.45	Halewood
15.40 Rowsley			19.15		(Forward at 20.40)
				19.20	Heaton Mersey
				19.30	Stuart Street
		19.30			Blackwell (Alfreton)
(13.17 Kirkby)				19.40	Ashton Road
16.30 Chesterfield (Avenue)			19.47		
19.42 Bredbury (trip)	20.14				
19.30 Heaton Mersey	20.35				
(15.40 Rowsley)				20.40	Trafford Park
19.35 Philips Park	20.45				(Forward at 21.25)
20.14 Peak Forest (S) trip			20.52		
17.55 Ashton Road (trip)	21.11				
(19.35 Philips Park)		21.25			Kirkby (Mansfield)
		21.55			Chesterfield (Avenue)
18.50 Blackwell (Alfreton)			21.55		

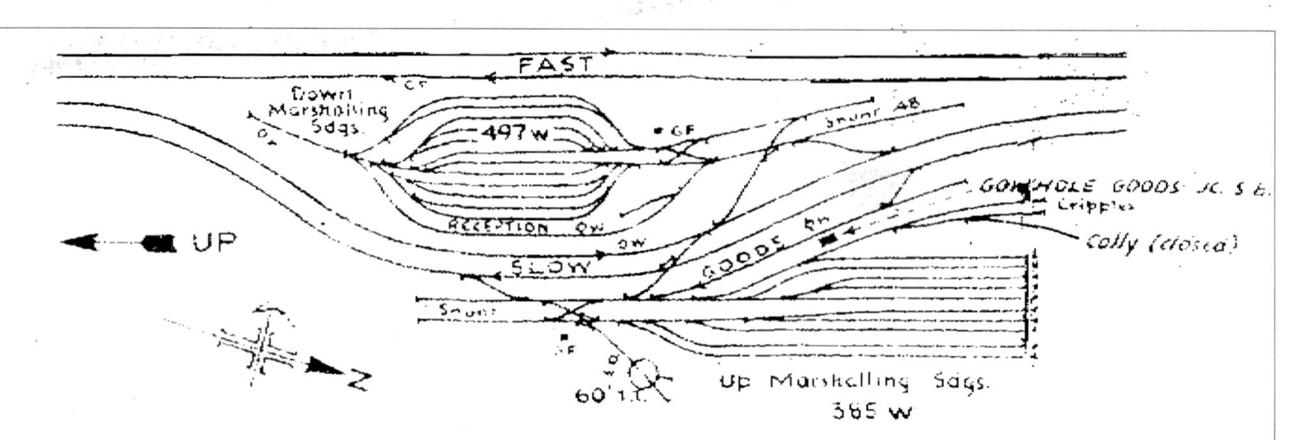

The diagrams provided by the LMS were functional rather than artistic as the above example, rescued from the former Gowhole control, shows. Down trains arrived on the shunt neck and were reversed onto the reception road to be broken up and remarshalled in the down yard. Up services ran via the goods line to one of two reception roads before being reversed into the up sidings. Loco facilities were primitive and the yard was wholly dependant on Belle Vue and Heaton Mersey for motive power.

An 'Austin 7' 0-8-0 comes to a stand at the south end of Gowhole up sidings on 6th April 1946 with a train from Brewery Sidings on the L&Y section in North Manchester. The shunter is standing by the brake-van and will indicate to the driver when he is ready for the engine to start to propel the train into the sidings, most of the movement being accomplished by gravity.

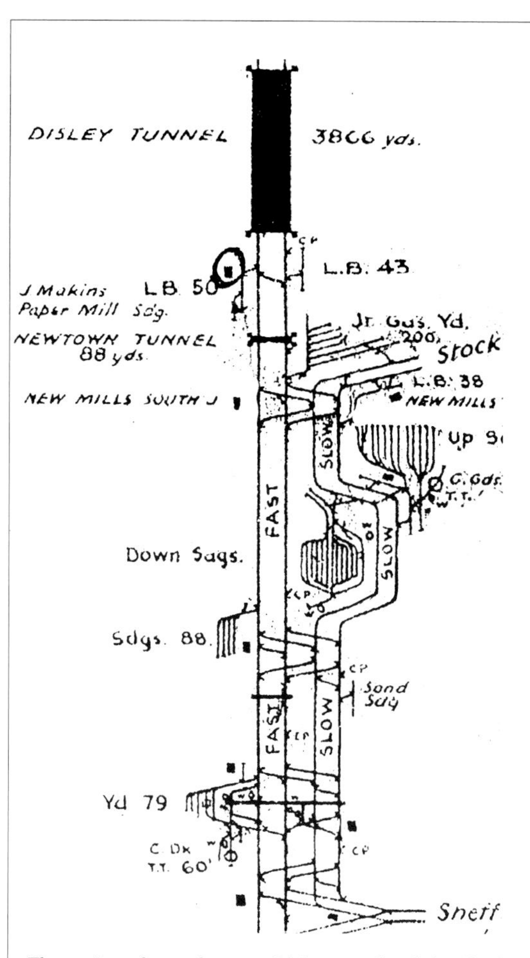

The section of route between Disley tunnel and the Chinley junctions. The old route via Stockport (Tiviot Dale) joins the line at New Mills South Junction and forms the slow lines which deviated through Gowhole Yard and diverged towards Sheffeld at Chinley North Junction. (LMS chart courtesy P. Webb.

88 wagons (8F 2-8-0) to 50 for a 3F 0-6-0. The standard load, insofar as there was such a thing, was the 60 vehicles permitted behind a 4F 0-6-0 and any Class H train exceeding this in the northbound direction had to have a banking engine on the rear of the train from Rowsley to Peak Forest.

Great attention had to be paid to the small print in the loading regulations (known, prosaically, as BR31162/5) since it diluted almost everything that was to be found in the tables of loadings. For example, if a Garratt locomotive was turned out for a train, it could take the load of a 4F 0-6-0 plus that for a 3F 0-6-0 (and not, as is popularly believed, the equivalent of two 'Crab' 2-6-0's) provided that a maximum of 90 loaded (100 empty) wagons was not exceeded and that any other local restrictions were observed. Similarly a 9F 2-10-0 could take one-tenth more than an 8F up to the limits that applied to a 2-6-6-2 unless the train concerned was operating between Rowsley and Cheadle in which case no engine could take more than the load permitted for a 4F 0-6-0.

To confuse matters even further any wagon other than the most commonplace had to have its equivalent in goods or mineral units calculated separately. Five 16-ton loaded mineral wagons were equal to 6 standard 13-tonners whilst a dead 0-6-0 tender engine was the equivalent of four. There were 38 calculations of

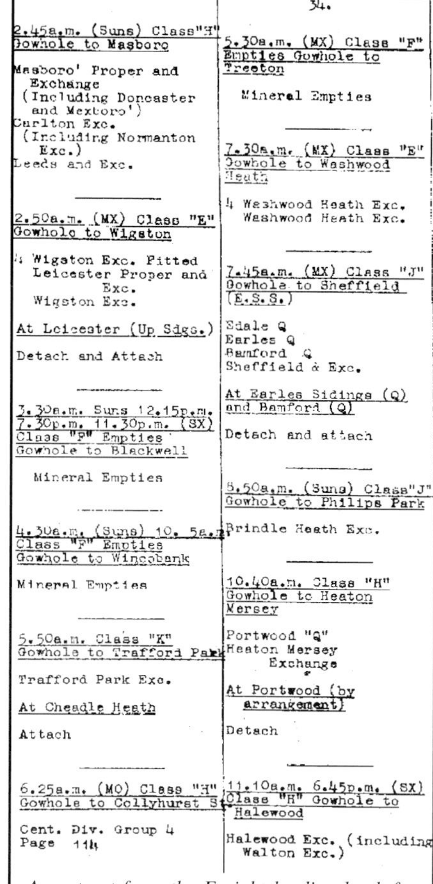

34.

2.45a.m. (Suns) Class "H"
Gowhole to Masboro

Masboro' Proper and Exchange
(Including Doncaster and Mexboro')
Carlton Exc.
(Including Normanton Exc.)
Leeds and Exc.

2.50a.m. (MX) Class "E"
Gowhole to Wigston

4 Wigston Exc. Pitted
Leicester Proper and Exc.
Wigston Exc.

At Leicester (Up Sdgs.)

Detach and Attach

3.30a.m. Suns 12.15p.m.
7.30p.m. 11.30p.m. (SX)
Class "F" Empties
Gowhole to Blackwell

Mineral Empties

4.30a.m. (Suns) 10. 5a.m.
Class "F" Empties
Gowhole to Wincobank

Mineral Empties

5.50a.m. Class "K"
Gowhole to Trafford Park

Trafford Park Exc.

At Cheadle Heath

Attach

6.25a.m. (MO) Class "H"
Gowhole to Collyhurst St.

Cent. Div. Group 4
Page 114

5.30a.m. (MX) Class "F"
Empties Gowhole to Treeton

Mineral Empties

7.30a.m. (MX) Class "E"
Gowhole to Washwood Heath

4 Washwood Heath Exc.
Washwood Heath Exc.

7.45a.m. (MX) Class "J"
Gowhole to Sheffield (E.S.S.)

Edale Q
Earles Q
Bamford Q
Sheffield & Exc.

At Earles Sidings (Q) and Bamford (Q)

Detach and attach

8.50a.m. (Suns) Class "J"
Gowhole to Philips Park

Brindle Heath Exc.

10.40a.m. Class "H"
Gowhole to Heaton Mersey

Portwood "Q"
Heaton Mersey Exchange

At Portwood (by arrangement)

Detach

11.10a.m. 6.45p.m. (SX)
Class "H" Gowhole to Halewood

Halewood Exc. (including Walton Exc.)

An extract from the Freight loading book for 1954. It was issued to Yard Inspectors as a guide to the sectionalising of trains but gave no indication as to the number of vehicles conveyed by each service; something that had to be calculated for each individual train, the limit depending on the type of engine and the route to be covered. (Courtesy P. Webb)

Most of the northbound trains which came into Gowhole avoided Peak Forest and ran via the Hope Valley line to take advantage of the more generous loadings allowed via Hathersage. Stanier 8F 2-8-0 8493 arrives at Gowhole with the 10.05 ex Staveley on 6th April 1946.

equivalents plus a mass of footnotes, none of which help in terms of clarification, and not even brake-vans were excluded since trains over certain routes, and especially those over the Peak District, had to be provided with 20-ton vans.

BELLE VUE: ENGINE MOVEMENTS (1953)

Target	Off Shed	Dest	Train
91	02.00	Gowhole	03.30 Ancoats
	02.52	Ashton Rd	03.25 Rowsley
85	03.33	Ashton Rd	local trips
	04.20	Gowhole	05.40 Rowsley
	04.47	Philips Park	05.45 Gowhole
84	04.55	Ashton Rd	Pilot
86	06.09	Ashton Rd	06.45 Gowhole
	06.28	Philips Park	07.10 Beswick
87	07.41	Ashton Rd	08.10 Gowhole
	07.45	Belle Vue	08.02 Kirkby (Mansfield)
	08.18	Collyhurst St	09.25 Gowhole
	11.28	Ashton Rd	Pilot
	12.00	Philips Park	13.20 Kirkby (Mansfield)
	12.15	Gowhole	13.45 Brewery
82	16.40	Ancoats	17.15 Park station
88	17.25	Ashton Rd	17.55 Gowhole
87	19.00	Bredbury	19.42 Gowhole
	19.05	Ancoats	19.30 Rowsley
	20.10	Ancoats	20.45 Carlisle
	20.10	Ancoats	21.20 Rowsley
	21.00	Gt Rocks	23.35 Heysham
	21.28	Ancoats	22.00 St Pancras
	21.28	Ancoats	22.40 Rowsley
	21.50	Ashton Rd	22.30 Carlisle
	23.30	Ancoats	Pilot
89	23.55	Ashton Rd	00.32 Heaton Mersey

Some trains were excluded altogether from the normal loading calculations and amongst these were the I.C.I trains which operated between Tunstead Sidings, Peak Forest and Northwich, Hartford and Wallerscote. These trains consisted of 43.5 ton vacuum-fitted hoppers running under class H conditions and could load to 16 vehicles when worked by a Stanier 8F 2-8-0 and routed via Disley. If a class 4F 0-6-0 worked the train the load had to be reduced to 11 vehicles whilst a 9F 2-10-0 could take 19 and in all cases the workings had to be banked from Tunstead to Peak Forest North Junction. The booked route was via the main line to Cheadle Heath but the alternative via Marple and Stockport could be used provided the services were reduced by two vehicles.

There were so many variables involved in marshalling goods trains that not even a Philadelphian lawyer could have been at home with the regulations and, for the majority of trains (which conveyed predictable commodities), a precis of the loading book was exhibited in the Yard Inspectors office to serve as an aid-memoir. If one had been at a place like Gowhole for twenty years experience taught one most of the possible permutations of loadings although a surprise special (a diverted train for Hellifield, for example) could throw one into a state of panic for quite a while as one tried to piece together the various sections of line involved and the loading requirements for each. Typically the Inspector would arrive at a solution, have the train marshalled to his orders only to find that the Hellifield guard knew better at which point an unholy row would break out with no-one in a position to act as arbiter......

It was not just Yard Inspectors who could be confused by the loading book and one worthy recalls being taken to task, it being claimed that a train to an unusual destination did not take its full load. In his defence the Inspector asked his interrogator what the load should have been and received an answer.....three days later. It took that long for someone to be certain of their facts.

It is often supposed that the control organisation - said to have been originated by the Midland Railway although in truth most railways had evolved some sort of traffic control system as soon as the telephone became a practicable means of communication - was designed to eradicate some of the excessive hours worked by train-crews on the Midland Railway and whilst this was one of the reasons for a broad supervision of train movements, it was far from being the only one and the fact that a control office was instituted at Gowhole suggests that traffic considerations rather than those of the paybill played a strong part in the introduction of the control system.

On the Midland Railway and the L.M.S. the district controllers did not normally interfere to any great extent with trains once they were on the main-line, the regulation of trains being left to the judgement of signalmen and station-masters. The function of the district controller was to see that the general strategy laid down in the timetable - especially that of freight trains - ran properly and to take any steps that were available in the way of correction when things went awry.

He also played a key role in the running of goods trains and one of his first tasks upon taking duty was to establish from the Yard Inspectors the volume and destination of traffic that they had on hand. This would be reported as, for example, No1 down siding: 60 Ashton Road, No.2 down siding: 46 Brewery, No 5: Siding: 3 Brindle Heath and so on until a clear picture had been established of the stock position in the yard. (It was commonplace practice in marshalling yards to allocate a siding to a particular destination). To these figures he would have estimate the volume of traffic that was 'in the pipeline', that is, en route to the yard in trains and likely to be ready for forward movement from Gowhole within the coming few hours.

Having estimated thus the volume of traffic needing to be moved the controller would then allocate train loads to departures to see how the booked train service was likely to cope. Having gaind a broad idea of how the service was going to cope he then turned his attention to see what services were going to run, some-

MIDLAND JUNCTION (1953)

Northbound	Time	Southbound
	00/41	23.38 Moston - Rowsley
22.18 Grimesthorpe - St H. Jcn	01/15	
	01/22	20.35 Heysham - Tunstead
01.00 Heaton Mersey - Hellifield	02/07	
	02/32	02.25 Philips Park - Ancoats
23.45 Grimesthorpe - Edge Hill	02/36	
23.35 Tunstead - Heysham	02/47	
	03/12	22.40 Hellifield - Heaton Mersey
	04/29	03.15 Hollinwood - Gowhole
02.32 Rowsley - Brewery	04/30	
05.35 Ashton Road - Hope Street	05/48	
	06/00	05.45 Philips Park - Gowhole
05.45 Ancoats - Brewery	06/02	
06.00 Belle Vue - Brindle Heath	06/14	
04.05 Rowsley - Brindle Heath	06/28	
	06/45	06.00 Moston - Gowhole
	07/06	06.28 Moston - Ashton Road
07.40 Ashton Rd - Park Station	07/52	
07.16 Gowhole - Brewery	08/07	
	08/45	08.35 Philips Park - Ashton Rd
	08/52	01.25 Carlisle - Ancoats
08.20 Heaton Mersey - Hellifield	09/28	
	09/39	09.25 Collyhurst St - Gowhole
	09/49	08.18 Moston - Gowhole
09.30 Gowhole - Collyhurst St	10/28	
10.30 Ashton Rd - Park Station	10/47	
10.00 Gowhole - Brindle Heath	10/54	
	11/05	10.57 Philips Park - Ashton Rd
12.25 Ashton Rd - Philips Park	12/35	
12.10 Gowhole - Brindle Heath	12/58	
	13/28	13.20 Philips Park - Kirkby
	14/00	13.50 Philips Park - Rowsley
13.45 Gowhole - Brewery	14/38	
	14/56	13.40 Brindle Heath - Gowhole
	15/09	14.18 Hartford - Gowhole
14.20 Gowhole - Collyhurst St	15/11	
	16/49	16.43 Philips Park - Ashton Rd
17.15 Ancoats - Park Station	17/50	
10.23 Codnor Park - Agecroft	18/10	
18.30 Gowhole - Brewery	19/16	
	19/20	19.05 Oldham Road - Ancoats
	19/44	19.35 Philips Park - Rowsley
19.30 Gowhole - Stuart Street	20/21	
	20/52	17.05 Blackburn - Ancoats
	21/06	20.25 Moston - Rowsley
20.45 Ancoats - Carlisle	21/08	
	21/38	21.30 Philips Park - Belle Vue
22.30 Ashton Road - Carlisle	22/50	
20.10 Rowsley - Brindle Heath	22/56	
22.10 Gowhole - Brindle Heath	23/02	

Midland Junction was the northern limit of the Midland Railway in Manchester and the point at which it made an end-on connection with the Lancashire & Yorkshire Railway. As the Midland's only point of contact between its Manchester interests and the northwest it was heavily used; the above list detailing the services which passed through the junction. It was also the only practicable means of connecting with the Settle & Carlisle and the long distance through trains between Manchester and Carlisle used this route to regain Midland metals at Hellifield.

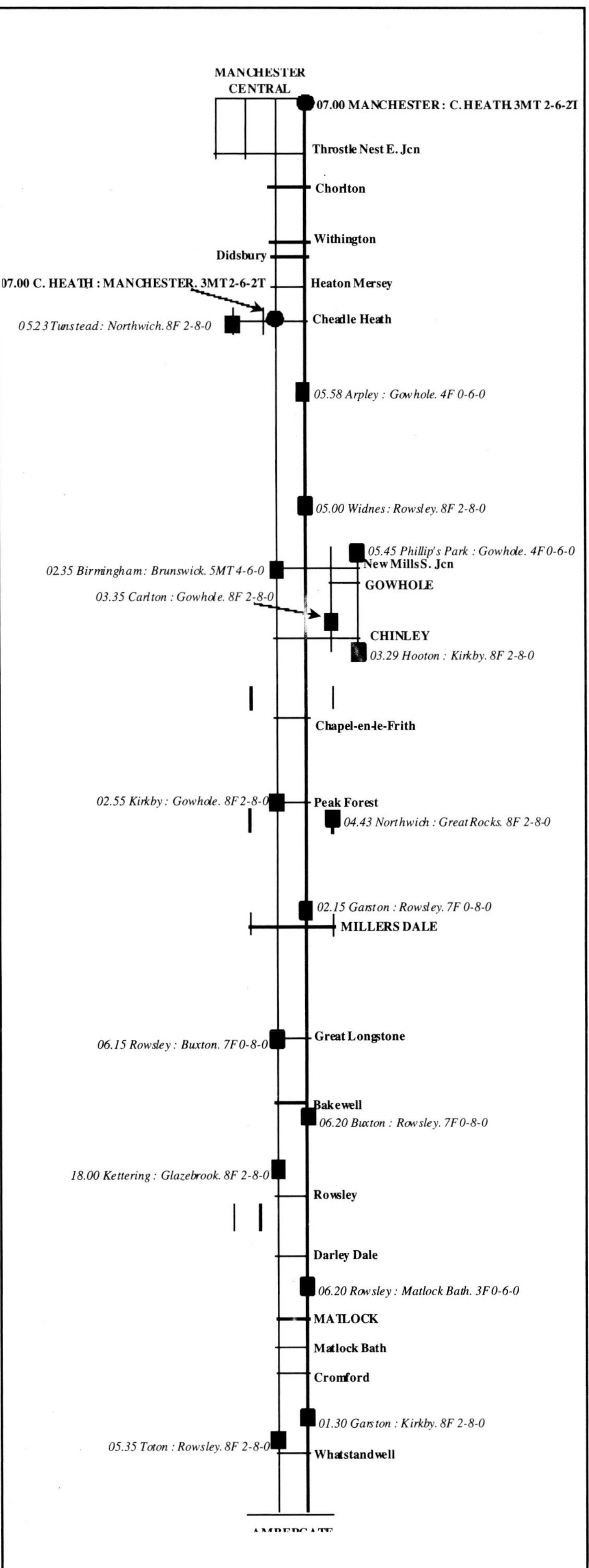

The line position at 07.00, an hour into the early turn, and the route is already well filled with goods trains. The telephone lines will be buzzing with regulation instructions very shortly since the 06.05 Manchester - Millers Dale/Buxton is due off the Stockport loop at New Mills South whilst the first express of the day for St Pancras will be pulling out of Manchester in 15 minutes time.

Stanier 8F 2-8-0 48327 of Buxton stands on the Gowhole turntable whilst its crew take breakfast prior to returning home with a service via Peak Forest. By the time of the photograph, 12th May 1966, Rowsley yard had been closed for two years and traffic flows had changed considerably as a result. One outcome was a rerouting of Buxton traffic direct to Gowhole with four trains per day in each direction. The motive power position had also changed during this period, dieselisation and the loss of traffic to the roads releasing greater number of Stanier 2-8-0's, although the 4F 0-6-0 was still in evidence on many local workings, especially in the Manchester area. With the closure of Gowhole Buxton men had their horizons broadened even further and could be seen working through to Warrington, Dewsnap, Guide Bridge and Moston which not only accelerated traffic but begged the question why it hadn't been implemented years before

thing that was critical at Gowhole where all outward workings depended on inward services. The workings covered by the various Manchester depots - Belle Vue, Heaton Mersey and Trafford Park - were not too difficult to arrange since Gowhole control had some jurisdiction over the work encompassed by their engines but workings by engines and men from beyond the district were a vwery ifferent matter and if a service from,say, Sheffield to Gowhole was cancelled the result was that Gowhole lost the return working and there was very little that Gowhole could do about it. The higher categories of goods trains, classes C,D, and E usually ran as booked in the fashion of passenger trains but F, H and J workings were highly fluid and could be altered or diverted at the drop of a hat. Thus the controller at Gowhole spent a considerable amount of time in 'negotiating' trains with adjacent area's although some comfort could be gleaned from the fact that there were a number of 'control order' engines and men at Heaton Mersey who started duty at fixed times but worked to whatever instructions they were given by the control in the course of their shift. (These adhoc trains did not run to any fixed timings but simply took their turn in the queue. If, for example, Gowhole 'lost' the 02.30 to Walton he might, if all else failed, order the 03.00 Heaton Mersey control order set to run light to Gowhole to work a special (circa 04.00) Class J to Walton, returning as ordered (which could be light engine or with a load of traffic back to Heaton Mersey or Gowhole) by the Liverpool district.

BELLE VUE (26G) : ALLOCATION (1950)

Class	Engine
1F 0-6-0T	41690
	41702
	41814
3F 0-6-0	43612
	43630
	43638
4F 0-6-0	43756
	43927
	43952
	44019
	44022
	44025
	44040
	44114
	44119
	44486
5MT 4-6-0	44803
	44845
	44921
	45031
	45226
	45284
	45450
3F 0-6-0T	47336
	47440
8F 2-8-0	48330
	48348
	48349
	48531
	48714
	48715
2F 0-6-0ST	51484

The first half-hour or so of a shift would therefore be spent in building up a plan of campaign for the coming eight hours although when it was complete considerable attention (which required a nose for trouble) would be expended on reviewing affairs at frequent intervals to see what adjustments were required in the light of events.

Although the running of trains on the running lines was left to the outside staff, a careful watch had to be kept on turn-round times at station yards and sidings and at Gowhole in particular. Reference has been made to the reaction of crews at being delayed on the way in but at the other end of the scale there were train-crews who would invoke overtime by losing time all the way into Gowhole - claims of poor steaming were difficult to counter unless one happened to have an inspector on hand to investigate - and then taking an extraordinary time to work out. In the majority of workings an allowance for a meal break would be given between workings at Gowhole and some crews would extend this as far as possible. Clearing the smokebox or fires that suddenly needed cleaning were pretty cast iron guarantees of overtime and the controller had to keep a close eye on turn-round times, despatching a motive power inspector to sort things out if matters looked as though they were getting out of hand.

It was essential at Gowhole to keep things moving since, the loss or heavy delay of a train from Gowhole brought with it the threat of congestion since the number of sidings was not great and keeping room available for approaching services was a priority if congestion on the main lines was to be avoided.

When it appeared that the flow of trains was going to overwhelm the yard the controller, after discussion with the Assistant Yard Master, could telegraph to all districts and stations the coded message BYRAG GOWHOLE which meant that no service terminating at Gowhole was to be started unless the control at Gowhole had given it individual acceptance. In extreme circumstances the phrase GOSLING GOWHOLE would be sent which meant that no trains were to be despatched to Gowhole. Neither of these steps were taken lightly but the fact that Gowhole was dependent on external resources for its trains resulted in Byrag restrictions being issued more frequently than was normally the case for a yard of its size. It

For reasons best known to the Commercial Manager of the day, every night the Buxton - Millers Dale push & pull took a trip down the main line to New Mills Central, leaving Buxton at 16.25 and returning at 17.24. It is difficult to see any justification for the service, particularly since the down service preceded the 17.22 Manchester - Buxton by only a quarter of an hour and made the same stops. It did, on the other hand, provide one more dimension to the already rich tapestry of motive power which used the Midland and Stanier 2P 0-4-4T 41906 is seen passing Gowhole with the up train in 1954. The down yard can be seen to the right of the train and the goods lines, which slewed to the east, are just visible above the wagons.

HEATON MERSEY (9F) : ALLOCATIONS 1950 (MR)

Class	Engine
Stanier 3MT 2-6-2T	40089
	40113
	40118
	40124
3F 0-6-0	43811
4F 0-6-0	43836
	43945
	44080
	44090
	44144
	44178
	44286
	44407
	44421
	44593
8F 2-8-0	48089
	48099
	48127
	48134
	48154
	48155
	48190
	48208
	48220
	48275
	48315
	48316
	48329
	48406
	48503
	48527
	48557
	48676
	48682
	48683
2F 0-6-0	58128
	58303

had to be remembered that any limitation on the acceptance of trains at Gowhole very quickly reacted back onto other sidings which quickly filled up with trains that were terminated on the road and was liable to do as much harm as good. (In actual fact most yards took a pride in avoiding the use of Byrags and Goslings and would use them as a last resort. The exception was the new (1960's) yard at Tinsley, Sheffield which, sent out a Byrag every time - so it was said - the AYM sneezed.

Whilst the district controller spent most of his time in the arranging of trains and traffic his assistant had the task of monitoring movements on the main line and generally keeping an eye on the state of the main line. Telephoned reports were received from the more important signalboxes as trains passed them and these were recorded by the controller on the train cards which held the details of the trains schedule, its load and engine. (An interesting aspect was the method by which signalmen identified trains when reporting to the controller. The Midland did not use train reporting numbers on a wide scale and very often all the signalman knew about a goods train was its destination. The I.C.I trains were recognisable enough for a signalman to report 'Northwich down the main at '29' whilst the identity of a train of mineral empties bhind a 4F 0-6-0 was less obvious. In these cases the report would focus on the engine number '4236 up at '44' which told the controller all he needed to know).

To assist in gaining an overall position the controller maintained a peg-board upon which pegs, representing the trains under his control, were moved on a geographical representation of the line under his supervision. It was not usual to 'peg' passenger trains since these moved too rapidly through the district although their passing times were recorded on a delay sheet along with any explanations of time lost. (On the LMR the district controllers did not normally interest themselves in train regulation and it was usually accepted that such matters fell within the responsibility of the signalmen. The controller did, however, have the authority to give instructions to signalmen on matters of train regulation although in practice this was usually only done in moments of real crisis. With only an up and a down main line the scope for regulation was, in any event, minimal). Gowhole control also had to make sure that its resources were used sensibly. If it transpired, for example, that the down pick-up - the 15.40 Rowsley - Trafford Park - had a full load on leaving Peak Forest and was unable to clear Chapel-en-le-Frith, the controller would have to search round and find a solution pretty quickly. Stopping a through freight was usually out of the question since they already conveyed a full load whilst to use a control order set from Heaton Mersey would mean utilising an engine and crew for little more than an hour with a great deal of light engine running. A better solution was to examine the various trip services that were already at work in the district and to divert one of them to Chapel without prejudicing the activities it was al-

HEATON MERSEY (9F) : ALLOCATIONS 1950 GREAT CENTRAL

Class	Engine
D16 4-4-0	62609
D11 4-4-0	62663 Prince Albert
	62665 Mons
J39 0-6-0	64727
	64733
J10 0-6-0	65132
	65135
	65144
	65145
	65146
	65154
	65157
	65160
	65178
	65181
	65185
	65188
	65193
	65194
	65197
	65198
	65200
	65209
N5 0-6-2T	69276
	69317
	69328
	69331
	69332
	69359

ready engaged in. Most experienced controllers carried their workings in their heads and could resolve most of the difficulties that arose in the course of a shift with (apparent) ease.

Much of the traffic dealt with at Gowhole was low category since wherever possible high value goods was moved from depot to depot by express goods services running under much the same rules that applied to passenger trains. The exceptions were wagonloads of goods based on wayside stations which were not served by through services and these tended to turn up at places such as Gowhole where they commanded a higher priority than the run of the mill traffic more normally dealt with.

Most of the general goods traffic from Manchester originated from either Ancoats or Ashton Road and was worked out in an impressive series of night trains to London, Carlisle (two trains) and Rowsley, the last mentioned being for traffic that could not be dealt with by a direct service. There were also a number of trip workings to local stations in the area and to yards on adjacent systems for exchange purposes; these - and the main-line services - running as per timetable after the fashion of passenger trains. All in all there were 42 arrivals and departures on the Ancoats branch daily excluding the frequent series of local movements that took place between Ancoats and Ashton Road.

The motive power depot which looked after affairs at Ancoats was Belle Vue which, like Gowhole, has never received much in the way of public attention.

Its origins went back to the days when the Midland had used the Great Central part of London Road. When passenger traffic transferred to Manchester Central in 1880 the company found its freight and passenger terminals on different sides of the city with no direct connection between them. Trafford Park therefore was used to house the passenger locomotives for the mainline passenger work on the Derby route whilst resources for the Ancoats branch remained at Belle Vue. In palmier days the shed had played a part in the suburban service which operated between Manchester (Victoria) and the Midland main-line, running to places such as Chinley and Buxton - through coaches between Blackburn and St Pancras were for a long time features of the line - but such workings were hit hard by the cuts of the Great War whilst the few that survived into the grouping disappeared during the last war leaving only a section of the overnight London - Manchester parcels train that continued to run between Stockport and Manchester Victoria.

The Midland cross-Manchester service had never been particularly frequent, apart from any other considerations its trains had to cross the Great Central main-line at Ashburys and this coupled with dense movement of goods traffic between the Midland and the Lancashire & Yorkshire prevented its expansion. It is an interesting feature of pre-grouping times that cross-city connections for passengers were poor in all the major British conurbations and contrasted curiously with the otherwise highly co-operative working that prevailed generally.

Whilst it lasted the service did provided a useful connection between south and north Manchester for long distance travellers with the six trains which ran from Chinley to Victoria in 1909 all conveyinged through coaches from St Pancras, three having portions for Blackburn. By 1932 there were only two trains running; the Victoria sections of the midnight and 10.25 expresses from St Pancras whilst by nationalisation only the night train, which conveyed parcels traffic, remained.

In freight terms on the other hand both Belle View and the link to the L & Y via Midland Junction remained busy with over fifty goods services a day (plus a good deal of light engine movements) passing between the two systems. The traffic that moved over the link was varied and ranged from exchange trips between the Ancoats branch and various yards on the Lancashire & Yorkshire to long distance express goods services between Ancoats to Carlisle.

The majority of these cross-Manchester trains came within the purview of Belle Vue MPD which had an allocation of 32 locomotives the largest of which were five Stanier 5MT 4-6-0's which were used for the night fitted freights to London and Carlisle. In addition the shed had a solitary 4MT 2-6-4T used for the Stockport - Victoria parcels together with fourteen goods engines (eight 4F 0-6-0's and six 8F 2-8-0's) employed on the Gowhole and Ancoats freight services. It also possessed ten 0-6-0 tanks of various types for shunting duties, most of which involved working the network of sidings in the Ancoats and Ashton Road complex.

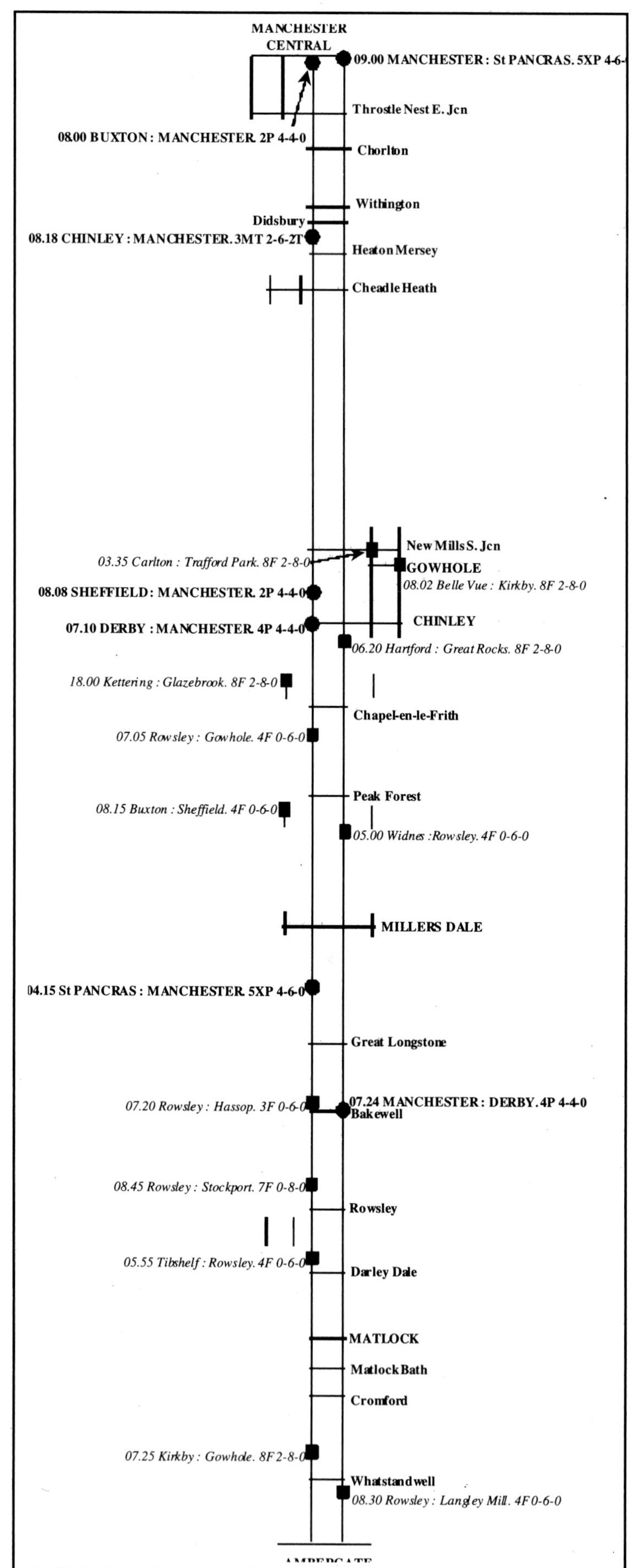

At 09.00 the emphasis is on down traffic with five passenger trains approaching Manchester and having to be weaved through a concentration of freight traffic which has to be held back on the loops and slow lines between Chapel-en-le-Frith and Gowhole. An interesting passenger movement has just taken place at Chinley, the 07.10 Derby - Manchester arriving at 08.54 and standing for eleven minutes during which time the 08.08 'express' from Sheffield stops and overtakes, allowing transferring passengers to reach Manchester at 09.24; forty-two minutes ahead of the Derby service which runs via Stockport. In the up direction the line has been cleared of most goods trains for the passage of the 09.00 Manchester - St. Pancras.

A Midland outpost, Belle Vue survived the grouping period as an outpost of Sheffield (Grimethorpe), being transferred to the Newton Heath district at nationalisation where it remained until 1956 when it closed, its engines and men being transferred to the parent L&Y shed.

The other flows of traffic northwards from Gowhole were to Trafford Park and the Cheshire Lines Committee, trains to the latter either travelling via Romily Junction and Heaton Mersey or - if a full load for a Merseyside destination could be put together - via Cheadle Heath. Excluding the through services which called in for relief before proceeding forward, Gowhole was responsible for twenty-eight northbound workings, the majority of which went either to Heaton Mersey (7 trains) or the Lancashire & Yorkshire (9 services). The remainder consisted of three workings to the CLC, three to the Ancoats branch, two to Trafford Park plus four local trips.

The trains to Heaton Mersey and the Ancoats terminals were worked by Heaton Mersey and Belle Vue sheds respectively who had a combined allocation of twenty-one 0-6-0 tender engines - mostly 4F's - for the purpose. The length limit (i.e. the maximum number of empty standard wagons that could be taken by a class J train) on most of the Midland routes into and around Manchester was sixty but in actual fact trains conveyed very much less than this, partly because the extra weight of loaded traffic but also because of the class 4F engines that the system rejoiced in, 38 wagons being the maximum to Trafford Park and 35 to Ancoats. Heaton Mersey services were even more restricted since the short stretch between Romily and Brinnington Junctions allowed a 4F to take no more than 29 vehicles.

Matters to the south of Gowhole were on an entirely different scale, all but three of the twenty-six departures being routed via Grindleford running under class F conditions which permitted an 8F 2-8-0 to take seventy empty wagons and a Garrett eighty-eight. (The difference between a large and a small engine on this route was marked since a 4F was permitted a load of no more than 48 empties). Hasland MPD, which worked most of the Avenue trains had an allocation of ten 2-6-6-2 Garratts for this traffic, whilst most of the other workings across the Hope Valley were handled by 2-8-0's from Staveley and Westhouses sheds.

Southbound freight services over Peak Forest tended to be through workings from the CLC or Manchester, returning empties to their point of origin, and only three services a day started from Gowhole, all of which ran to Rowsley. This tended to ease the congestion on the main line since the considerable amount of traffic which ran through from the CLC and Manchester to Peak Forest, Rowsley and beyond was added to by a not inconsiderable amount of

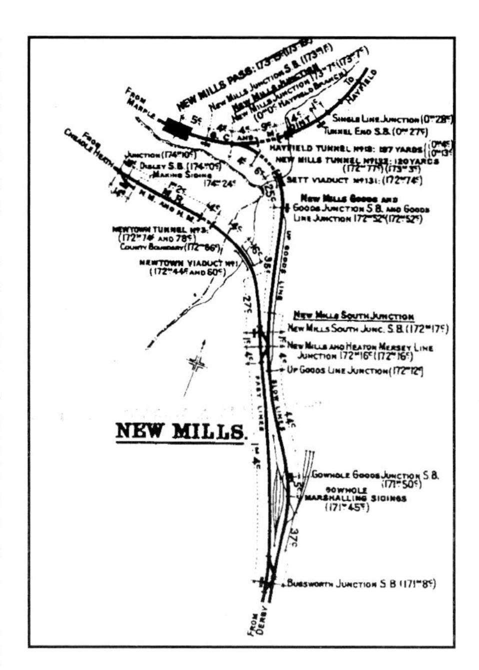

goods traffic from the Buxton route which joined the mainline a short distance north of Millers Dale. To these movements the frequent movement of bankers returning to Rowsley from both Peak Forest and Buxton had to be added and the sum of these workings added up to an extremely busy mainline and one of the most important freight arteries in the country.

Peering rather anxiously from the cab, the driver of 7F 49560 attempts to centre his engine on the Gowhole turntable before returning to the L & Y with a trip to Brewery Sidings. Not only have the crew got one of the ugliest engines ever to turn a wheel, but the tender is full of dust and the engine has no vacuum brake which means turning it the hard way. The class was a Fowler development of the LNWR 0-8-0 but did not live up to its promise of becoming a standard LMS goods engine.

CHINLEY

If few people had heard of Gowhole and Belle Vue, Chinley, at any rate, was a name known to most since it was the first junction of note outside the Manchester area on the Midland route and was the first stop for most of the London expresses.

In common with other Midland stations, Chinley was a substantial structure with five running lines - the fifth was a down loop which ran round the back of the station - and a bay at the south end from which the occasional Sheffield service departed. The facilities provided for passengers - and most of the patronage came from changing trains - were generous for a place of its size and although the refreshment rooms had been a pre-nationalisation casualty, the scale of the station was of the spaciousness that was the hallmark of the Midland Railway - who would have built a cathedral to serve the needs of a chapel - whilst the waiting rooms were provided with coal fires that were regularly attended. Happily it survived, more or less in its original form, until quite recent times and a cynic might have commented that the only major alteration ever inflicted upon it was the substitution of electric lighting for gas at about the time steam was giving way to diesel.

With a population of only 2,200 it was surprising that Chinley featured as prominently in the timetable as it did, yet all but two of the London trains made a stop whilst some of the Manchester suburban services terminated there. In addition the station played host to the Shef-

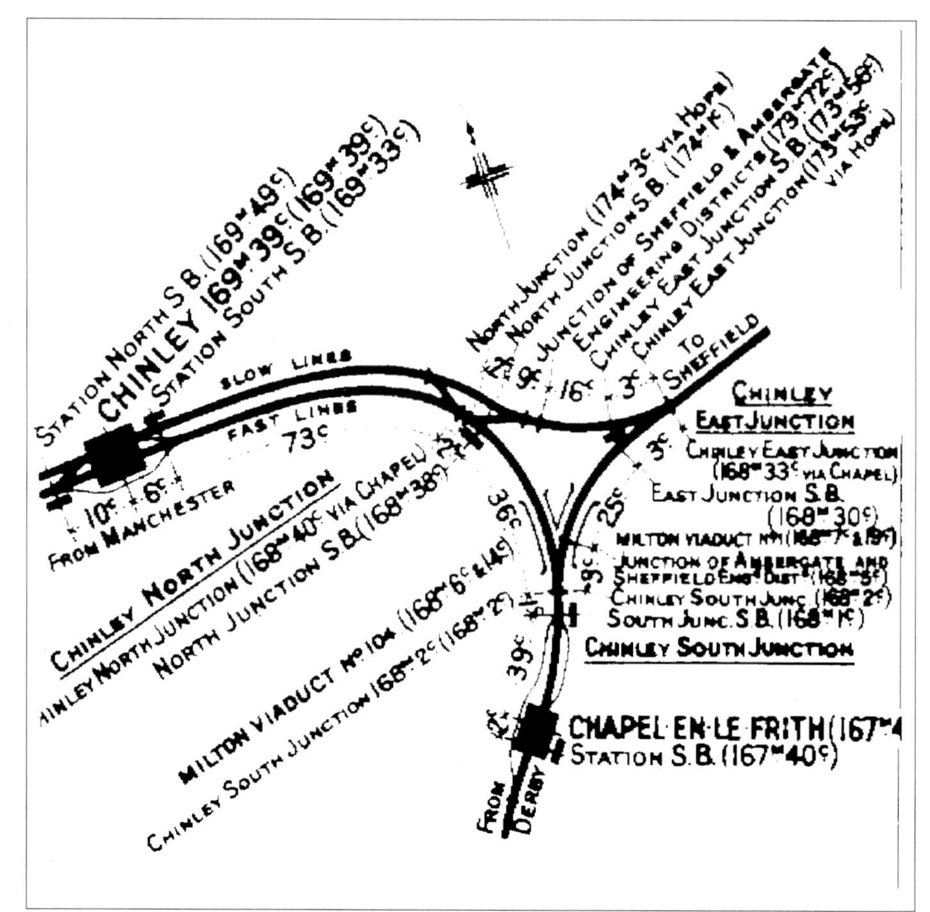

Recently displaced as pride of the line by the new 5XP Jubilee 4-6-0's, compound 1088 finds itself relegated to carriage shunting duties at the north end of Chinley on 29th May 1938. The usual four coach formations used on local trains in the area were ample for most demand and were reasonably easy on the 4-4-0 engines generally used. The complexity of the carriage workings, however, resulting in a considerable amount of balancing which saw trains, such as the one being formed, consisting of eight vehicles which were not only expensive to work but must have cost a fortune in associated shunting movements.

The 2P 4-4-0's led remarkable and long lives as one of the Midland's principal express classes until the arrival of the Stanier 4-6-0's, after which they were relegated to stopping trains for many years until, in 1957, being resurrected as main line locomotives to assist the Jubilee 4-6-0's on the accelerated timings introduced that year. In quieter times, 4th August 1951, 40486 blows off furiously whilst waiting to leave Chinley with an afternoon stopping train for Manchester (Central) via Stockport (Tiviot Dale). The engine was something of a stranger to the district, being allocated to Birmingham (Saltley) and has probably worked into the area by piloting a passenger train from Derby. In later years it was allocated to Bristol from where it was withdrawn in 1957.

In contrast to the usual class J mineral train with its 4F 0-6-0 some of the flows in the district were years ahead of their time and none more so than the I.C.I trains which were based at Tunstead, Peak Forest, and ran to Northwich, Hartford and Wallerscote. Powered by Stanier 8F 2-8-0 locomotives, the trains consisted of 16 fully fitted 43.5-ton hoppers which survived in traffic until recent times. Above, Northwich 8F 48340 approaches Chinley from the south under caution, the brakes being applied in anticipation of a signal stop at the north end of the station. These workings were the envy of other crews who had to put up with the burden of unfitted trains yet it was not until after dieselisation that it came home to the footplatemen of these services how fortunate they had been with the Stanier 8's which, thanks to their magnificent brakes, allowed absolute control of the trains to be maintained even on the most adverse of gradients.

The 10.10 Rotherham (Masboro') - Blackpool North heads north from Chinley on Sunday 29th May 1938 behind almost-new Stanier 5MT 4-6-0 5342.

CHINLEY STATION : 1953(NIGHTS)

Train	Arr	Dep	Destination	Train	Arr	Dep	Destination
20.20 (J) Rowsley	*21.58*	*22.03*	*Heaton Mersey*	*01.45 (F)Gowhole*	*01.58*	*02.00*	*Leeds (Hunslet)*
20.25 (F) Moston		*22/03*	*Rowsley*	*21.16 (F) Garston*		*02/04*	*Rowsley*
21.55 (F) Gowhole		*22/08*	*Avenue*	*22.35 (H) Nottingham*		*02/20*	*Brunswick*
20.08 (J) Grimesthorpe		*22/17*	*Gowhole*	*20.35 (H) Heysham*		*02/25*	*Great Rocks*
21.20 (E) Ancoats		*22/20*	*Rowsley*	*23.38 (H) Moston*		*02/27*	*Rowsley*
21.24 Sheffield	**22.26**			*00.55 (H) Grimesthorpe*		*02/40*	*Gowhole*
21.30 Manchester*	**22.35**			*23.55 (H) Brunswick*		*02/40*	*Derby (Spondon)*
18.40 ST PANCRAS	**22.40**	**22.41**	**MANCHESTER**	*01.35 (E) Rowsley*		*02/41*	*Ancoats*
		22.46	**Manchester***	*02.30 (F) Gowhole*		*02/44*	*Avenue*
		22.46	**Sheffield**	*01.24 (F) Partington Jcn*	*02.53*	*02.55*	*Avenue*
22.0 (D) Tunstead		*22.54*	*Hartford*	*23.30 (F) Beeston*	*TThS*	*02/59*	*Trafford Park*
22.00 (C) Ancoats		*22/56*	*St Pancras*	02.00 Derby (Parcels)		03/08	Manchester*
20.45 (H) Rowsley		*23/01*	*Garston*	*22.55 (F) Walton*		*03/12*	*Sheffield*
21.40 (F) Trafford Park		*23/07*	*Rowsley*	*00.50 (D) Hartford*	*03.15*	*03.17*	*Great Rocks*
19.35 (E) Derby		*23/10*	*Warrington*	*01.10 (J) Avenue*		*03/30*	*Gowhole*
22.17 (Light) T. Park		*23/17*	*Grimesthorpe MPD*	*02.32 (E) Rowsley*		*03/43*	*Brewery*
21.00 (J) Rowsley		*23/23*	*Belle Vue*	*03.45 (H) Gowhole*		*03/57*	*Chesterfield*
23.20 (F) Gowhole		*23/32*	*Blackwell*	*01.30 (F) Garston*		*04/00*	*Kirkby*
22.35 (F) Heaton Mersey		*23/38*	*Rowsley*	*03.00 (H) Rowsley*		*04/10*	*Heaton Mersey*
22.18 (F) Grimesthorpe	*00.01*	*00.06*	*St Helens Jcn*	*02.45 (F) Glazebrook*		*04/17*	*Clay Cross*
23.55 (F) Gowhole		*00/07*	*Staveley*	*21.35 (C) Somers Town*		*04/26*	*Ancoats*
23.35 (J) Tunstead	*TWTh*	*00/15*	*Heysham*	*03.25 (F) Ancoats*		*04/40*	*Rowsley*
22.50 (F) Grimesthorpe		*00/30*	*Walton*	*03.40 (F) Rowsley*		*04/46*	*Ancoats*
20.30 (J) Kirkby		*00/36*	*Ashton Road*	*02.20 (J) Wincobank*		*04/54*	*Gowhole*
12.00 MANCHESTER		**00/40**	**ST PANCRAS**	*04.40 (Light) Tunstead*		*05/03*	*Belle Vue MPD*
21.05 (E) Huskisson		*00/42*	*Rowsley*	*03.05 (J) Avenue*		*05/12*	*Gowhole*
21.10 (J) Avenue		*00/44*	*Gowhole*	*04.05 (f) Rowsley*		*05.14*	*Brindle Heath*
22.40 (H) Ancoats		*00/59*	*Rowsley*	*01.50 (F) Ellesmere Part*		*05/20*	*Rowsley*
23.25 (F) Chesterfield		*01/00*	*Gowhole*	*05.10 (F) Gowhole*		*05/22*	*Avenue*
12.55 (F) Gowhole		*01/10*	*Wincobank*	*04.15 (E) Rowsley*		*05/25*	*Walton*
23.45 (H) Grimesthorpe		*01/30*	*Edge Hill*	*05.30 (F) Gowhole*		*05/41*	*Wincobank*
00.40 (Light) H. Mersey		*01/31*	*Tunstead*	*05.40 (F) Gowhole*		*05/53*	*Rowsley*
21.00 (H) Dundas		*01/40*	*Rowsley*				

** :Trains via Stockport. / : passing time*

field services; an infrequent working of trains most of which consisted of four corridor coaches hauled, usually, by a 2P 4-4-0 which took well over an hour to accomplish the 25 mile journey. There was only one concession to speed and that was the 08.05 from Sheffield Midland which ran non-stop to Hope - fifteen miles in twenty-seven minutes - and then from Chinley to Manchester Central in twenty-six minutes; the fastest working of the day and a minute better than the booked timing for the London trains. Not only was this working quite out of keeping with the rest of the service but it bettered, by a considerable margin, the GC timings at that time of day whose 08.43 and 09.10 departures from Victoria took 99 and 98 minutes to reach Central and London Road respectively.

Curiously there was no return working via Hope and the only express alternative to the 17.22 Manchester - Buxton, which involved a change at Chinley, was the 17.35 ex Central (16.30 Liverpool - Hull) which, with two stops, reached Sheffield Victoria in eighty-seven minutes. Although it was only four miles longer than the GC route - and rather less mountainous - the Midland never seemed to view its Manchester - Sheffield line as much more than a branch and its services rarely reflected the fact it connected two of the most important cities in the north of England. The 08.05 survived as an express until the completion of the GC electrifica-

It was generally reckoned by crews from other railways that nothing could move on the LM until it was blowing off furiously and Stanier 2-8-0 48275 does nothing to counter the allegation. In mitigation the Buxton 8F has been commandeered to take over from a failed 5XP and the fireman is 'getting some rock in' ready for the long slog to Peak Forest. The small driving wheels will ensure time being kept to the summit but the riding thereafter will be lively to say the least. Note the GWR vehicle next to the engine and the Austerity 2-8-0 (also blowing off) on the up slow. Summer 1955.

tion after which it was downgraded to an ordinary stopping service with an extra fifteen minutes being inserted into its schedule.

Prior to the Great War the normal time by a fast train was about 85 minutes although one service, the 13.50 from Manchester, managed the run in seventy minutes inclusive of a stop a Chinley where a section from Liverpool, via Cornbrook Junction, was attached. At that time there were three daily workings from Liverpool to Sheffield and two in the reverse direction. The eastbound trains all left Merseyside in the morning whilst the return services left Sheffield in the evening. Life at Chinley in those days could be quite exciting, especially when London coaches from Manchester Victoria and Liverpool Central had to be attached to a Manchester - St Pancras express in the short period that the express was in the station. Typical of the period were the complications attending the 13.50 from Manchester Central which was allowed no more than five minutes for the attachments. The first part of the drama took place at 13.55 with the arrival of the 13.15 ex Victoria which included, at its head, a through coach from Blackburn (12.15) to London. The train ran into the down slow platform where the St Pancras coach was uncoupled and taken forward by the train engine to wait the arrival of the main section from Manchester Central. Thirteen minutes later the Liverpool train, with its St Pancras coach next to the engine, arrived at 13.55 but ran through the station to reverse into the bay at the south end, the engine uncoupling and running off light to the turntable to prepare for its next working. At 14.21 the express proper ran in on the up main, the engine promptly being uncoupled in order to run across

CHINLEY STATION : 1953 (EARLY)

Train	Arr	Dep	Destination	Train	Arr	Dep	Destination
02.50 (H) Garston		*06/03*	*Staveley*	*09.40 (F) Gowhole*		*09/51*	*Avenue*
05.23 (J) Tunstead		*06/04*	*Northwich*	*18.00 (J) Kettering*		*09/52*	*Cheadle Ex*
01.40 (J) Kirkby		*06/17*	*Gowhole*	*09.00 (H) H. Mersey*		*09/55*	*Rowsley*
03.10 (J) Lt Eaton Jcn		*06/38*	*Gowhole*	*09.47 (D) Tunstead*		*10/23*	*Wallerscote*
04.43 (D)Northwich		*06/42*	*Great Rocks*	*09.20 (E) Rowsley*		*10/30*	*Ancoats*
03.35 (J) Blackwell		*06/43*	*Gowhole*	*10.25 (F) Gowhole*		*10/37*	*Staveley*
02.35 (F) W. Heath		*06/53*	*Brunswick*	*08.00 (J) Avenue*		*10/55*	*Gowhole*
03.29 (H) Hooton		*06/58*	*Kirkby*	*09.05 (F) Walton*	*10.56*	*10.58*	*Clay Cross*
03.35 (J) Carlton	*07.01*	*07.05*	*Trafford Park*	**09.06 NOTTINGHAM**	**11.03**	**11.05**	**LIVERPOOL**
06.00 Sheffield	**07.06**			*10.50 (H) Gowhole*		*11/08*	*Rowsley*
		07.09	**Sheffield**	*09.25 (J) Grimesthorpe*		*11/22*	*Gowhole*
06.05 Manchester*	**07.18**	**07.23**	**Buxton**	*08.45 (D) Wallerscote*		*11/28*	*Great Rocks*
05.00 (F) Widnes		*07/27*	*Rowsley*	*07.25 (J) Kirkby*		*11/32*	*Gowhole*
07.05 Buxton	**07.32**	**07.34**	**Manchester**	*11.25 (F) Gowhole*		*11/36*	*Staveley*
		07.38	**Sheffield**	*11.04 (D) Tunstead*		*11/40*	*Hartford*
04.45 (J) Avenue	*07.40*	*07.42*	*Gowhole*	*00.57 (F) Brent*		*11/50*	*Brunswick*
07.35 (J) Gowhole		*07/48*	*Sheffield*	**10.55 Sheffield**	**12.00**		
02.55 (J) Kirkby		*07/50*	*Gowhole*	**10.50 Manchester***	**12.01**		
07.15 MANCHESTER		**07/51**	**ST PANCRAS**	**11.35 Manchester**	**12.08**	**12.10**	**Nottingham**
05.43 (J) Staveley		*08/05*	*Gowhole*	**10.24 Derby**	**12.12**		
07.02 Sheffield	**08.13**	**08.18**	**Manchester ***			**12.18**	**Sheffield**
07.24 Manchester	**08.16**	**08.19**	**Derby**	*09.55 (J) Grimesthorpe*		*12/19*	*Gowhole*
08.10 (F) Gowhole		*08/23*	*Avenue*	*12.15 (F) Gowhole*		*12/27*	*Blackwell*
08.00 Buxton	**08.25**	**08.28**	**Manchester**	*11.48 Cheadle Ex.*		*12/38*	*Roundwood*
08.05 SHEFFIELD	**08.56**	**08.58**	**MANCHESTER**	**08.15 ST PANCRAS**	**12.39**	**12.41**	**MANCHESTER**
06.20 (D) Hartford		*09/00*	*Great Rocks*	*12.30 (K) Gowhole*	*12.30*		*(To Yard)*
07.10 Derby	**08.54**	**09.05**	**Manchester***			**12.50**	**Manchester***
09.05 (F) Gowhole		*09/18*	*Blackwell*	*10.05 (J) Staveley*		*12/53*	*Gowhole*
04.15 ST PANCRAS		**09/26**	**MANCHESTER**	*10.55 (F) Northwich*		*12/59*	*Great Rocks*
08.25 Manchester*	**09.27**			*12.02 (H) Rowsley*	*13.18*	*13.20*	*Walton*
07.05 (J) Rowsley		*09/27*	*Gowhole*	*13.08 (H) Gowhole*		*13/20*	*Rowsley*
09.00 MANCHESTER	**09.36**	**09.38**	**ST PANCRAS**	*09.15 (H) Walton*		*13/32*	*Rowsley*
09.15 Buxton	**09.37**	**09.39**	**Manchester**	*10.02 (J) Carlton*		*13/35*	*Gowhole*
08.2 Belle Vue		*09/42*	*Kirkby*	*13.28 (H) Gowhole*		*13/40*	*Sheffield*
		09.43	**Sheffield**	**12.35 Sheffield**	**13.41**		
07.20 (J) Staveley		*09/50*	*Gowhole*				

** :Trains via Stockport. / : passing time*

Although nearly twenty years had passed since the Compounds were relegated from pride of place by the Stanier regime, 1953 saw large numbers still at work including 41154 of Trafford Park as it waits for the right-away from Chinley with a slow train for Sheffield. (Further south they continued to have an express working, the 15.40 St Pancras - Leicester being diagrammed for a Compound until 1956). The four coach set in the bay platform waits to form the next day's 07.09 to Sheffield; a Buxton 2P 4-4-0 duty

CHINLEY STATION : 1953 (LATE)

Train	Arr	Dep	Destination	Train	Arr	Dep	Destination
10.15 ST PANCRAS	**14.04**	**14.06**	**MANCHESTER**	**17.24 New Mills**	**17.37**	**17.45**	**Buxton**
(12.30 trip ex Gowhole)		*14.10*	*Chapel en le Frith*	**16.10 Derby**	**17.56**	**17.59**	**Manchester***
13.04 Manchester*	**14.11**			**17.22 Manchester**	**18.00**	**18.02**	**Buxton**
13.45 MANCHESTER	**14.18**	**14.20**	**ST PANCRAS**			**18.05**	**Sheffield**
10.23 (J) Codnor Park		*14/20*	*Agecroft*	**14.15 ST PANCRAS**	**18.08**	**18.10**	**MANCHESTER**
		14.23	**Sheffield**	*13.58 (J) Codnor Park*	*18.15*	*18.17*	*Gowhole*
10.30 (J) Kirkby		*14/29*	*Ashton Road*	**17.50 MANCHESTER**	**18.23**	**18.26**	**ST PANCRAS**
14.06 (D) Tunstead		*14/42*	*Northwich*			**18.31**	**Sheffield**
13.20 (F) Philips Park		*14/42*	*Kirkby*	*18.20 (F) Gowhole*		*18/36*	*Avenue*
11.05 (F) Garston		*14/54*	*Rowsley*	**17.32 Sheffield**	**18.42**	**18.52**	**Manchester***
12.08 (F) Avenue		*15/00*	*Gowhole*	*18.42 (F) Gowhole*		*18/54*	*Wincobank*
13.05 Derby	**15.02**	**15.06**	**Manchester***	*18.10 (D) Tunstead*		*18/54*	*Hartford*
12.40 (D) Hartford		*15/14*	*Great Rocks*	*15.40 (J) Rowsley*	*18.28*	*19.02*	*Trafford Park*
13.10 (J) Avenue		*15/18*	*Gowhole*	**18.00 Sheffield**	**19.13**		
13.24 (J) Rowsley		*15/19*	*Garston*	*17.00 (D) Hartford*		*19/32*	*Great Rocks*
13.50 (H) Philips Park		*15/22*	*Rowsley*	*16.30 (J) Avenue*		*19/35*	*Gowhole*
15.15 (F) Gowhole		*15/29*	*Staveley*	*15.50 (F) Toton*		*19/43*	*Trafford Park*
15.25 (F)Gowhole		*15/37*	*Wincobank*	*19.30 (F) Gowhole*		*19/43*	*Blackwell*
13.05(J) Blackwell		*15/42*	*Gowhole*	**18.45 Sheffield**	**19.57**		
12.30 (J) Walton		*15/46*	*Kirkby*	**18.45 Manchester***	**19.59**		
14.30 (H) Rowsley		*15/55*	*Trafford Park*	*04.35 (J) Corby*	*20.15*	*20.17*	*Glazebrook*
14.50 Manchester*	**15.58**	**16.03**	**Derby**	**19.35 Manchester**	**20.12**	**20.19**	**Derby**
14.10 (J) Wincobank		*16/15*	*Gowhole*	**16.15 ST PANCRAS**	**20.21**	**20.23**	**MANCHESTER**
15.43 (D) Tunstead		*16/19*	*Wallerscote*			**20.26**	**Manchester***
13.17 (F) Garston		*16/30*	*Danesmoor*			**20.27**	**Sheffield**
16.00 MANCHESTER		**16/32**	**ST PANCRAS**	*19.30 (E) Ancoats*		*20/30*	*Rowsley*
14.45 (J) Rowsley		*16/32*	*Gowhole*	*20.14 (J) Peak Forest*		*20/40*	*Gowhole*
14.15 (J) Avenue		*16/37*	*Gowhole*	*19.00 (H) Trafford Pk*		*20/44*	*Rowsley*
03.35 (J) Kettering	*16.46*	*16.48*	*Glazebrook*	*11.55 (H) Chesterfield*		*20/48*	*Cheadle Exchange*
16.25 Buxton	**16.52**	**17.03**	**New Mills**	**19.16 Derby**	**21.04**	**21.07**	**Manchester***
13.17 (J) Kirkby		*17/12*	*Ashton Road*	*18.10 (F) Huskisson*		*21/25*	*Rowsley*
16.03 Manchester*	**17.11**	**17.15**	**Sheffield**	*19.35 (H) Philips Park*		*21/39*	*Rowsley*
17.10 (F) Gowhole		*17/21*	*Avenue*	*18.50 (J) Blackwell*		*21/41*	*Gowhole*
15.30 LIVERPOOL*	**17.20**	**17.22**	**NOTTINGHAM**	*18.50 (F) Halewood*	*21.44*	*21.46*	*Avenue*
14.45 (J) Blackwell		*17/28*	*Gowhole*	*20.10 (J) Rowsley*		*21/50*	*Brindle Heath*
16.30 Sheffield	**17.35**			*19.05 (J) Staveley*		*21/55*	*Gowhole*

to the bay where it coupled to the Liverpool vehicle. Simultaneously the Blackburn coach was reversed onto the Manchester section. The main line engine then drew forward with its Liverpool coach and, as soon as the L&Y locomotive had moved away, backed on to its train, coupled up and, a mere five minutes after it had arrived, was off. Years later when scientific (sic) methods were applied to scheduling with a minute being allowed for the engine being uncoupled, another minute to run forward and so on, the whole thing was declared impossible and such feats disappeared with nationalisation. Impossible or not, they took place day after day in an age when people pulled their weight and took a pride in meeting a challenge.

The Manchester - Derby stopping trains (five down per day and four up) probably added more to the tapestry of the line that to its passenger receipts although it must be remembered that such long-distance 'parliamentary' services (as they were still known on the GN) were run for parcels traffic as much as anything else. A few bags of mail here and a consignment of dogs there helped to make them pay their way and they remained a feature of the route until it closed. Not all of them were local to the line and one, the 11.35 from Central) started from Liverpool Central (10.30) and continued through to Nottingham where it arrived at 14.41. (If this seemed sedate, the alternative was no better, being the 12.30 'express' from London Road which, in spite of its designation, still took all but three hours to reach Nottingham Victoria). Happily the Derby stoppers remained loco-hauled until the end and one remembers catching an example from Manchester early on a Sunday morning during the mid-sixties. Banished to the outside platform nine

The only engines on the Midland given the distinction of names were the 5XP Jubilee's which, appropriately, worked the top services until the late-1950's. It was unusual for anything else to work a St Pancras - Manchester express; the workings normally being divided between Trafford Park and Kentish Town. On this occasion a foreign engine had been slipped into the diagrams as 45594 'Bhophal' of Millhouses runs downhill into Chinley with a train from London in 1953. The authorities at Manchester will have to decide whether to cut the engine out of the working at Manchester and return it to Sheffield on a stopping train or to allow it to remain in the working and send it back to London so that someone else can deal with it.

with its wooden platforms the three coaches were still genuine LMS specimens and, as a reminder of better days, included buttons which invited one to summon a steward. At least one passenger tried to order a coffee in this way but arrived in Derby thirsty.

Some of the stoppers performed the most irritating breaks in their running as passengers from Rowsley to Tiviot Dale discovered if they used the 11.20 (10.24 ex Derby) service which shunted at Chinley for no less than thirty-eight minutes, partly to connect with the 08.15 express from St Pancras but also to clear a way for the many goods trains that needed a path through the station. The distance from Rowsley to Stockport was just over thirty miles yet the journey took more than two hours.

Unfortunately not all the activity at Chinley was recorded in the detail that researchers would wish for and although the volume of traffic on the line was as heavy as any main line, the trains lacked some of the glamour that was evident on other routes in the Manchester periphery and it is a fact of life that enthusiasts in the area tended to be drawn to the magnetic influence of locations such as Crewe or Derby where more prestigious motive power was to be found in greater quantities.

Jubilee's apart, the motive power at Chinley may have been a little on the humdrum side but the variety of trains was a different matter giving the staff, especially those in the signalling environment, plenty to think about with little time in which to reflect before making operating decisions and whilst time spent on the platforms was rewarding enough with an average of one train every seven minutes, a visit to one of the signalboxes was essential to a clear understanding of the effort expended in keeping so many trains on the move.

The key to good signalling - safety being taken as read - was to keep trains moving and with the volume of traffic through Chinley this was not always an easy result to achieve. Even the basics of signalling were made difficult by the number of trains that had to be dealt with and not only did every service have to be formally accepted, signalled and offered on but almost every step in the procedure had to be recorded currently in writing.

It was not necessary for a signalman to know the full description of each train that was offered onto him - its point of origin for example was largely irrelevant - but he had to know where it was going (or which route it was taking) and its speed. Southbound trains coming onto the district at New Mills South would be 'wired forward' by word of mouth over the telephone, the information being expanded by Gowhole Goods Junction who only signalled the slow lines but added a good many trains to the sequence. Buxworth Junction was the first signalbox to have a full picture of what was going on and he would relay this to Chinley Station North who in turn would pass it on. Typical of the style would be a message from Buxworth Junction saying "London up the fast, Kirkby up the goods followed by one for the Dore and Totley...". The recipient would make a note on the back on a cigarette packet, see how the news was likely to effect his local strategies and then pass the information forward to the box in advance. The speed or class of a train would be notified when it was put on the block and anything else that the signalman needed out know would be given to him by the controller. (Drivers were supposed (sic) to give a whistle-code on the approach to certain signalboxes to advise the signalman of the route they were supposed to take. This depended on drivers remembering to whistle, remembering the code and presumed that the signalman had the luxury of the time to listen and be able to distinguish one engine's whistle from another. The notion, which pre-dated the telephone, maintained a number of clerks in employment to keep the lists up to date but performed little else in the way of value).

The regulation of trains was almost always a matter of judgement, decisions being made on

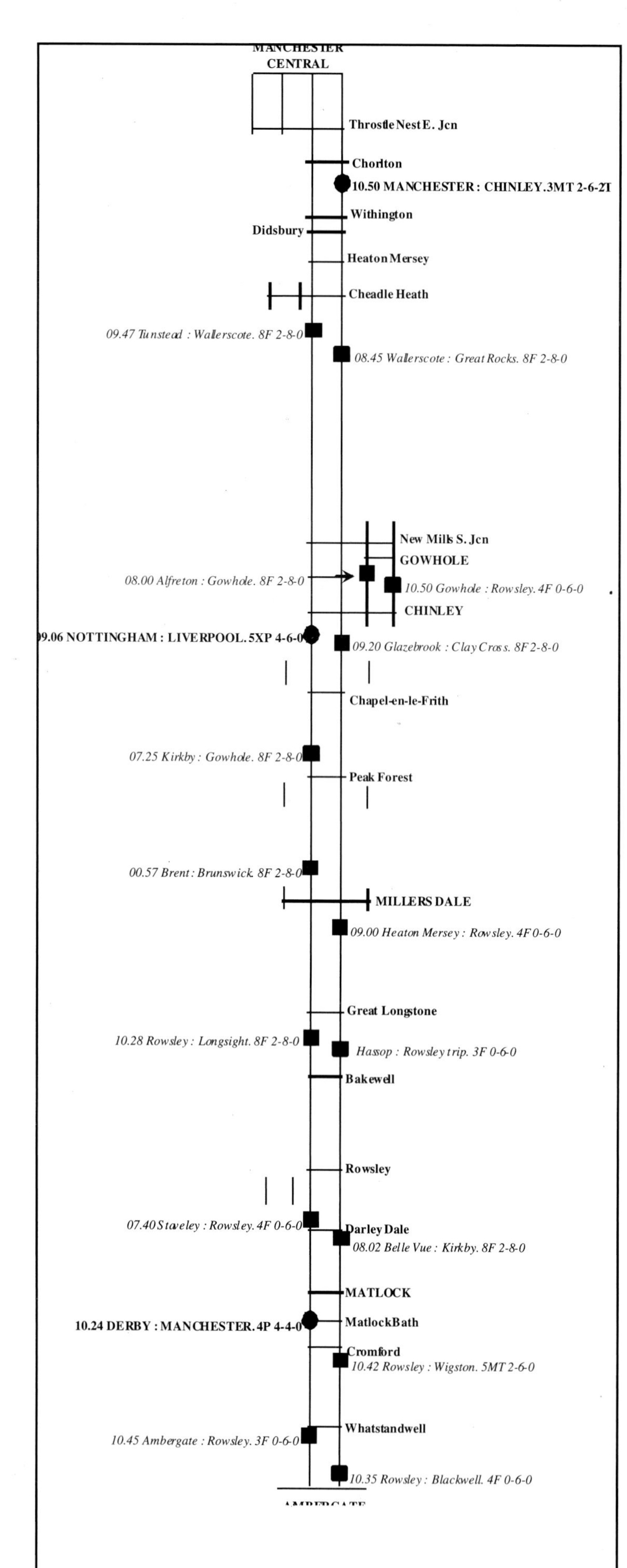

The line situation at 11.00 with the line well occupied by trains. The diagram shows how lightly the section between New Mills and Manchester was used and, apart from the odd gods train which avoided Heaton Mersey by running direct to the CLC via Disley and Cheadle Heath, it was left to the handful of local suburban workings and the London expresses. South of New Mills the situation is very different with a continuous procession of trains in each direction.

the spot. Trains were given a path and a running line in the working timetable but such plans were made on the assumption that everything ran to time. In reality trains from Gowhole heading for the Sheffield district were run on the slow lines with up freight services via Peak Forest coming out on the main line provided they had a sufficient margin ahead of the next passenger train. For example the late turn signalman at Chinley had a gap between booked passenger trains for the Derby line of nearly two hours after the departure of the up Palatine and this was a useful period during which any workings for the Peak Forest direction could be plucked from the queue of Avenue trains waiting to proceed up the Hope Valley and given a run towards Chapel-en-le-Frith.

The nigger in the wood-pile was the handful of goods trains that stopped in the station for relief since any slip-up in the arrangements could block the line for a considerable period of time. A typical case was the 03.35 Iron Ore from Glendon to Glazebrook for which a set of Heaton Mersey men travelled to Chinley, relieving the train in the platform. Although it could not always be avoided, it was not a good idea to schedule trains to be relieved away from a motive power depot since it rendered trains vulnerable to delay and the service to blockage when things went wrong.

Under normal circumstances the Heaton Mersey men would sign on and travel to Chinley by the 14.50 ex Manchester. On reaching their destination they would report to the inspector who would find out where the train was and remind the signalman that it was to be relieved in the station.

When everything ran to time there was usually little to worry about but one had to be on guard for the unexpected. For example the relief controller might decide to use the Heaton Mersey men to conduct a special freight from Heaton Mersey to the south, conducting it as far as New Mills South but continuing with it as far as Chinley to take up their booked working. On paper the special would have plenty of time to get to Chinley in time for the Heaton Mersey men to relieve the Glazebrook service but, the laws of perversity being what they are, the special would probably sit at New Mills South for an age waiting for a path and then be pushed up the slow line behind a queue of trains for Gowhole and the Dore road.

In the meantime the Glazebrook would be enjoying a good run over the Peak, romping into Chinley well ahead of time and coming to a stand with the expectation of being relieved immediately whilst in reality the crew to take it forward were still the wrong side of Gowhole, presuming that someone, somewhere, was taking care of things.

The inward crew, anxious to have a brew before returning south as passengers on the 15.30 Liverpool - Nottingham, would ask the signalman where their relief had gone to and the signalman in turn, not being either required or expected to know the details of crewing diagrams, would ask control what was happening. The controller would ask the relief controller who would reply that they were conducting the 3.30pm Heaton Mersey - Corby special to New

Another foreign Jubilee - 45562 'Alberta' of Leeds (Holbeck) - lopes into the station with an express from London on 19th April 1954. Midland engines rarely shone with cleanliness but the Jubilee's invariably exhibited an oily green appearance sufficient to show their express passenger status. 45562, however, looks as though a good clean would do it no harm.

Although normally a quiet location from the point of view of passenger services, there were several times a day when the coincidence of connecting passenger trains gave Chinley an air of bustle as in this mid-1950's scene with BR5 4-6-0 73013 waiting on the down slow line at the head of a Sheffield service as Stanier 4MT tank 42466 arrives with a local service from Manchester (Central) via Cheadle Heath. A down train for Manchester stands in the down fast platform. To assist with the transfer of connecting passengers and to prevent them having to climb the overbridge, up Sheffield services were permitted to start from the down platforms. It might be thought that with the numbers of Stanier Black 5's available, the Midland would have had sufficient 5MT locomotives for its needs but the line accepted the new standard 5MT's in considerable numbers which, if regarded as having less 'punch' than the Stanier engines, did nothing to lessen the variety of motive power to be seen in the area.

Mills and were probably fast asleep in Chinley buffet. Meanwhile the Glazebrook train, whose Derby crew were not prepared to work forward and in any case only knew the road as far as Cheadle, simmered away on the down fast with no-one to work it and completely blocking the down main until its crew belatedly arrived (wondering, in all innocence, what had been done with the train they were supposed to relieve...).

Such things could happen and more than occasionally did.

It might be fairly asked why signalmen were not expected to take an active role in the organisation of railway matters - such as crew relief - and the simple answer is that at a busy box they had quite enough to do as it was and to add to their workload would be to place an unreasonable burden of responsibility upon them. Their primary role was the safety of trains and to give them concerns that diverted attention from this aspect could have prejudiced the very high record of safety that the railways had. (It should be added that in addition to signalling trains signalman were also required to watch them as they passed, alert for any signs of danger and, above all, to ensure that the train was complete and had not become divided. This factor alone limited the amount of time signalmen at busy locations had for additional responsibilities).

After the closure of the smaller control rooms such as Gowhole and Rowsley, a number of section controllers were based in key signalboxes in order to act as a coordinator between the traditional control structure and the outside world. For some reason the Midland was the only part of BR which adopted this approach.

Locomotive facilities at Chinley were rather basic and consisted of little more than a turntable and water columns together with a small ash pit for any fireman who felt energetic enough to use it during turn-round times. As in the case of Gowhole, Chinley had no shed or engine allocation and power for its trains were provided in the main by back workings of inward services or, for starting turns, engines which ran light from Buxton, twelve miles to the south. Needless to say, if a passenger engine was declared a failure on arrival at Chinley, some pretty urgent thinking was required by the district controller in order to find a substitute.

A mile south of the station the Sheffield and Derby lines parted company and it was always a dramatic experience to rush through Chinley and round the broad curve at the junction where the Sheffield line diverged and, a minute later, the south curve line came in; both lines being supported by very impressive viaducts.

Interesting though it might have been for the observer, traffic working between Chinley and the North Junction was a serious business and a close eye had to be kept on the approach of trains, especially those from the north, since misjudgement could cause problems which would take some time to rectify. As a general rule goods traffic for the Sheffield lines used the slow lines whilst Derby trains took the fast but since most of the passenger trains were booked to run over the slow line between the North Junction and Chinley station, there were often times when the signalmen at either end had to extemporise. The worst problems could be caused by mineral trains for Rowsley from the north which approached Chinley on the up slow line at a time when the up fast was occupied by passenger trains. To hold the train until a path became available on the up main was not always wise since it would effectively block the slow line for everything in its wake whilst sending it forward to Chinley North Junction would merely transfer the problem a mile to the south. Equally bringing the train out onto the main line meant obstructing the down slow for five or more minutes whilst the train crawled across te layout plus a measure of negotiation with the boxes up the line. (Bringing a steam-hauled mineral train off one line and across another was always an unpredictable business. Some would walk across without any problem whilst another would take an eternity). A margin of twenty-five minutes was needed to clear a class J train from Chinley to Peak Forest - if the weather was clear and the engine steaming well - and if that was not available it could only be run as far as the goods line at Chapel-en-le-Frith provided, of course, that there was room to accept it. Decisions of this sort were made continuously and any delay - especially that which reacted back onto passenger trains - aris-

In 1957 the Midland's passenger services received their first substantial acceleration since the war; a step which produced timings which were at the very limits of Jubilee haulage. Initial thoughts on their replacement brought the interesting possibilities of West Country light Pacifics and Gresley V2 locomotives working between Manchester and St Pancras but in the event the authorities elected to transfer a number of 7P Royal Scot 4-6-0's from LNWR sheds; the largest passenger engines seen on the line up to that time. The number of Royal Scot's available proved insufficient for the Midland's needs and in June 1958 six Britannia Pacifics (2 from Stewarts Lane, 3 from Canton and 1 from Stratford) were sent to Trafford Park to work between Manchester and St Pancras. One of the former SR locomotives. 70014 'Iron Duke' is seen at Chinley on an express for London shortly after its arrival from Stewarts Lane. The engine had a chequered career at Manchester, parting from its tender at speed near Cheadle Heath on one occasion and, on another, spending some time in the Bridgewater canal after 'getting away from its crew' at Trafford Park MPD. The pacifics produced a good deal of useful work on the Midland but were unsuited to the Derby - Manchester section. The curves between Ambergate and Chinley caused loosening of the joints between their smokeboxes and saddles with the result that the Pacifics were moved to other parts of the region; Royal Scots returning to the line until dieselisation in 1962.

Reduced in circumstance but still in steam 5XP 4-6-0 45565 'Victoria' pulls away from Chinley in 1962 with the 18.55 Chinley to Manchester. By the time of the photograph steam was fast being displaced from the Midland express workings although the Jubilee's continued to work some of the Buxton and Sheffield trains for another three years.

A Stanier 8F 2-8-0 clanks cautiously through Chinley station on the down slow line with the 13.17 Kirkby - Ashton Road) class J coal train during the long summer of 1959.

ing from misjudgement was liable to result in the receipt of a critical letter (a 'please explain') with the possibility of an uncomfortable fifteen minutes in front of the Station Master.

The problems involved with keeping traffic on the move at Chinley were countless yet to the bystander it seemed to work like a well oiled machine; something that was a compliment to those who worked on the line. It was a fascinating location to work at but it was an equally rewarding place to simply sit and watch the railway go by. Train after train would struggle through on the slow line, long hauls of wagons moving up the hill at about 20 mph behind a Garratt or 8F 2-8-0 from Gowhole or somewhere in the Manchester area to the North Erewash Valley with almost equally long strings of loaded coal in the opposite direction, buffers ringing and engines clanking slowly through the station, hopeful of a clear run.

On the fast lines it was occasionally possible to return a generation to the past as was the case when a Sheffield train arrived behind a 2P 4-4-0 just as a Derby slow was running into the station behind a Midland Compound. More modern times were reflected in the London trains which appeared more or less hourly in one direction or the other, usually behind a Jubilee 4-6-0 which, thanks to the cyclic diagramming the LMS had adopted, might come from almost any shed on the system.

A visit today brings a lump to the throat for, although the station (just) remains the handsome expresses between Manchester and St Pancras finished years ago as did the heavy mineral traffic to and from Hasland, Kirkby and Sheffield. The Sheffield line remains however although an unholy union has been created between the Midland route and the LNWR Buxton branch from Stockport which has resulted in the return of the CLC Liverpool - Sheffield trains. Alas, however, these services are but ghost trains formed of soulless railcars and make a detour via Manchester. It is all very sad.

A mile south of Chinley station, the slow lines diverged from the Derby main line at Chinley North Junction, running to Sheffield via Hathersage. In addition to a rather desultory passenger service - enlivened by the use of 2P 4-4-0's throughout the 1950's - the Hope Valley carried a very heavy service of goods trains from Avenue sidings and Staveley in the North Derbyshire coalfield. Garrett 2-6-6-2 locomotives from Hasland MPD were the regular engines for the Avenue trains and most of the class could be seen from the platforms of Chinley. Above, 5MT 44662 of Leeds (Holbeck) deputises for a Jubilee with a Manchester - London train on 17th July 1955. The pub survives unto this day.

PEAK FOREST

CHINLEY N.JCN - BUXTON JUNCTION

Although it is 5th March 1961 and most local trains in the country have been taken over by multiple-units, it is still possible to travel from Chinley in a passenger train behind a 4F 0-6-0. 44212 of Grimesthorpe passes Chinley East Junction with a Sunday evening stopping train for Sheffeld (Midland).

Although the line had been climbing steeply since Cheadle Heath, the really mountainous section of the route started at the Chinley South Junction where the Sheffield branched trailed in to join the double-tracked mainline from Manchester for the climb up to Peak Forest summit. Traffic - all of it freight - leaving the Sheffield line for the south was nothing like as heavy as that which ran towards Gowhole and consisted of five trains in each direction and although they added insufficient traffic to warrant any additional running lines on a grand scale, up and down goods lines were provided between the junction and Chapel-en-le-Frith to allow some scope for regulation before they started the worst of the climb to the summit.

In view of the difficulties involved in getting freight trains up the hill and to ease the congestion that accompanied the heavy flow of traffic coming southwards from Gowhole and the north, permissive block signalling was authorised for the Chapel-en-le Frith goods line - which usually , and inaccurately, referred to as 'the loop' - to allowed goods trains to queue up behind one another within the capacity of the line.

The difference goods lines, loops and slow lines often causes confusion - in some minds they are one and the same thing - and a word or two of explanation may not be out of place

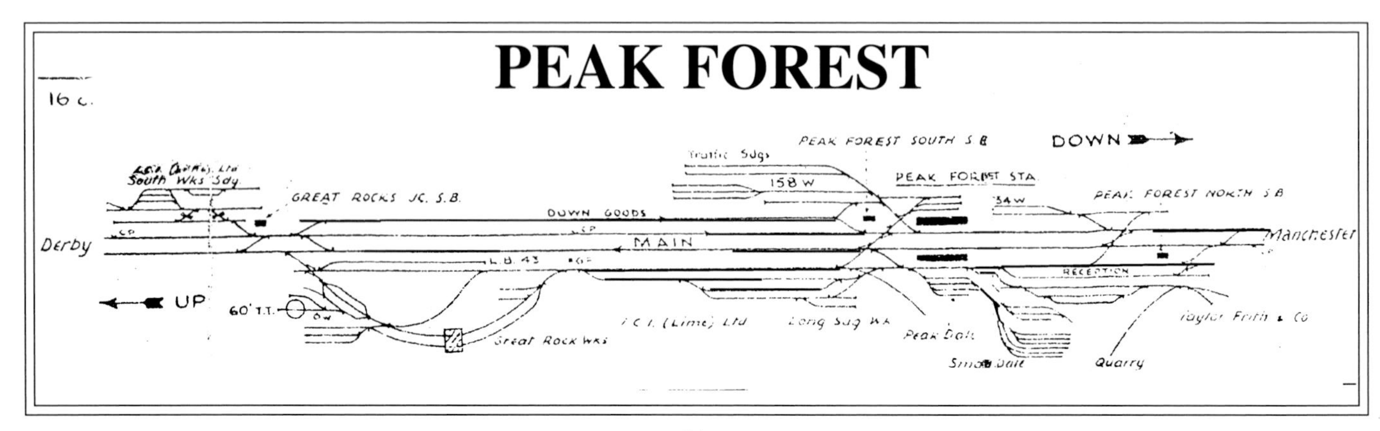

PASSENGER SERVICES : CHAPEL-EN-LE-FRITH (1953)

Train	Central	South	Destination
07.09 Buxton		07.20	Manchester (LR) 08.13
07.05 Buxton	07.27		Manchester (C) 08.08
06.05 Manchester (C)	07.31		Buxton 08.10
07.30 Buxton		07.41	Manchester (LR) 08.29
07.50 Buxton		07.59	Manchester (LR) 08.45
08.00 Buxton	08.20		Manchester (C) 09.0
07.24 Manchester (C)	08.26		Derby 10.03
07.27 Manchester (LR)		08.28	Buxton 08.45
08.34 Buxton		08.45	Manchester (LR) 09.32
07.10 Derby	08.49		Manchester (C) 10.06
09.05 Buxton		09.14	Manchester (LR) 09.48
09.15 Buxton	09.33		Manchester (C) 10.09
09.00 Manchester (LR)		10.04	Buxton 10.21
10.30 Buxton		10.41	Manchester (LR) 11.28
10.24 Derby	12.07		Chinley 12.12
11.35 Manchester (C)	12.18		Nottingham 14.41
12.10 Manchester (LR)		13.09	Buxton 13.24
13.10 Buxton		13.21	Manchester (LR) 14.17
13.05 Derby	14.57		Manchester (C) 16.07
14.50 Manchester (C)	16.10		Derby 18.24
16.29 Buxton		16.40	M'ter (Mayfield) 17.37
16.25 Buxton	16.47		New Mills 17.12
16.00 Manchester (LR)		16.57	Buxton 17.06
16.45 Manchester (LR)		17.29	Buxton 17.43
15.30 Liverpool (C)	17.30		Nottingham 19.29
17.40 Buxton		17.51	Manchester (LR) 18.49
16.10 Derby	17.51		Manchester (C) 18.59
17.24 New Mills	17.53		Buxton 18.18
17.05 Manchester (LR)		18.01	Buxton 18.16
17.22 Manchester (C)	18.10		Buxton 18.33
17.50 Manchester (LR)		18.47	Buxton 19.02
18.40 Buxton		18.51	Manchester (LR) 19.45
18.20 Manchester (LR)		19.15	Buxton 19.30
19.00 Manchester (LR)		19.59	Buxton 20.13
19.35 Manchester (C)	20.27		Derby 21.58
19.16 Derby	20.59		Manchester (C) 22.07
20.20 Manchester (LR)		21.17	Buxton 21.32
21.45 Buxton		21.56	Manchester (LR) 22.50
21.06 Manchester (LR)		22.03	Buxton 22.18
22.37 Manchester (LR)		23.38	Buxton 23.53

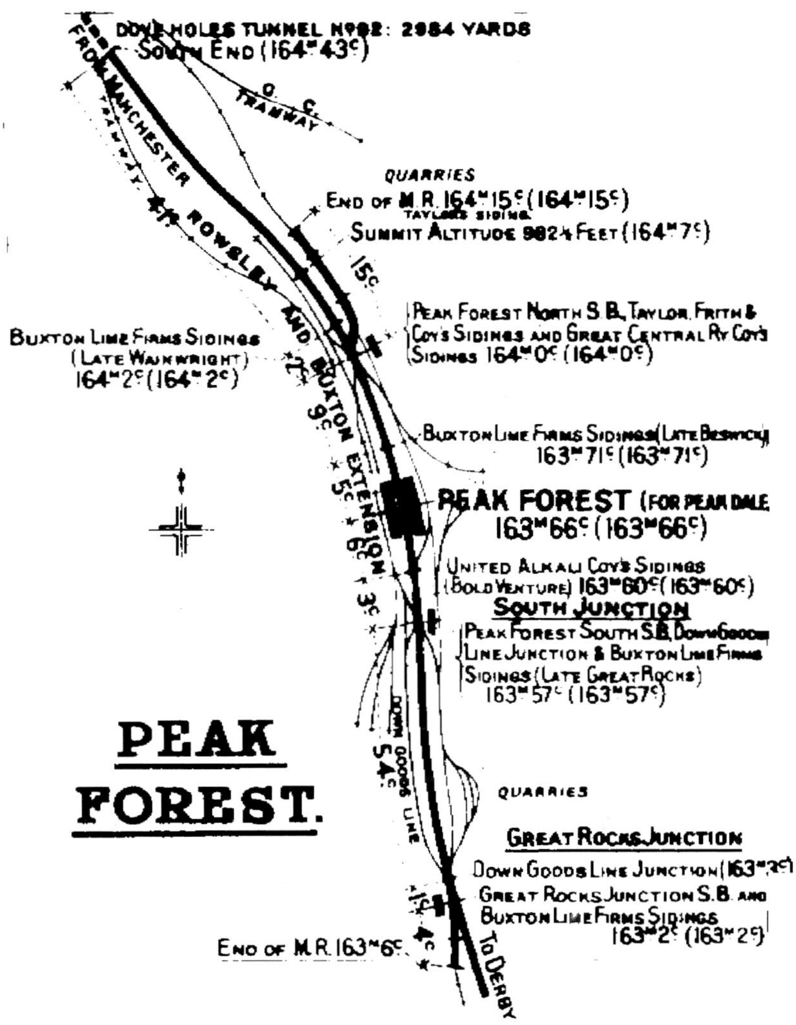

since the difference between them was fundamental.

A loop was a section of line where the entrance and exit was controlled by the same signalbox whereas a line was an extended loop where beginning and end was controlled by separate signalboxes, the line being operated under strict signalling principals.

Whether a loop or line was for goods, passenger or both depended upon the signalling which, in turn, reflected the use to which it was likely to be put and very often, a goods loop/line would be signalled permissively so that more than one train could use it at the same time. A slow line, which could be used by both passenger and goods trains, would be signalled under the absolute block arrangements in which only one train could be accepted in each block section. Passenger loops or lines were usually found in major through stations and were often signalled under the permissive arrangement, especially in the case of very long platforms where two or more passenger trains had to be accommodated.

As trains climbed towards Dove Holes and Peak Forest, it was possible to catch an occasional glimpse of the LNWR's Buxton branch which crossed the Midland twice, once on the short tunnel to the north of Dove Holes signalbox and again over Dove Holes tunnel itself.

Although depicted in the public timetable as a purely local line between London Road, Manchester, and Buxton, the line was actually a freight route of some importance and carried a steady flow of 7F and 8F worked services running from the LNWR yards around Stockport to Rowsley. Trains had to be banked from Stockport and it is believed that the Buxton line was the longest section of line upon which trains were assisted in this manner. It was also the route that the Midland had originally aspired to use and one wonders what sort of motive power would have been needed to drag the nine or so coaches of their expresses up the bank from Stockport to Buxton.

Under any ordinary circumstance Chapel-en-le-Frith with its population of only 6,000 would only just have warranted one railway station but thanks to the reluctance of the LNWR to reach an agreement with the Midland, it ended up with two; each of the companies having their own.

The LNWR or South station, which survived the Beeching era, was situated some distance from the town centre and at the top of a steep hill and was not therefore particularly convenient for passengers travelling either to Manchester or Buxton. The Midland station was the more centrally located of the two although the LNWR gave the better service of the two especially during the rush hour when it provided four services to Manchester, each taking about three quarters of an hour plus an express, taking only 34 minutes, for those who started work at ten. (For some unfathomable reason the return working of the express - the 17.40 from Manchester - ran non-stop between Whaley Bridge and Buxton, missing

DOVE HOLES TUNNEL (NORTH) : 1953 (NIGHTS)

Train	*Down*	*Up*	*Destination*
21.00 Belle Vue MPD		*22/04*	*Great Rocks*
20.45 (H) Rowsley	*22/08*		*Garston*
20.25 (F) Moston		*22/14*	*Rowsley*
18.40 ST PANCRAS	**22/35**		**MANCHESTER**
22.00 (D) Tunstead	*22/42*		*Hartford*
21.20 (E) Ancoats		*22/46*	*Rowsley*
21.00 (J) Rowsley	*23/07*		*Belle Vue*
22.00 (C) Ancoats		*23/15*	*St Pancras*
21.40 (F) Trafford Park		*23/25*	*Rowsley*
22.35 (F) Heaton Mersey		*23/52*	*Rowsley*
23.35 (J) Tunstead (TWTh)	*23/56*		*Heysham*
20.30 (J) Kirkby	*00/16*		*Ashton Road*
00.00 MANCHESTER		**00/45**	**ST PANCRAS**
21.05 (E) Huskisson		*01/02*	*Rowsley*
22.40 (H) Ancoats		*01/12*	*Rowsley*
21.00 (H) Dundas		*01/57*	*Rowsley*
22.35 (H) Nottingham	*02/12*		*Brunswick*
21.16 (F) Garston		*02/25*	*Rowsley*
01.35 (E) Rowsley	*02/34*		*Ancoats*
20.35 (H) Heysham		*02/37*	*Great Rocks*
23.55 (H) Brunswick		*02/52*	*Derby (Spondon)*
02.02 DERBY (pcls)	**03/02**		**MANCHESTER**
23.38 (H) Moston		*03/05*	*Rowsley*
00.50 (D) Hartford		*03/27*	*Great Rocks*
02.32 (E) Rowsley	*03/32*		*Brewery*
03.00 (H) Rowsley	*04/02*		*Heaton Mersey*
01.30 (H) Garston		*04/17*	*Kirkby*
03.30 (J) Buxton	*04/29*		*Sheffield*
03.40 (F) Rowsley	*04/39*		*Ancoats*
04.40 (Light) Tunstead	*04/52*		*Belle Vue*
04.05 (F) Rowsley	*05/07*		*Brindle Heath*
03.25 (F) Ashton Road		*05/10*	*Rowsley*
04.15 (E) Rowsley	*05/17*		*Walton*
01.50 (F) Ellesmere Port		*05/36*	*Rowsley*
05.23 (J) Tunstead	*05/48*		*Northwich*
01.40 (J) Kirkby	*05/54*		*Gowhole*

DOVE HOLES TUNNEL (NORTH) : 1953(EARLY)			
Train	Down	Up	Destination
05.40 (F) Gowhole		06/04	Rowsley
0325 (J) Grimesthorpe		06/20	Buxton
03.10 (J) Little Eaton Jcn	06/22		Gowhole
02.55 (F) Washwood Heath	06/38		Brunswick
03.43 (D) Northwich		06/53	Great Rocks
03.29 (H) Hooton		07/10	Kirkby
07.05 BUXTON	**07/21**		**MANCHESTER**
06.05 MANCHESTER		**07/34**	**BUXTON**
02.55 (J) Kirkby	07/36		Gowhole
07.15 MANCHESTER		**07/55**	**ST PANCRAS**
18.00 (J) Kettering	08/01		Glazebrook
08.00 BUXTON	**08/16**		**MANCHESTER**
07.24 MANCHESTER		**08/29**	**DERBY**
05.00 (F) Widnes		08/40	Rowsley
07.10 DERBY	**08/46**		**MANCHESTER**
07.05 (J) Rowsley	08/59		Gowhole
06.20 (D) Hartford		09/11	Great Rocks
04.15 ST PANCRAS	**09/18**		**MANCHESTER**
09.15 BUXTON	**09/29**		**MANCHESTER**
09.00 MANCHESTER		**09/44**	**ST PANCRAS**
08.05 (J) Buxton	09/54		Sheffield
08.2 (H) Belle Vue		09/54	Kirkby
09.00 (H) Heaton Mersey		10/07	Rowsley
09.47 (D) Tunstead	10/12		Wallerscote
09.22 (E) Rowsley	10/22		Ancoats
09.06 NOTTINGHAM	**10/54**		**LIVERPOOL**
07.25 (J) Kirkby	11/10		Gowhole
10.50 (H) Gowhole		11/25	Rowsley
11.04 (D) Tunstead	11/29		Hartford
00.57 (F) Brent	11/39		Brunswick
08.45 (D) Wallerscote		11/40	Great Rocks
10.24 DERBY	**12/03**		**CHINLEY**
11.35 MANCHESTER		**12/21**	**NOTTINGHAM**
08.15 ST PANCRAS	**12/30**		**MANCHESTER**
12.02 (H) Rowsley	13/08		Walton
10.55 (F) Northwich		13/15	Great Rocks
10.23 (J) Codnor Park	13/32		Agecroft
13.08 (H) Gowhole		13/32	Rowsley
09.15 (H) Walton		13/45	Rowsley
10.15 ST PANCRAS	**13/55**		**MANCHESTER**
11.18 (J) Grimesthorpe		13/57	Buxton

Chapel-en-le-Frith giving commuters something of an unbalanced day although for those who worked very short hours there was a 16.45 departure from London Road which made limited stops and reached Chapel in 44 minutes).

The Midland services were less frequent, there were only two rush hour trains in the morning - each taking about forty minutes to reach Manchester Central - whilst the evening service back was worse with trains at 16.32 and 17.22 and nothing else until the late evening Derby slow.

On the other hand the Midland trains were, from the enthusiasts point of view, markedly more interesting than those of the LNW which, day in day out, were handled by commonplace 2-6-4 tanks which could be seen almost anywhere. On the Midland, motive power was far less predictable and ranged from Compound 4-4-0's to Jubilee's with the possibility, from the early 1950's, of one of the new BR standard 5MT 4-6-0's.

From the operators perspective passenger trains were viewed with mixed feelings. Dealing with express passenger trains gave one a sense of being part of an first-division system - a train that ran to or from London conveyed a certain status - whilst at the same time they played havoc with the general flow of goods traffic. A St Pancras express leaving Manchester was heralded by goods trains being shunted away from the up main for miles ahead which was something of a nuisance when you wanted goods trains to run to Rowsley or Peak Forest as quickly as possible so that their crews would have no excuse not to work back. It was especially irritating when traffic for miles around had to be recessed for the sake of a three-coach stopping train whose passenger complement probably did not exceed the vehicles making up the train. On the other hand the mixed timetable provided an interesting challenge in trying to run passenger trains punctually with the minimum of disruption to other trains although if things went wrong and a passenger train was delayed there was the devil of a row afterwards at the inquest.

Up through trains coming onto the mainline at New Mills South were allowed about three-quarters of an hour to get to the summit at Peak Forest - there was no banking in the up direction - and it sometimes came as a surprise to be reminded that the distance was only eight and a half miles. On a bad night with a wet rail the allowance simply became apocryphal as engines slogged and slipped their way up the bank running at average speeds that didn't even approach double figures whilst the district controller would be staring at the trains represented on his peg board, willing them to clear the section ahead so that they could get to Rowsley in time to work a return load.

Ulcerous as it could be for the district control, for the train crew it could be a nightmare in all kinds of weather and typically a crew on an unfitted train would pull out of Gowhole, creep up the slow line behind a queue of Erewash trains only to find that by the time they should have been passing Millers Dale they were being 'put in' (i.e. run from main to goods) at Chinley South Junction, the subsidiary signal advising them that they were following another goods train on the same line in the same section.

DOVE HOLES TUNNEL (NORTH) : 1953(LATE)			
Train	Down	Up	Destination
10.30 (J) Kirkby	14/11		Ashton Road
13.45 MANCHESTER		**14/26**	**ST PANCRAS**
14.06 (D) Tunstead	14/31		Northwich
13.05 DERBY	**14/53**		**MANCHESTER**
13.20 (F) Philips Park		15/00	Kirkby
13.24 (J) Rowsley	15/05		Garston
11.05 (F) Garston		15/10	Rowsley
12.40 (D) Hartford		15/23	Great Rocks
13.50 (J) Buxton	15/32		Wincobank
13.50 (H) Philips Park		15/34	Rowsley
14.30 (H) Rowsley	15/42		Trafford Park
15.36 (J) Chapel		15/44	Peak Forest
12.30 (J) Walton		15/58	Kirkby
15.43 (D) Tunstead	16/08		Wallerscote
14.50 MANCHESTER		**16/14**	**DERBY**
14.45 (J) Rowsley	16/16		Gowhole
03.35 (J) Kettering	16/26		Glazebrook
16.00 MANCHESTER		**16/37**	**ST PANCRAS**
16.25 BUXTON	**16/41**		**NEW MILLS**
13.17 (J) Kirkby	16/56		Ashton Road
15.40 (J) Rowsley	17/07		Trafford Park
15.30 LIVERPOOL		**17/34**	**NOTTINGHAM**
15.03 (H) Grimesthorpe		17/44	Peak Forest
16.10 DERBY	**17/47**		**MANCHESTER**
17.24 NEW MILLS		**17/57**	**BUXTON**
14.15 ST PANCRAS	**17/59**		**MANCHESTER**
17.22 MANCHESTER		**18/14**	**BUXTON**
17.50 MANCHESTER		**18/32**	**ST PANCRAS**
18.10 (D) Tunstead	18/35		Hartford
18.55 (J) Peak Forest	19/08		Wincobank
16.23 (J) Grimesthorpe		19/21	Buxton
17.00 (D) Hartford		19/41	Great Rocks
04.35 (J) Corby	19/49		Glazebrook
16.15 ST PANCRAS	**20/12**		**MANCHESTER**
20.14 (J) Peak Forest	20/27		Gowhole
19.35 MANCHESTER		**20/31**	**DERBY**
19.30 (E) Ancoats		20/41	Rowsley
19.16 DERBY	**20/54**		**MANCHESTER**
19.00 (H) Trafford Park		20/56	Rowsley
20.10 (J) Rowsley	21/32		Brindle Heath
18.10 (F) Huskisson		21/36	Rowsley
20.20 (J) Rowsley	21/43		Heaton Mersey
19.35 (H) Philips Park		21/51	Rowsley

At times like this the crew of this most humble of trains would have to exercise talent of a kind that no top-link express driver was ever called upon to use and that was to control the speed of an unbraked train of many hundred tons weight in such a way that it (just) kept on the move but could be stopped at a moments notice.

On a falling gradient maintaining a walking pace with an unfitted train in order to stop without much in the way of notice called for an

TRAFFIC MOVEMENTS : PEAK FOREST (1953): MORNINGS				
Train	Arr	Yard	Dep	Destination
		P.Forest	00.32	LE Rowsley
21.30 (F) Chaddesden MWFO	00.20	Tunstead		
		Tunstead	01.50	LE Derby MPD (TThSO)
00.40 LE Heaton Mersey MPD	02.00	Gt Rocks		
20.35 (H) Heysham	02.58	Gt Rocks		
00.50 (D) Hartford	03.55	Gt Rocks		
03.30 LE ex Buxton MPD (78 trip)	04.08	P. Forest Sth		
		Gt Rocks	04.40	LE Belle Vue MPD
		P. Forest	04.50	LE Tunstead (78 trip)
04.50 LE Peak Forest (78 trip)	04.55	Tunstead		
		Tunstead	05.23	Northwich (J)
		P.Forest	05.53	LE Rowsley
05.25 LE ex Buxton MPD (79 trip)	05.55			
04.43 (D) Northwich	07.10	Gt Rocks		
		P. Forest	07.54	Two LE's Rowsley
		P.Forest	09.15	LE Tunstead (78 trip)
06.20 (D) Hartford	09.26	Gt Rocks		
		P. Forest	09.40	Two LE's Rowsley
		Tunstead	09.47	Wallerscote (D)
		Gt Rocks	10.12	LE Tunstead
10.12 LE ex Gt Rocks	10.17	Tunstead		
		P. Forest	10.32	Peak Forest Jcn (J): 78 trip
10.32 (J) Peak Forest (78 trip)	10.40	P. F. Jcn		
		P. Forest	10.50	LE Tunstead (79 trip)
10.50 LE ex P. Forest (79 trip)	10.56	Tunstead		
		Tunstead	11.04	Hartford (D)
08.45 (D) Wallerscote	12.00	Gt Rocks		

especially reliable engine brake - such as that of the Stanier 8F - years of skill and a guard who could read the drivers mind. On a rising track such as the goods line at Chapel-en-le-Frith it was just as difficult except that one was balancing the effects of gravity with the inertia of the train, the trick being to reduce steam gradually until the train came to a stand at which time the brake would be applied. It was then necessary to ease back a little - without sending the train into reverse - in order to pick up the couplings so that when the time came to start, the engine could take up the strain gradually and not attempt to lift the entire train at one go.

It was all very tricky and never more so than in goods lines worked under the permissive arrangement which allowed goods trains to queue up, one behind the other. The idea was to creep up the line until the lights on the brakevan of the train ahead came into sight and to pull up just short of it

After a wait of some time a passenger train would rattle by and with a quiet lurch the goods in advance would follow it, the next train in line carefully proceeding down to the exit signal to wait its turn to come out onto the up main. Another passenger would roar by and after it had cleared the block section ahead to Dove Holes the signal would come off and the goods would crawl out onto the main and, taking the greatest care to keep the wagon couplings taut in order to prevent a divided train, would attempt to make the best speed possible - which, given the weight of the train and the 1/90 gradient, would probably yield second place to a competent cyclist.

TRAFFIC MOVEMENTS : PEAK FOREST (1953): AFTERNOON

Train	Arr	Yard	Dep	Destination
		P. Forest Jcn	12.01	P. Forest Sth (J) : 78 trip
		P. Forest	*12.03*	*LE Rowsley*
		P. Forest	12.32	LE Tunstead (79 trip)
12.32 LE ex P. Forest (79 trip)	*12.40*	*Tunstead*		
10.55 (F) Nothwich	13.37	Gt Rocks		
		Tunstead	14.06	Northwich (D)
11.33 (K) Rowsley	15.10	P. Forest Jcn		(Fwd at 15.30)
		P. Forest	*15.27*	*3 LE's Rowsley*
		P. Forest Jcn	15.30	Gt Rocks (11.33 ex Rowsley)
11.33 (K) Rowsley	15.40	Gt Rocks		(Fwd at 16.07)
12.40 (D) Hartford	15.40	Gt Rocks		
		Tunstead	15.43	Wallerscote (D)
15.36 (J) Chapel en le Frith (94 trip)	15.56	P.Forest		
		Gt Rocks	16.07	P. Forest Sth (11.33 ex Rowsley)
11.33 (K) Rowsley	16.15	P. Forest Sth		
		P. Forest	*16.25*	*LE Rowsley*
		P. Forest	*16.52*	*LE Rowsley*
		P. Forest Sth	17.00	Rowsley (J)
16.45 (J) Buxton	17.12	P. Forest Jcn		(Fwd at 18.30)
		P. Forest	*17.18*	*LE Tunstead (78 trip)*
17.18 LE ex P. Forest (78 trip)	*17.25*	*Tunstead*		
		P. Forest	*17.42*	*LE Rowsley*
15.03 Grimesthorpe	17.55	P. Forest Sth		
		Tunstead	18.10	Hartford (D)
(16.45 ex Buxton)		P. Forest Jcn	18.30	P.Forest Sth (J)
(16.45 ex Buxton)	18.46	P. Forest Sth		
		P. Forest Sth	18.55	Wincobank (J)
		P. Forest	*19.40*	*LE Rowsley*
17.00 (D) Hartford	19.58	Gt Rocks		
		P. Forest Sth	20.14	Gowhole (94 trip)
18.50 Buxton (K)	20.35	P. Forest Sth		
		P. Forest	*20.58*	*LE Buxton MPD (78 trip)*
		P. Forest	*21.23*	*LE Tunstead (79 trip)*
21.23 LE ex P.Forest (79 trip)	*21.30*	*Tunstead*		
		Tunstead	22.00	Hartford (D)
		P. Forest	22.06	Buxton (J)
21.00 LE Belle Vue MPD	*22.15*	*Gt Rocks*		
		P Forest	*22.43*	*LE Buxton MPD (79 trip)*
		P. Forest	*23.07*	*Two LE's Rowsley*
		Tunstead	23.35	Heysham (J) MWFO

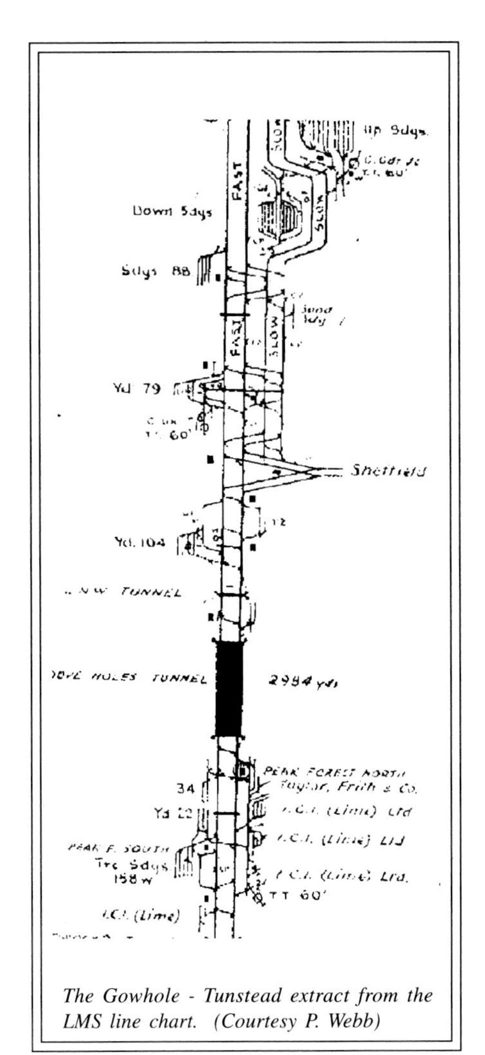

The Gowhole - Tunstead extract from the LMS line chart. (Courtesy P. Webb)

Eventually with the regulator wide open and the lever as far forward as it could be set without lifting the fire through the tubes, there was little more the driver could do other than contemplate his fireman, who would be working like a navvy, and to look back now and again to make sure the train was following in one piece.

The worst was yet to come and as the train barked its way through the long bridge/short tunnel carrying the LNWR overhead all three crewmen would be giving some thought to the state of Dove Holes tunnel and mentally counting the number of trains that had passed through it in the previous thirty minutes or so. In this case there was an express, a goods and a local at the very least all of which added up to an atmosphere that was going to be almost as solid as the tunnel lining.

For the occasional traveller - the fortunate enthusiast - who curried enough favour to get a footplate pass a trip on a steam engine through Dove Holes tunnel was probably a thrill that could compare with any except for the fact that he would almost certainly be doing it on a passenger train which would mean the two mile bore would be navigated in a matter of a few minutes; the high speed of an express doing something to sweep clear some of the smoke from the cab interior, especially if the engine was a Stanier type with their well protected cab and tender.

On a 4F 0-6-0 at less than ten miles per hour with the engine barking loudly enough to waken the dead and adding to the considerable fug left by the preceding trains, it was a different matter especially when one did it day in, day out. There were no windows to close on a 4F and the low tender seemed designed to catch the exhaust and direct it straight forward into the footplate area. The only defence or protection was to crouch as low as possible on the engine, face wrapped in a cloth or handkerchief, hoping that the track was dry enough to prevent the engine slipping and bringing the train to a stand or - even worse - to snatch it badly enough to break a coupling: something that would be murder to rectify in the sulphurous murk of the tunnel. Thoughts often turned to half-forgotten tales told about trains somewhere on the Continent which disappeared into tunnels only to be found hours afterwards with their crews suffocated to death on the footplate. Could it happen here...?

Apart from the smoke - which was a feature of any busy tunnel - Dove Holes had a consistency in that whatever the weather it was, at best, a tricky section of line to work and, at worst, downright dangerous. In the summer months the heat on the footplate was indescribable - especially if one had already been shovelling coal for some hours - whilst in the winter icicles of unbelievable size hung down from the tunnel roof and if one was unfortunate enough to be working the first train through on a Monday morning after the line had been quiet for some time, it paid to keep your head well inside the cab since collisions with icicles were by no means an unknown occurrence. In all weathers the track could be wet in certain parts of the tunnel and constant vigilance had to be paid to the working of the engine to arrest any signs of slipping.

When diesels were introduced to the line the dangers of the tunnel increased and there were a number of incidents in which ice com-

Framed in the wilderness of the high peak and with some climbing yet to do, Fowler 'Crab tank' 2-6-4T 42365 of Buxton passes Chinley South Junction en route for home with the two-coach 17.24 ex New Mills on 7th August 1951. This train was usually worked by an 0-4-4T as part of the Buxton - Millers Dale diagram.

pletely smashed and knocked out cab windows. One Trafford Park driver suffered serious injuries in such an accident and this lead to the Buxton-based independent snow-ploughs being fitted with special ice clearing devices.

Occasionally alarms had an interesting outcome for some of the individuals concerned as happened in October 1954 when 4F 0-6-0 43400 of Rowsley was working a special from Gowhole to Peak Forest and emerged from Dove Holes tunnel with bricks on the boiler - probably brought down by the blast of the exhaust. The driver raised the alarm and the permanent way were summoned to examine the tunnel during which time the line was closed to all traffic. The 10.15 ex St Pancras stood at Peak Forest North for just over thirty minutes - which suggests good work by the tunnel inspectors - and the 13.50 Manchester to London was diverted via Dore & Totley. How it came to be present is not related but one of the Derby officers saloons happened to be in the locality and was pressed into service to convey the stranded up line passengers from Millers Dale and Matlock to Ambergate where the 13.50 made a special stop. Most people couldn't get a ride in a saloon for love or money.

If goods engines and their crews had to work close to the limits of performance on the climb to Peak Forest it was only slightly less so for passenger trains and with the standard nine coach load being worked by a 5XP 4-6-0, the fourteen and a half minutes booking from New Mills South Junction to Peak Forest called for a constant output of just under 1200 drawbar horsepower which, as the equivalent of 1600 bhp, was just about the maximum the class was capable of and very similar to the output of the two LMS diesel-electrics (10000/1) which worked on the line for a short time during the late 1940's.

It was not without reason that the Midland looked down its nose at the Great Northern which, Midland men said, was a waste of space. The reasoning was that the GN ran through great tracts of desolate countryside - a 'green fields' railway - without serving any industry worthy of the name whilst on the Midland it was difficult to travel a mile without meeting some private siding or other.

And it was quite true. Most of the goods moved by the Great Northern originated on another system whilst even in the high desolation of the Derbyshire hills at Peak Forest the Midland served not just an occasional trader but part of the industrial fabric of Imperial Chemicals; one of the giants of British industry. The area was also a highly lucrative part of the Midland and if the receipts fell short of paying for the whole of the Derby - Manchester route, they certainly underwrote a good proportion of it and local railwaymen were aware of it for once a week a clerk from ICI would walk up to the station and hand over to the stationmaster a cheque for a quarter of a million pounds (occasionally more) with less ceremony than he would have employed in buying a day return to Millers Dale.

The sidings and yards of Peak Forest were spread over an area of about two miles and commenced, going from north to south, at Peak Forest North with Taylor, Frith & Co's sidings on the up side and a collection of sidings on the down side for general use. Peak Forest south controlled the station goods yard and general

PEAK FOREST : BANKING ENGINES

Train	Arr	Return
01.40 Kirkby - Gowhole	05.44	05.53
03.10 Lt Eaton - Gowhole	06.12	07.54
02.55 Kirkby - Gowhole	07.27	07.54
18.00 Glendon - Glazebrook	07.51	09.40
07.05 Rowsley - Gowhole	08.45	09.40
07.25 Kirkby - Gowhole	11.00	12.03
10.23 Codnor Park - Agecroft	13.23	15.27
10.30 Kirkby - Ashton Rd	13.36	15.27
13.24 Rowsley - Garston	14.37	15.27
14.45 Rowsley - Gowhole	16.06	16.25
03.35 Glendon - Glazebrook	16.16	16.52
13.17 Kirkby - Ashton Rd	16.35	17.42
15.40 Rowsley - Trafford Park	16.55	17.42
04.35 Corby - Glazebrook	19.34	19.40
20.10 Rowsley - Brindle Heath	21.21	00.32
20.20 Rowsley - Heaton Mersey	21.33	Q
20.45 Rowsley - Garston	21.55	23.07
21.00 Rowsley - Belle Vue	22.57	23.07
20.30 Kirkby - Ashton Rd	00.06	00.32

Q: Bank when needed. Return to Rowsley @ 23.07

On 1 March 1961 one of the brand-new Sulzer Type 4 2500hp diesel electrics, which within a couple of years were to oust steam from all mainline duties, makes an appearance. D51 negotiates the 10 mph restriction at Chinley North Junction with a Sunday St Pancras - Manchester express, diverted via Chesterfield and Hathersage.

sidings on the down side whilst on the other side of the line there were the Small Dale, Peak Dale and Long Siding works of ICI, part of nine yards which extended most of the way to Tunstead.

A glance at the traffic working charts will confirm that Peak Forest was a busy location and that its workings included the celebrated block trains which ran to and from the Northwich area and consisted of sixteen vacuum-braked 43.5 ton bogie hoppers hauled throughout by Stanier 8F 2-8-0's based at Northwich MPD. There were six such workings daily, for which Northwich had an allocation of twelve 8F's, each taking about three hours in each direction and running via the mainline, switching to the CLC at Cheadle Heath.

Although limestone had been moved in train loads for many years between Peak Forest and Northwich, it was not until the mid-1930's that the idea of doing it in fully-fitted block trains formed of high capacity wagons was conceived and in 1937 the initial batch of 84 wagons was received from Charles Roberts of Wakefeld, the first train operating in November of that year. (Subsequent batches of wagons were received from time to time until the fleet eventually stood at 152 vehicles). For the first year or so of operation the workings were handled by 4F 0-6-0's, each handling trains of eleven wagons,

Freight trains for the Ambergate road which lacked a margin to climb to Peak Forest could be 'put in' at Chinley South Junction to wait on the goods line for a path up the hill. The exit was controlled by Chapel-en-le-Frith and the goods lines worked under the permissive block arrangements which allowed goods trains to follow each other in the same block section as depicted above with Stanier 8F 2-8-0 on the 12.30 Walton - Kirkby empties and a second goods train buffering up to its brake-van. By the time the Kirkby train had followed an express through Dove Holes tunnel, a mile to the south, the crew of the second freight would find an atmosphere they could cut with a knife.

In fair weather......Jubilee 4-6-0 45618 'New Hebrides' arrives at Chapel-en-le-Frith (Central) with the 15.30 Liverpool (Central) Nottingham (Midland) in the summer of 1955.

....and foul. Several inches of snow does nothing to deter a pair of young enthusiasts at Chapel-en-le-Frith (Central) during the winter of 1955. The object of attention is Stanier 5MT 45273 (Bristol) as it thunders through with an express for St Pancras.

Diluting the Stanier look is BR standard 5MT 4-6-0 73001 of Derby as it pulls away from Chapel-en-le-Frith (Central) in 1954 with the 07.24 Manchester - Derby stopping train.

With their remarkable braking characteristics - not to mention their haulage powers - the Stanier 8F 2-8-0's might have been tailor-made for the lines over the Peaks. 48443 of Royston passes under the LNWR Buxton - Stockport line a mile to the south of Chapel-en-le-Frith (Central).

until sufficient numbers of Stanier 8F 2-8-0 locomotives became available, allowing train loads to increase to 16 vehicles and annual tonnages to double by the 1950's to 1.5 million tons per annum. (The gross load of each service, excluding engine and brakevan was 1072 tons, making them one of the heaviest, if not the heaviest, train in BR service).

The proper system of working took a little time to get into service, being dependent upon the supply of wagons from the builders and initially the 4F 0-6-0's used the few available as a fitted head on trains otherwise made up of conventional wagons. When the 8F's started to take over in 1938, loadings were initially set at 18 wagons per train, the sets being reduced soon after to 16.

During the first ten years of operation the working of the trains was shared by Northwich and Heaton Mersey, the former being a satellite depot of the other. The Heaton Mersey crews suffered the disadvantage of picking up the trains half-way through their workings and because of the longer terminal times at Northwich were unable to work a service for its complete cycle. Thus, at the time of nationalisation, the work was transferred to Northwich MPD whose men were able to work through to Peak Forest and back without having to be relieved.

The use of Stanier 2-8-0's was not a foregone conclusion and in the early days of the hopper traffic when 0-6-0's were the usual form of power, trials were held with a 2-6-6-2 Garratt whilst after the war an Austerity 2-8-0 was also tried. At the other extreme and during times of motive power shortages during the war, GCR J10 and J11 0-6-0's occasionally found themselves pressed into service on the trains.

At Great Rocks inward limestone trains would run across the down main and into the sidings where the 2-8-0 would be replaced by one of the eight industrial saddle tanks used by ICI for shunting in the area. The 8F would then reverse over to the up side loco sidings, where it would turn and water and, after the crew had had their break, back down to Tunstead where a loaded train would be waiting. The turnround time for each train was only about an hour and a half and allowed the Northwich crews to encompass a return trip within each turn of duty.

The working methods used by ICI were nothing if not a pointer to the future and it was by no means unknown for a train of empties to be loaded and taken back to Northwich by the same engine and crew that had brought them in less than two hours earlier.

The most difficult part of the entire circuit came in starting the loaded trains from Tunstead where the adverse gradient of 1/90 required the use of an assisting engine as far as the summit of the line at Peak Forest South. Because the sidings at Tunstead were of the dead-end type, assistance from the rear could not be given and the 0-6-0 had to double-head the 8F as far as Peak Forest. (In the 1950's the geometry of Tunstead was revised in order to allow assistance to be given

The engines that won the war! A statement often repeated by LMS locomen when asked to describe the Black 5, and evidently the Running Foreman at Trafford Park on 15th February 1953 was of the same mind since he seems happy to have substituted 44938 in place of the usual 5XP for the up Palatine, 13.45 Manchester - St Pancras.

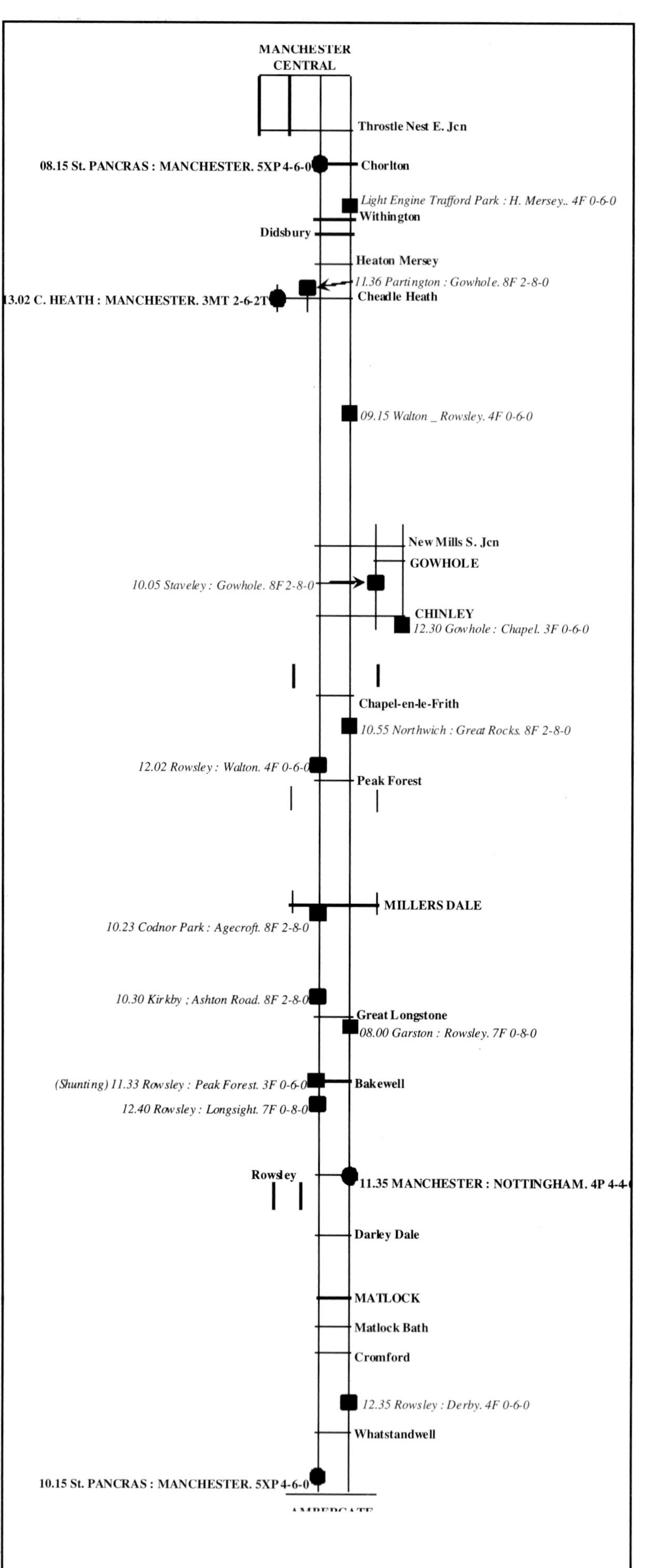

The 13.00 line position. It was not often two down London trains appeared on the section at the same time but the 10.15 from Pancras passed Ambergate just as the 08.15 was ending its journey. The earlier of the two was not especially fast and called at most major intermediate stations whilst the 10.15 called only at Leicester and Loughborough before reaching Derby and was thus twenty-five minutes faster.

After a long innings, Buxton's 4-4-0 passenger engines were replaced by a number of Fowler 2-6-4 tanks and - later in the day - a trio of Ivatt 2MT 2-6-0's of which 46465 is seen waiting to pass through Dove Holes tunnel on its way back to Buxton on 10th June 1964. Although formerly a Cambridge engine, 46465 was no stranger to the Midland having been employed for many years on the Cambridge - Kettering branch services. The working in which the engine is taking part started at 05.36 with a light engine run to Chinley prior to working the 07.00 all-stations to Sheffeld Midland. The 2-6-0 then turned and worked back with the 09.39 stopping train, returning light to Buxton after a spell of shunting at Chinley. The tunnel in the rear of the view is the short bore - 304ft - over which the LNWR Stockport - Buxton line ran.

4F 0-6-0 4170 of Burton powers a down fitted express goods past Peak Forest North towards the summit of the long climb from Rowsley. Behind the signalbox is the Peak Forest Pyramid, a geometric pile of waste which, when it was eventually disposed of, was of sufficient volume to fill an adjacent disused quarry.

With the end of the climb in sight, Black 5 4-6-0 44658 of Kentish Town roars through Peak Forest station at the head of a relief St Pancras - Manchester express on 6th October 1951. 44658 was one of the last conventional engines of the class to be built.

Stanier 8F 2-8-0 48743 of Liverpool (Speke Junction) puts in an uncommon appearance at Peak Forest with a southbound train of empties on 2nd March 1952. The scene behind the train depicts a typically busy day in the Taylor-Frith yard - or Taylor's Bank as it was known - with a back-cabbed 4F 0-6-0 from Buxton shunting the sidings. The shunter in charge can be seen standing by the shunting frame cabin, referred to those in the know as the 'shut-eye' since it was one of the few places around Peak Forest where shunting was not continuous and an uninterrupted forty winks could be obtained.

Buxton driver Ball and fireman Orritt smile for the camera as their 3F 0-6-0 43562 lends a hand to a Stanier 8F 2-8-0 in getting a loaded Tunstead - Northwich train up to the summit. The method of working was not satisfactory since the train had to come to a stand at Peak Forest North to uncouple the 0-6-0, after which the 8F had to restart its train without assistance. A few years after this view was taken, 6th October 1951, a revised procedure was introduced allowing the Buxton 0-6-0's to bank from the rear, thus giving assistance all the way to the summit without the need to restart the train.

from the rear, a move which spared the trains from having to stop and restart at Peak Forest.).

This starting assistance was given to each train by one of the two Buxton-based trip engines that spent their time at Peak Forest. Designated as trip (or target) 78 and 79, the 4F 0-6-0's arrived from Buxton between four and five in the morning, No.78 arriving at the head of the 03.30 Buxton - Sheffield class J goods which it double-headed as far as Peak Forest South whilst its companion followed on a couple of hours later, running light from Buxton shed. When not engaged with the Northwich trains the two trip engines were kept busy in running ad-hoc services between the various yards that made up the Peak Forest conglomeration. (Some of this work was supposed to have been done by ICI with their allocation of industrial engines but the local BR staff, who regarded ICI as a valued customer, instigated a tradition of doing the work for them with the result that normally only two of the eight industrial engines were ever in steam at one time. (At about the time the Beeching report was being prepared some economists from Marylebone Road discovered the Spanish customs that prevailed in and around Peak Forest and put a stop to them by costing the work and sending ICI a bill for the gratuitous shunting).

Although spared the worst of Dove Holes tunnel since their trains were going with the gradient, the Northwich crews did not escape the effects of suffocation entirely as they had to blast their way through the Tunstead tunnel which was situated at the point where the 2-8-0 and its assistant were beginning to get hold of the train. The tunnel was short but this was of little comfort to the crews on the 8F who not only had their own exhaust to breath through but that of the 0-6-0 as well and patent respiratory methods were generally the order of the day, especially if the two engines were working chimney to chimney.

Once over the top the skill in running the train depended to a great extent in the control of the vacuum brake and it was not until diesels had taken over the workings that drivers really started to appreciate quite how good the brakes on the 8F 2-8-0's had been. (One would have given a good deal to have been on the footplate of the Garratt when it was tried. For all their sixteen wheels their brake power was negligible and there must have been a few raised hairs before the test train got to Cheadle Heath).

One local trip paid a visit to the area and this was Heaton Mersey-based target 94, the 4F 0-6-0 ringing off shed at 05.50 and running light to Cheadle Heath for its first working, the 06.20 class K goods to Trafford Park, clearing any traffic that had arrived overnight. After a spell of shunting the trip returned south with the 09.15 class H to Gowhole, proceeding to Peak Forest - worked by Gowhole men - with the 12.30 trip from Gowhole, which included a lengthy spell at Chapel-en-le-Frith where it shunted the yard and picked up any traffic that was on hand. The 4F spent the afternoon and evening in making up its return working at Peak Forest, leaving for Gowhole at 20.14 after which the engine returned light to Heaton Mersey where it arrived back after some sixteen hours in traffic.

In common with most of the traffic points on the route there were no motive power facilities at Peak Forest, other than the turntable and water column at Great Rocks, and locomotives for starting trains had to be supplied from a variety of depots, one such being Belle Vue which sent an 8F 2-8-0 light on three nights a week to work the 23.35 Heysham service from Tunstead, the engine returning some twenty-seven hours later before returning light to Belle Vue after disposing of its train. Unlike the Northwich workings, the locomen did not work through on this service but manned the train only between Peak Forest and Belle Vue. Because the northbound Heysham train departed after the Buxton bankers had returned to their depot, the train was assisted as far as Peak Forest South by the Rowsley 4F 0-6-0 which had banked the 20.10 Rowsley to Brindle Heath to the summit.

Other than the Northwich workings the only other foreign service which worked into the area was an afternoon train from Grimesthorpe

After years of struggling across the hills with 3F and 4F 0-6-0's, Rowsley finally received some modern replacements amongst which was Caprotti-fitted BR5 4-6-0 73141 - made redundant on the Derby - London semi-fast trains by diesel traction - which is seen backing onto the 17.00 Peak Forest - Rowsley on 8th June 1961. The train has been drawn into the station by 4F 0-6-0 44339 which was working one of the two Buxton trip duties.

which worked back in the evening with a load of lime for the steel industry in Sheffield.

The majority of trains from the south had to be assisted by a banking engine - a Rowsley-based 3F or 4F 0-6-0 - as far as Peak Forest and a key element in the operation of the line was the attention given to the return of these engines without which Rowsley was unable to make trains up to anything like a respectable load. So urgent was the matter considered that returning engines were allocated a path in the timetable and given the same priority as a train.

BUXTON JUNCTION : 1954 (Nights)

Train	Down	Up	Destination
22.00 BUXTON		22/06	MILLERS DALE
22.25 MILLERS DALE	22/28		BUXTON
22.06 (J) Peak Forest	*22.37*		*Buxton*
22.43 (LE) Peak Forest	*22/53*		*Buxton MPD*
21.58 (J) Rowsley	*23/02*		*Edge Hill*
22.40 (J) Rowsley	*23/45*		*Ash Bridge*
23.55 (J) Rowsley	*00/56*		*Longsight*
00.25 (J) Rowsley	*01/25*		*Buxton*
18.50 (F) Latchford		*01/39*	*Rowsley*
01.07 (2 LE's) Dove Holes LNW		*02.02*	*Rowsley banker*
22.14 (H) Heaton Norris		*02/13*	*Rowsley*
21.25 (F) Garston		*03/15*	*Rowsley*
03.15 (J) Buxton		*03/31*	*Rowsley*
03.30 (J) Buxton		*03/49*	*Sheffield*
00.05 (F) Garston		04/35	Rowsley
03.50 (J) Rowsley	*04/45*		*Buxton*
05.25 (LE) Buxton MPD		05/42	Peak Forest

Note: Trains from Buxton = Up, Trains to Buxton = Down

This was unusual since it was quite common elsewhere to assume that bankers would be returned immediately upon arrival and their movements were not included in the timetable.

The Rowsley bankers were in a class of their own because of the distance over which they had to assist trains and the fact that the time spent away from Rowsley was critical. Each engine had its own working - bankers were not provided on a haphazard basis - and without them the yard was severely handicapped in the loadings that could be sent up the bank to Millers Dale. In addition a number of engines and men were able to cover two banking trips per shift although this could only be accomplished if the first trip was performed punctually. Most engines, because of the times at which trains were booked to leave Rowsley, were only able to manage a single trip, the rest of their shift being occupied in whatever ad-hoc shunting requirements there happened to be at Rowsley. Even, however, on the single trip engines, it was essential that they were returned to Rowsley as quickly as possible since variations in working - late running, special trains - always dictated that a pool of banking engines should be on hand to cover any eventuality.

Work on the bankers was probably as unpleasant as any that could have been found in footplate circles and quite

BUXTON JUNCTION : 1954 (Early)

Train	Down	Up	Destination
06.20 (J) Buxton		*06/35*	*Rowsley*
05.35 (J) Rowsley	*06/38*		*Buxton*
02.15 (F) Garston		*06/55*	*Rowsley*
03.25 (J) Grimesthorpe	*07.02*		*Buxton*
07.05 BUXTON		07/11	MANCHESTER
06.15 (J) Rowsley	*07/22*		*Buxton*
07.50 BUXTON		07/56	MILLERS DALE
08.00 MILLERS DALE	08/03		BUXTON
08.00 BUXTON		08/06	MANCHESTER
08.13 MILLERS DALE	08/16		BUXTON
08.16 BUXTON		08/21	MILLERS DALE
08.05 (J) Buxton		*08/35*	*Sheffield*
08.38 MILLERS DALE	08/41		BUXTON
08.46 BUXTON		08/52	MILLERS DALE
08.55 (2 LE's) Buxton		*09/09*	*Rowsley*
09.13 MILLERS DALE	09/16		BUXTON
09.15 BUXTON		09/21	MANCHESTER
08.45 (J) Rowsley	*09/45*		*Edgeley Jcn*
09.40 BUXTON		09/46	MILLERS DALE
10.05 MILLERS DALE	10/08		BUXTON
10.25 BUXTON		10/31	MILLERS DALE
10.48 MILLERS DALE	10/51		BUXTON
10.55 (2 LE's) Buxton MPD		*11/05*	*Rowsley*
10.28 (J) Rowsley	*11/27*		*Longsight*
11.30 BUXTON		11/36	MILLERS DALE
11.35 (H) Buxton		*11/51*	*Rowsley*
12.05 BUXTON		12/11	MILLERS DALE
11.15 (J) Rowsley	*12/17*		*Buxton*
12.25 MILLERS DALE	12/28		BUXTON
08.00 (J) Garston		*12/35*	*Rowsley*
12.40 MILLERS DALE	12/43		BUXTON
11.27 (LE) Bibbington Jcn		*13/03*	*Rowsley banker*
12.55 (H) Buxton		*13/12*	*Rowsley*
13.20 BUXTON		13/26	MILLERS DALE
12.40 (J) Rowsley	*13/40*		*Longsight*
13.50 MILLERS DALE	13/53		BUXTON
13.25 (J) Buxton		*13/56*	*Millers Dale*

Note: Trains from Buxton = Up, Trains to Buxton = Down

The Ivatt 4MT 'clodhopper' 2-6-0's were introduced in 1947 with the object of replacing the Midland 0-6-0's. In the event only 162 moguls were built and the 0-6-0's survived unscathed leaving the LM with the question of what to do with the Ivatt engines. Their biggest impact was made on the Midland & Great Northern system, which the class monopolised; the remaining engines being scattered throughout the LM. One of the class had a regular duty, alternating with a Compound 4-4-0, on the 15.40 St Pancras - Leicester semi-fast express otherwise their duties were of a very humdrum nature. They made only infrequent visits to the Derby - Manchester line, occasionally turning up on the Sheffield - Buxton freights, although the incidence increased as the 0-6-0's were withdrawn towards the end of steam. On March 27th 1965 43048 tops the bank at Peak Forest South with a Rowsley to Heaton Mersey goods.

With the worst of the climbing over and having had the benefit of a wait to be overtaken by a passenger train, 8F 2-8-0 48774 of Newton Heath drags a Rowsley - Brewery goods out of the down loop at Peak Forest South on 28th May 1964.

During the 1950's diesels were a novelty - there were only seven main-line locomotives - and most spent some time on the Midland system; the Peak route being a convenient testing route for Derby works. On 30th June 1950 the smallest of the BR diesels, 827hp 10800, was caught on camera as it passed Great Rocks at the head of a dynamometer test train on one of its earliest outings.

Although a single representative of the class - 45509 - had been resident at Derby for some years it was reserved for services to the west of England with the result that appearances by Patriot class engines on the London - Manchester route were extremely uncommon. Thus the sighting on 30 June 1960 of a Patriot 5XP 4-6-0 at Great Rocks on a St Pancras - Manchester express was doubly momentous since 45518 'Bradshaw' was an Edge Hill locomotive and well away from its normal haunts. The level of coal in the tender suggests that the engine took over the train at Derby and may have been used to relieve one of the Metrovick Co-Bo 1200hp diesels that were being used at the time and which had already gained a reputation for unreliability. In the background 4F 0-6-0 44554 of Heaton Mersey, which has worked the afternoon trip in from Gowhole has just been turned and is about to run forward to the water column, where the fireman stands waiting.

A good southerly general view of Great Rocks as it was in 1958 with a Northwich 8F 2-8-0 climbing towards Peak Forest summit, assisted in rear by 4F 0-6-0 44339 of Buxton. The line into the ICI private sidings can be seen on the right, where arriving empty hoppers gained access to the works. Trains would pick up an ICI shunter - whose task it was to set the road in the sidings - from a nearby cabin which was known locally as the 'Dogs Home'.

BUXTON JUNCTION : 1954 (Late)

Train	Down	Up	Destination
13.50 (J) Buxton		*14/18*	*Wincobank*
11.18 (J) Grimesthorpe	*14/20*		*Buxton*
14.22 BUXTON		14/28	MILLERS DALE
14.45 MILLERS DALE	14/48		BUXTON
15.20 (J) Millers Dale	*15/30*		*Buxton*
09.35 (J) Dundas Sidings		*15/45*	*Kirkby*
16.03 BUXTON		16/11	MILLERS DALE
16.18 MILLERS DALE	16/21		BUXTON
16.25 BUXTON		16/31	NEW MILLS
16.33 BUXTON		16/39	MILLERS DALE
16.56 MILLERS DALE	16/56		BUXTON
16.45 (J) Buxton		*17/08*	*Peak Forest*
16.20 (J) Rowsley	*17/19*		*Edgeley*
17.20 BUXTON		17/26	MILLERS DALE
17.46 BUXTON		17/51	DERBY
17.53 MILLERS DALE	17/56		BUXTON
17.24 NEW MILLS	18/11		BUXTON
17.22 MANCHESTER	18/27		BUXTON
18.25 BUXTON		18/31	MILLERS DALE
17.20 (H) Rowsley	*18/37*		*Garston*
18.35 (J) Buxton		*18/50*	*Rowsley*
18.55 MILLERS DALE	18/58		BUXTON
19.10 (2 LE's) Buxton MPD		*19/20*	*Rowsley*
19.20 (LE) Buxton MPD		*19/32*	*Rowsley*
16.23 (J) Grimesthorpe	*19/44*		*Buxton*
19.40 BUXTON		19/46	MILLERS DALE
18.50 (K) Buxton		*20/05*	*Peak Forest*
20.07 MILLERS DALE	20/10		BUXTON
20.24 BUXTON		20/30	MILLERS DALE
20.55 MILLERS DALE	20/58		BUXTON
20.58 (LE) Peak Forest	*21/08*		*Buxton MPD*
21.05 (2 LE's) Buxton		*21/25*	*Rowsley*
20.35 (J) Rowsley	*21/34*		*Edgeley*

Note: Trains from Buxton = Up, Trains to Buxton = Down

apart from spending half a working life breathing another engines' smoke, the other half was spent returning to base tender first which, given the extremes of weather found on the Dales, was anything but invigorating. Prior to the installation of the turntable at Great Rocks in the 1930's, the only way of avoiding extensive tender-first running was to turn the engines on the angle at Peak Forest Junction; an uncertain arrangement which depended on the goodwill of signalmen, a lull in traffic and local officialdom which was prepared to turn a blind eye to the ten minutes or so that the operation took. More often than not it was less troublesome to cover the fourteen miles tender first although eventually feelings came to a head; a confrontation that was quelled in Midland Railway times by the allocation to Rowsley of 3F 0-6-0's equipped with tender cabs. The intention was sound if the practice was not and, more often than not, a crew would take duty on a banker only to find that their tender-cab engine was in Derby works and its replacement was one of the conventional type.

It was not just the trains to Peak Forest that had to be banked but those from Rowsley to Buxton. The common perception of the Buxton branch was that of a rural branch which supported the Millers Dale shuttle plus a handful of through services to and from Manchester. In fact passenger traffic accounted for only 46% of the movements on the branch and the majority of traffic activity came from Rowsley which despatched fourteen services daily, eight of which worked through to the LNWR - chiefly the Stockport area - over gradients which if anything were more severe than those up to Peak Forest.

Although off the beaten passenger track, Buxton was no backwater so far as goods traffic was concerned since it was the only point of interchange with the LNW for traffic destined for the south Manchester area. Most of the traffic on the Rowsley - Buxton - Stockport (LNW) axis was worked by Buxton engine and men, the shed having a large allocation - 55 engines - for a town of its size.

It was also one of the few locations in which some of the pre-grouping distinctions had been removed between the LNWR and the Midland - the lines of the two systems were so closely intertwined that, locally at any rate, the distancing of the two had been an absurdity - when the motive power depots merged in 1935; the combined establishment coming under the aegis of Longsight (LNWR). Moves of this sort rarely gain approval from the individuals effected and the Buxton merger was no exception and the Midland men complained for some time that the merger preferred former LNWR staff. On the other hand it did provide an opportunity for the Midland to be shown that there was more to life than a 3F 0-6-0 and the pooling of the two allocations resulted in many of the Buxton turns to Rowsley being worked by LNWR 0-8-0 locomotives. By nationalisation about half the allocation consisted of eight-coupled locomotives - 19 Stanier 8F 2-8-0's and 8 LNWR 0-8-0's - with the number of Midland

The star of the 4P Compound 4-4-0's began to wane in the mid 1950's as the influx of BR standard locomotives started to encroach upon their traditional duties and by the latter part of the decade they had become an uncommon sight in the passenger field. They remained useful stand-by engines for a few years - six of the class were still in existence as late as 1960 - and 41157 of Derby was caught on the 19.35 Manchester - Derby slow at Great Rocks during the summer of 1957. Although produced from a design which dated back to the turn of the century, it is sometimes forgotten that most of the class was introduced two years after the appearance of the first Gresley Pacifics.

Journeys end for Stanier 8F 2-8-0 48605 as it crosses from the up main to enter the ICI sidings at Great Rocks with 17.00 empty hoppers from Hartford in 1959. Upon arrival the 8F engine will hand over the train to an ICI locomotive.

Having handed its train over to an ICI engine, 48605 recrosses to the up side and turns on the 60' table at Great Rocks. Many turntables were equipped with a device which enabled power to be obtained from the vacuum brake of the engine as it was being turned, but on this example the engine had to be carefully balanced after which the crew, as shown above, would apply Newton's third principle in its most primitive form. During the worst months of the winter Northwich crews would give it up as a bad job and turn on the angle at Millers Dale Junction.

Untimetabled trips between yards in the Peak Forest area were continuous and worked by two Buxton-based 0-6-0's which shunted for about 30 engine-hours daily and banked the Northwich hopper trains as far as Peak Forest summit. This 1962 view shows the two trip engines meeting, the photograph being taken by the fireman of 44339 whilst his engine was waiting to enter the sidings to bank one of the hopper trains. Neither engine remained still for very long and both invariably returned to Buxton with empty tenders.

8F 2-8-0 48465 waits for the road at Peak Forest Junction with a Peak Forest - Buxton goods on 22nd August 1964. The signalbox can just be seen the far side of the short tunnel.

Peak Forest Junction as seen from the south in June 1937 with 5MT 4-6-0 5036 in charge of a special passenger working. On the right are in the ICI Central Works sidings which at the time were shunted by horse.

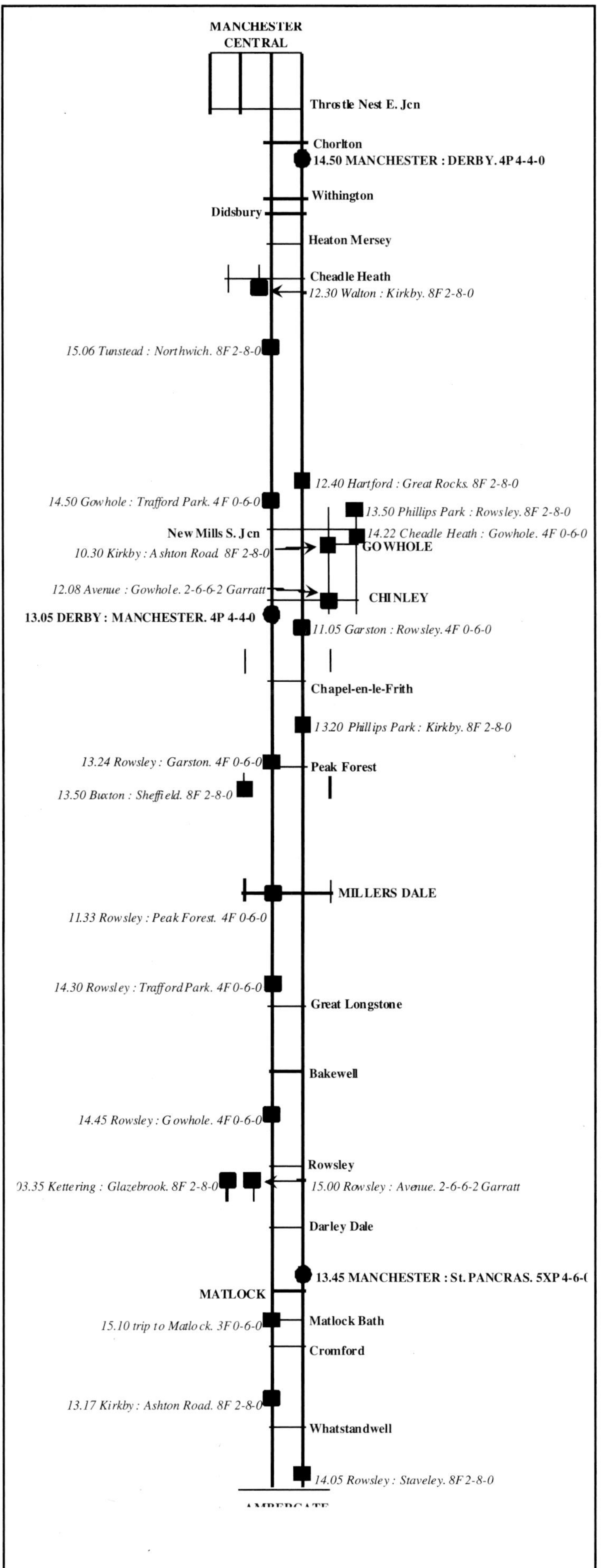

The line position at 15.00 As usual the number of trains is remarkable, 13 approaching Manchester and 10 leaving. The effect that an express passenger service had on freight traffic can be seen from the fact that whilst the up Palatine has passed Darley Dale, goods trains are only just beginning to move again with nothing south of Peak Forest in the up direction.

Taken from almost exactly the same spot as the previous photograph but after a lapse of twenty-two years, Kentish Town-based rebuilt Royal Scot 4-6-0 46142 'The York and Lancaster Regiment' speeds south with a Manchester - St Pancras express on 9th September 1959.

0-6-0's falling to 10, sufficient for those local trip workings which usually called for nothing larger.

Because of its relationship with the LNW, the Buxton - Rowsley workings were a remarkably cosmopolitan set of trains and although Buxton had the lions share of the diagrams, engines from Longsight and Stockport were booked to appear on some of the through workings whilst bankers on down trains from Rowsley came from as far afield as Saltley (05.35 ex Rowsley), Kirkby (11.15) and Longsight (16.20). The star turn was the 17.20 Rowsley - Garston on Saturdays when it was booked to be banked up to Bibbington Sidings by an engine from Birkenhead shed. To add to the colour, engines running from Buxton MPD to Rowsley to pick up, or bank, a northbound working, were often attached to up services at Buxton in order to save a path and to provide some additional braking power on the falling gradients.

Bankers also had to be provided on workings from Buxton to Peak Forest and beyond and were restricted to a class 4F load - 26 loaded mineral wagons - unless they were given assistance in which case a maximum of 37 wagons was permitted for services hauled by class 7F and 8F eight-coupled engines.

MILLERS DALE

LITTLE SWITZERLAND

Multiple units did not feature prominently in operations over the Peak District, the exception being the Millers Dale - Buxton shuttle which became DMU operated relatively early in the day; railcars replacing the steam motor train in 1958. For all their soullessness there were times when they proved useful, as in this view of 20th September 1959 when, because of engineering works, the shuttle was unable to run between Millers Dale and Buxton Junctions and had to be diverted via Peak Forest Junction where the driver simply walked from one end of the train to the other. In the view above the unit heads towards Peak Forest Junction, its usual route being visible above the train.

Whilst scenically satisfying, the route south of Tunstead was barren of originating traffic other than the relatively small quantities dealt with at the way stations and their sidings. It was not, however, completely devoid of operating interest since the section to Millers Dale had the triangular junctions with Buxton (and its connections to the LNWR) whilst Millers Dale itself, the most important station between Derby and Chinley, was the interchange point between the Buxton branch and the main line.

Up workings had finished their climbing but of course goods trains then had to be held back against the falling gradient, engaging in a struggle against gravity with the brake valve taking the place of the regulator. Guards and drivers more than ever had to work as a team even though they were separated by a quarter of a mile of train and devoid of any communication save for a handlamp in emergencies and no guarantee that any message would be received. Express passenger work received public recognition but in truth there was no driving skill that called for so much fine judgement as the task of guiding an unbraked goods train down a long and steep incline. The potential for trouble was always present and it is to the everlasting credit of such drivers that so many trains over the Peak arrived at their destinations in one piece.

Going north goods trains faced a long slog of 14 miles from Rowsley with many of the lower class services having to be banked throughout partly to keep the train on the move and partly to act as an anchor in the event of the train becoming divided; something that was uncommon rather than rare.

Assisting in the rear - banking - was not an operation that the railways had ever been very keen on and generally it was confined to short sharp sections of line such as the Lickey incline and the Folkestone Harbour branch. Neither was it an option that could be applied every time a yard inspector or district controller thought that a particular train might move a little faster with a bit of help from behind. The rules were strict and banking could only be resorted to on the sections of line for which specific permission had been granted, a list of such lines being given in the sectional appendix to the timetable together with any rules and regulations that applied.

For example a familiar form of banking could be seen at most London termini where the engine which had brought in the empty coaching stock gave the train engine a helping hand from the rear as it was leaving. It was not, however, a casual matter and had to be sanctioned in the appendix. In the case of trains leaving St Pancras assistance could be given to the home sig-

MILLERS DALE (North) : 1953

Train	Down	Up	Destination
22.00 BUXTON		**22.09**	
19.35 (H) Philips Park		22.10	Rowsley
18.40 ST PANCRAS	**22.20**		**MANCHESTER**
	22.25		**BUXTON**
21.00 (J) Rowsley*	22.32		Belle Vue
20.25 (F) Moston		22/35	Rowsley
21.58 (J) Rowsley*	22/53		Edge Hill via Buxton
21.20 (E) Ancoats		23/11	Rowsley
23.07 Peak Forest (LE)		23/27	Rowsley banker
22.40 (J) Rowsley*	23/31		Ash Bridge via Buxton
22.00 (C) Ancoats		23/37	St Pancras
20.30 (J) Kirkby*	23/43		Ashton Road
21.40 (F) Trafford Park		23/47	Rowsley
21.30 (F) Chaddesden	00/00		Peak Forest (MWFO)
22.35 (F) Heaton Mersey		00/14	Rowsley
23.55 (J) Rowsley*	00/46		Longsight via Buxton
00.00 MANCHESTER		**00/58**	**ST PANCRAS**
00.32 Peak Forest (LE)		01/07	Rowsley banker
00.25 (J) Rowsley*	01/15		Buxton
21.05 (E) Huskisson		01/23	Rowsley
22.40 (H) Ancoats		01/35	Rowsley
22.35 (H) Nottingham	01/48		Brunswick
18.50 (F) Latchford via Buxton		01/50	Rowsley
01.50 Peak Forest (LE) TThSO		02/02	Derby MPD
01.35 (E) Rowsley	02/12		Ancoats
01.07 Dove Holes (LNW) 2 LE's		02/12	Rowsley banker
22.14 (H) Heaton Norris via Buxton		02/23	Rowsley
21.00 (H) Dundas		02/32	Rowsley
21.16 (F) Garston		02/46	Rowsley
02.02 DERBY (PCLS)	**02/48**		**MANCHESTER**
02.32 (E) Rowsley	03/10		Brewery
23.55 (H) Brunswick		03/14	Spondon (Derby)
21.25 (F) Garston via Buxton		03/25	Rowsley
03.00 (H) Rowsley	03/38		Heaton Mersey
03.15 (H) Buxton		03/42	Rowsley
23.38 (H) Moston		04/01	Rowsley
03.40 (F) Rowsley	04/17		Ancoats
03.50 (J) Rowsley	04/35		Buxton
04.05 (F) Rowsley	04/44		Brindle Heath
00.05 (F) Garston via Buxton		04/45	Rowsley
01.30 (H) Garston		04/54	Kirkby
04.15 (E) Rowsley	04/55		Walton
01.40 (J) Kirkby*	05/08		Gowhole
03.25 (F) Ashton Road		05/32	Rowsley
03.10 (J) Little Eaton*	05/50		Gowhole
01.50 (F) Ellesmere Port		05/59	Rowsley

* : Banked in rear

MILLERS DALE (North) : 1953

Train	Down	Up	Destination
02.35 (F) Washwood Heath	06/12		Brunswick
05.53 Peak Forest (LE)		06.13	Rowsley banker
05.40 (F) Gowhole		06/25	Rowsley
05.35 (J) Rowsley*	06/26		Buxton
06.20 (J) Buxton		06/45	Rowsley
02.55 (J) Kirkby*	06/50		Gowhole
02.15 (F) Garston via Buxton		07/05	Rowsley
06.15 (J) Rowsley*	07/11		Buxton
18.00 (J) Kettering*	07/23		Glazebrook
03.29 (H) Hooton		07/32	Kirkby
06.05 MANCHESTER		**07.50**	**(Forms 08.00 Buxton)**
07.50 BUXTON		**07.59**	
(06.05 Manchester)	**08.00**		**BUXTON**
07.05 (J) Rowsley*	08.05		Gowhole
07.15 MANCHESTER		**08.08**	**ST PANCRAS**
	08.13		**BUXTON**
07.54 Peak Forest (2 LE's)		08/19	Rowsley bankers
08.16 BUXTON		**08.25**	
07.10 DERBY	**08.32**		**MANCHESTER**
	08.38		**BUXTON**
07.24 MANCHESTER		**08.45**	**DERBY**
08.46 BUXTON		**08.55**	
05.00 (F) Widnes		09/03	Rowsley
04.15 ST PANCRAS	**09.07**		**MANCHESTER**
	09.13		**BUXTON**
08.55 Buxton (2 LE's)		09/17	Rowsley
08.45 (J) Rowsley*	09/35		Edgeley Jcn via Buxton
09.40 BUXTON		**09.49**	
09.00 MANCHESTER		**09.57**	**ST PANCRAS**
09.20 (E) Rowsley	09/59		Ancoats
	10.05		**BUXTON**
09.40 Peak Forest (2 LE's)		10/06	Rowsley bankers
07.25 (J) Kirkby*	10/14		Gowhole
08.02 (H) Belle Vue		10/16	Kirkby
10.25 BUXTON		**10.34**	
09.06 NOTTINGHAM	**10.43**		**LIVERPOOL**
	10.48		**BUXTON**
09.00 (H) Heaton Mersey		10/54	Rowsley
00.57 (F) Brent	10/58		Brunswick
10.55 Buxton (2 LE's)		11/13	Rowsley bankers
10.28 (J) Rowsley*	11/17		Longsight via Buxton
11.30 BUXTON		**11.39**	
10.24 DERBY	**11.48**		**CHINLEY**
10.50 (H) Gowhole		11/49	Rowsley
11.35 (H) Buxton		12/01	Rowsley
11.15 (J) Rowsley*	12/07		Buxton
12.05 BUXTON		**12.14**	
08.15 ST PANCRAS	**12.19**		**MANCHESTER**
	12.25		**BUXTON**
12.03 Peak Forest (LE)		12/29	Rowsley banker
11.35 MANCHESTER		**12.35**	**DERBY**
	12.40		**BUXTON**
12.02 (H) Rowsley	12/44		Walton
08.0 (J) Garston via Buxton		12/45	Rowsley
10.23 (J) Codnor Park*	13/01		Agecroft
11.27 Bibbington Sdgs (LE)		13/12	Rowsley banker
10.30 (J) Kirkby*	13/15		Ashton Road
12.55 (H) Buxton		13/22	Rowsley
13.20 BUXTON		**13.29**	
12.40 (J) Rowsley*	13/31		Longsight via Buxton
10.15 ST PANCRAS	**13.44**		**MANCHESTER**
	13.50		**BUXTON**
13.08 (H) Gowhole		13/55	Rowsley

* : Banked from Rowsley

nal just beyond the station whilst at Kings Cross banking was prohibited except for exceptionally heavy trains from certain platforms which could be assisted for a couple of coach lengths and no more.

Rowsley to Peak Forest was an exceptional section since banking was allowed over such a long distance: 14 miles, and was one of the longest instances of continuous banking in the country. (The longest was not very far away and was over the 17-mile section of the LNWR between Stockport and Buxton). The potential for problems where long distance banking was concerned were legion since trains consisted of relatively unstable short wheelbase wagons, each with an individual resistance, being pulled at one end and pushed in the other by two engines of similar output without any communication between them.

Theory implied that the train engine kept going and that the banker kept up the rear until it was removed from the train at Peak Forest. Theory also hoped that the driver of the banking engine would have some idea of what his opposite number on the train engine might do in an emergency but did not say what. For example the driver of the train engine could spot some obstruction on the line - sheep and horses were not unknown - and ease the regulator in order to slow down or stop. Neither the guard or the driver of the banker - could have any idea of what was happening and both had to fall back on an intuition born of experience. If they was paying strict attention the crew on the banker might feel a lurch of resistance as the train engine slackened off and ease off whilst on the other hand, unaware of problems - especially if there was a reason to expect an increase in resistance, such as a steepening of gradient - they could continue blasting away behind the brakevan whilst the middle of the train rose like a pyramid to block both main lines for the next day and a half. Similarly if the banker thought that the train engine had slackened off, when it fact it hadn't, and shut off steam, the result could be a divided train; the train engine and front portion careering away uphill in happy oblivion of the fact leaving behind half a train with an engine on the wrong end. A great deal depended on the skill and experience on the part of the crews who worked the Rowsley trains and the fact that so many trains reached Peak Forest intact testifies not to the simplicity of the operation but to the expertise of the men involved.

Another problem which did nothing to diminish the difficulties of working the line was the acceptance of down goods trains at places like Great Rocks Junction where there were relatively long sections to the south - which meant that trains were well spaced out - but rather a congested area to the north with the shunting

Where every prospect pleases and only diesels are vile...... Dwarfed by the scale of the scenery, a diverted railcar reverses at Peak Forest Junction whilst en route from Millers Dale to Buxton during the diversions of 20th September 1959.

Ennui at Peak Forest Junction in 1962 as the 13.50 class J from Buxton to Sheffield waits for a path at Peak Forest Junction. Presumably advised by the signalman that a procession of trains from the Millers Dale direction will have priority, Driver Gyte abandons the heat of the footplate for a more comfortable seat on the grass whilst his fireman records the scene on camera. Stanier 8F 48389 passively simmers in the background. The crew did not work the train throughout but changed footplates with the 16.23 Grimesthorpe - Buxton at Earles Sidings.

MILLERS DALE (North) : 1953			
Train	Down	Up	Destination
13.25 (J) Buxton		*14.03*	
9.15 (H) Walton		*14/14*	*Rowsley*
*13.24 (J) Rowsley**	*14/14*		*Garston*
14.22 BUXTON		**14.31**	
13.05 DERBY	**14.38**		**MANCHESTER**
13.45 MANCHESTER		**14.39**	**ST PANCRAS**
	14.45		**BUXTON**
11.33 (K) Rowsley	*15.00*		*Peak Forest*
14.30 (H) Rowsley	*15/12*		*Trafford Park*
	15.20		*Buxton (J)*
13.20 (F) Philips Park		*15/28*	*Kirkby*
*14.45 (J) Rowsley**	*15/34*		*Gowhole*
11.05 (F) Garston		*15/37*	*Rowsley*
15.27 Peak Forest (3 LE's)		*15/47*	*Rowsley bankers*
*14.45 (J) Blackwell**	*15/54*		*Gowhole*
09.35 (J) Dundas via Buxton		*15/55*	*Kirkby*
13.50 (H) Philips Park		*16/04*	*Rowsley*
16.03 BUXTON		**16.12**	
*13.17 (J) Kirkby**	*16/12*		*Ashton Road*
	16.18		**BUXTON**
12.30 (J) Walton		*16.22*	*Kirkby*
14.50 MANCHESTER		**16.28**	**DERBY**
*15.40 (J) Rowsley**	*16/31*		*Trafford Park*
16.33 BUXTON		**16.42**	
16.00 MANCHESTER		**16.50**	**ST PANCRAS**
	16.56		**BUXTON**
16.25 Peak Forest (LE)		*16/59*	*Rowsley banker*
*16.20 (J) Rowsley**	*17/09*		*Edgley via Buxton*
17.00 (J) Peak Forest		*17/15*	*Rowsley*
16.52 Peak Forest (LE)		*17/22*	*Rowsley banker*
17.20 BUXTON		**17.29**	
16.10 DERBY	**17.32**		**MANCHESTER**
15.30 LIVERPOOL		**17.46**	**NOTTINGHAM**
14.15 ST PANCRAS	**17.48**		**MANCHESTER**
	17.53		**BUXTON**
17.46 BUXTON		**17.55**	**DERBY**
17.42 Peak Forest (LE)		*18/12*	*Rowsley banker*
*17.20 (H) Garston**	*18/25*		*Garston via Buxton*
18.25 BUXTON		**18.34**	
17.50 MANCHESTER		**18.45**	**ST PANCRAS**
	18.55		**BUXTON**
18.35 (J) Buxton		*19.00*	*Rowsley*
*04.35 (J) Corby**	*19/11*		*Glazebrook*
19.10 Buxton (2 LE's)		*19/30*	*Rowsley*
19.20 Buxton (LE)		*19/40*	*Rowsley banker*
19.40 BUXTON		**19.49**	
16.15 ST PANCRAS	**20.01**		**MANCHESTER**
	20.07		**BUXTON**
19.40 Peak Forest (LE)		*20/10*	*Rowsley banker*
20.24 BUXTON		**20.33**	
19.16 DERBY	**20.39**		**MANCHESTER**
19.35 MANCHESTER		**20.46**	**DERBY**
	20.55		**BUXTON**
*20.10 (J) Rowsley**	*20/59*		*Brindle Heath*
19.30 (E) Ancoats		*21/02*	*Rowsley*
*20.20 (J) Rowsley**	*21/09*		*Heaton Mersey*
19.00 (H) Trafford Park		*21/18*	*Rowsley*
*20.35 (J) Rowsley**	*21/22*		*Edgeley via Buxton*
21.05 Buxton (LE)		*21/33*	*Rowsley*
*20.45 (H) Rowsley**	*21/34*		*Garston*

** : Banked from Rowsley*

movements, etc, which were a continuous feature of life as far as Peak Forest.

Under normal circumstances no signalman could accept a train unless the line was clear for a distance of a quarter of a mile beyond his home signal at the time of acceptance and this requirement made life very difficult for signalboxes such as Great Rocks whose clearance (ie the quarter mile ahead of the home signal was almost continuously obstructed with shunting movements or light engines and meant that, so long as the usual regulations were applied, he could only accept a train from the south at the risk of paralysing all local movements. (It needs hardly be said that a class J train could take an extraordinary time to run from Peak Forest Junction, especially if it was an unbanked 4F 0-6-0 on a filthy night).

The quarter of a mile clearance was referred to as the 'regulation 4' acceptance but in cases such as that of Great Rocks Junction where the safety margin was outweighed by

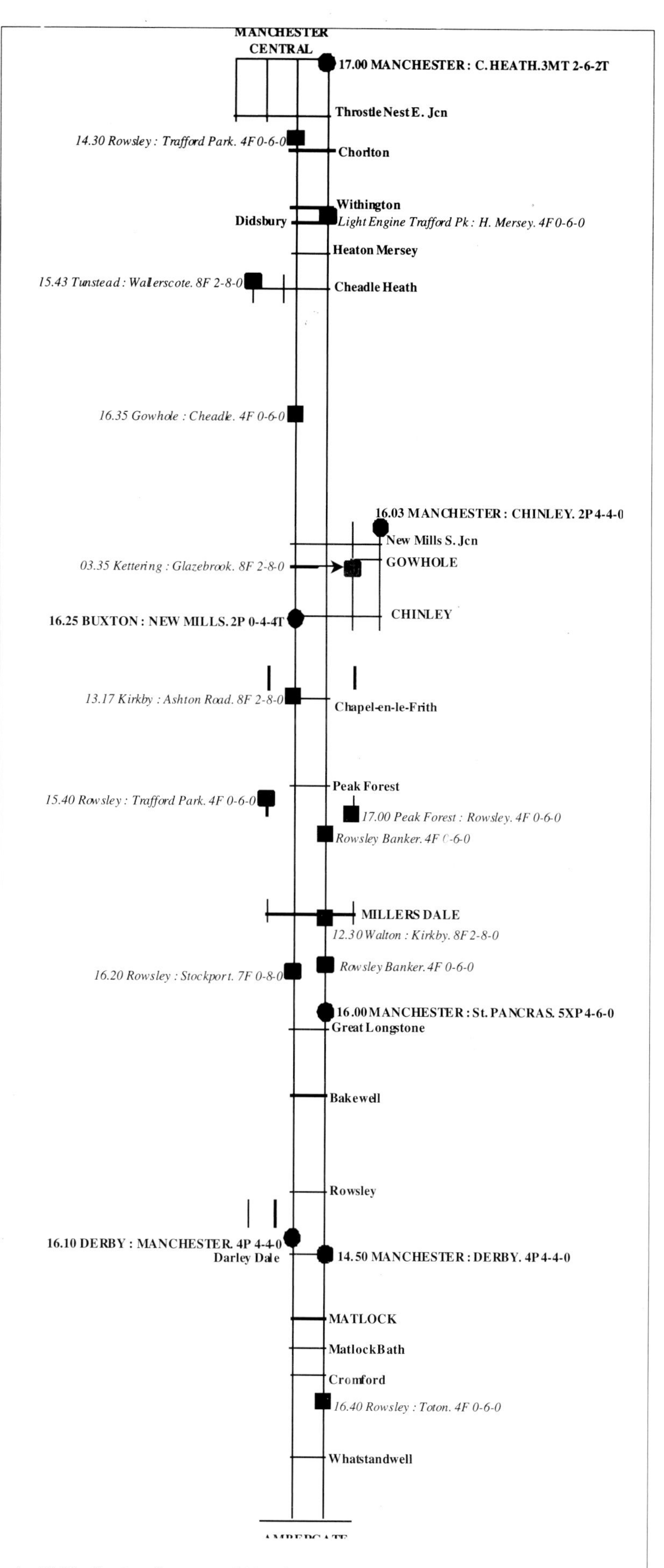

At 17.00 all other lines out of Manchester would be teeming with suburban passenger trains, the Midland being the exception; its prewar service of local trains never being revived whilst most of those that remained used the old road via Tiviot Dale such as the 15.30 Liverpool - Nottingham which is approaching Marple and the 16.30 slow from Central which is running into Stockport. Further south the afternoon stopping train to Derby is slowing to enter Darley Dale up loop where it will wait to be overtaken by the 16.00 Manchester - London express. As a result the two and a quarter miles from Rowsley were booked to take thirty-two minutes: probably a record.

It was unusual in itself to see a Stanier 2-8-0 on passenger work and unique to catch one in harness with the LNER beaver-tailed observation saloon. However on 25th September 1955 the saloon was used in an enthusiasts special from London to Buxton and whilst its passengers were being carted around the Cromford & High Peak in goods wagons, Stanier 8F 48519, which is seen at Buxton Junction, was delegated to turn the stock on the Blackwell Mill angle.

The nearest the LNER had to an all-purpose mixed traffic engine was the B1 4-6-0 which, whilst they did a great deal of invaluable work on their home metals, never approached the LMS Black 5 in terms of all round performance; something that was due to the LNER having an abundance of class 7 and 8P locomotives as opposed to the relatively small numbers possessed by the LMS. In the summer of 1948 a series of locomotive exchanges was arranged in order to demonstrate that it was perfectly possible for engines of one company to work satisfactorily on foreign metals. One of the LNER engines which took part was B1 4-6-0 61251 'Oliver Bury' of Kings Cross which is seen climbing the Derbyshire Alps at Blackwell Mill at the head of the 10.15 St Pancras - Manchester.

Risking confusion with scenery more usually associated with North American railways, 5XP 4-6-0 45639 'Raleigh' of Derby echoes its staccato three-cylinder beat from the hillsides as it attacks the climb through Blackwell Mill to Peak Forest with a Manchester-bound express from London on 15th May 1948. The Millers Dale - Buxton branch can be seen on the right.

The LNWR assessed its G2 0-8-0 locomotives as being the most efficient on the system and in 1929 the LMS sought to improve the type further. The result was the 'Austin 7' 7F 0-8-0 which were nothing like as successful as the design they were based upon. Most of the class ended up on the L&Y section including 9674 of Newton Heath which was captured working a Rowsley - Newton Heath goods on 15th May 1948.

A double for enthusiasts at Millers Dale Junction. Black 5's were commonplace on the Midland but the one above was from Stoke and had been commandeered by Derby to work an express forward to Manchester on 15th May 1948. Since the train was over the limit of nine coaches a pilot had to be provided and 2P 4-4-0 482 of Derby shed was the engine selected. Ten years later thes 2P's were still performing the same task since, after a decade of desultory existence, they were called back to the main line to assist with the 1957 accelerations whose timings were beyond the efforts of unpiloted 5XP 4-6-0's. The branch on the right is the line to Buxton.

An up express goods from the L&Y division to Rowsley approaches Millers Dale on 25th May 1964 behind 8F 2-8-0 48250 of Agecroft. The engine is about to take the fast line - the outermost tracks - through the station and the convergence of the down slow and main lines can be seen below the engine to the centre of the photograph. By the date of the picture diesel haulage was all but universal on passenger services although steam continued to be dominant on goods workings for a further twelve months.

This is the Millers Dale that most people remember - a procession of freight trains running hell-for-leather up the bank and usually with a minimum of two engines, one at each end of the train. In this case three engines have been called upon with 4F 0-6-0 43907 of Kirkby piloting 8F 2-8-0 48005 (Stourton) at the head of the train and a Rowsley 3F 0-6-0 banking in the rear.

The first visit by a Pacific to the Midland was in June 1948 when Bulleid light 4-6-2 No. 34005 'Barnstaple' of Exmouth Junction worked the 10.15 St Pancras - Manchester (Central) as its contribution to the locomotive exchanges. Understandably the West Country caused quite a stir in the area, partly because of its strength and performance but also - until the crews had mastered its subtleties - because of wild bouts of slipping in Dove Holes tunnel. On the occasion of the picture, the firemen is taking no chances with the climb ahead and has been doing some robust firing during the stop at Millers Dale. To the right of the express, in No.5 bay, the Buxton push & pull waits with a good head of steam to follow. By chance when the Midland realised, nine years on, that its expresses required something larger than the customary Jubilee 4-6-0, the possibility was mooted of acquiring a number of SR Pacifics but in the event less extreme measures were resorted to, with the transfer of Britannia 4-6-2's and Royal Scot 4-6-0's to Kentish Town and Trafford Park. The only large-scale invasion by foreign engines on the Midland took place in 1960 when a batch of A3 Pacifics were drafted to the Settle and Carlisle route for the final three years of steam working. LMS and BR standard types remained in force on the rest of the system until the arrival of diesels from 1962.

Relegated by Britannia's, Scots and Metrovick Co-Bo diesels and about to be ousted by the 2500hp Sulzer's, Jubilee 4-6-0 45561 ' Saskatchewan' of Trafford Park runs into Millers Dale in 1960 with a Manchester - London service formed, by all appearances, from a scratch set of seven coaches.

On a rather dull day in 1958 Stanier 5MT 4-6-0 44985 finds itself a long way from its Kentish Town base and runs into Millers Dale with a Derby - Manchester stopping train. A two-car multiple-unit waits in platform 5 with the connection for Buxton.

Originated by the LMS in 1938, the title 'Palatine' had originally been bestowed on the 16.30 from London and 10.00 ex Manchester whilst the 10.30 down and 16.25 had been christened the Peaks Express. Both names disappeared with the war and it was not until 1957 that any train over the route carried the distinction of a title when the Palatine was resurrected for the 07.55 from St Pancras and the 14.25 from Manchester. Above, Britannia 4-6-2 70042 'Lord Roberts' arrives with the down train whilst the diesel connection waits to follow from the bay platform.

Stanier 2P 0-4-4T No. 41905 propels its two-coach push and pull set from platform 1 across to platform 5 bay. The movement was an indication of the lengths to which the railway - locally at any rate - went to suit the convenience of the passengers. The train connected with an up express to London which called at platform 1 and, to save the passengers having to walk across the station, the Buxton train preceded the London train into platform 1 and then shunted across to the bay which was situated next to the down main platform. By 1951, when the photograph was taken, most push and pull trains on the LM were operated by new Ivatt 2-6-2 tanks but somehow the Buxton service escaped this reform. The 0-4-4 tanks were not actually as venerable as they looked and were a class of 10 engines built as recently as 1932 as replacements for the older types of 0-4-4T inherited by the LMS.

Although Millers Dale boasted four through platforms, it was not often that the inner or slow faces were used by passenger services simultaneously since in normal circumstances trains were not booked to overtake in the station. One long standing exception, however, was the mid-afternoon stopping train from Derby which was booked to be overtaken by the 14.25 St Pancras - Manchester express; the Derby train standing in platform 3 for nearly thirty minutes. The arrangement was probably convenient for the limited number of passengers travelling from places such as Great Longstone to Manchester but played havoc with the freight service since both down lines were effectively blocked for quite a long period. The scene above captures Midland Compound 1024 running in at the head of the 14.25 ex St Pancras whilst sister-engine 1021 waits patiently with the 15.47 Derby - Manchester slow. Both engines commenced their workings at Derby - through running between London and Manchester only commenced once the Stanier 4-6-0's had become established in the late 1930's. This did not mean that Midland engines did not stray far from their local districts, as for example was the case on the Great Northern, and every opportunity was taken to utilise engines to the maximum. Evidence of this is given by the presence of 1024 which was based at Bristol and had worked to Derby as part of a two day diagram. In order to keep the engine working it was allocated to a filling-in duty to Manchester , returning with the midnight St Pancras as far as Derby before working to Bristol. 1021 was allocated to Derby and was used on express or long distance stopping services on all the Midland lines radiating from Derby.

operational needs a concession was given, known as the 'regulation 5' acceptance which allowed the basic quarter-mile clearance point to be occupied without imposing any restrictions on the flow of traffic from the south.

This relaxation allowed signalmen - at locations where it was specifically authorised - to accept trains provided the line was clear only as far as the home signal which, in the case of Great Rocks Junction, meant that he could continue to authorise shunting movements, etc, whilst a train approached from the Buxton direction. (The regulation 4 clearing point was a safety margin and meant, in practice, that if a train over-ran the home signal it had a quarter of a mile in which to pull up before any great harm was likely to result. This did not protect the driver afterwards - passing a signal at danger was the nearest thing the railway had to a capital offence - since enquiries were searching and guilty parties tended to be dealt with severely).

Because the basic quarter-mile safety margin was compromised, special precautions had to be taken to ensure that the driver of a train concerned understood what was happening and much of this devolved upon the signalman at Tunstead when he was offering the train forward to Great Rocks Junction.

Normally a train would be offered on by the appropriate bell code (3-2 in the case of a class J) and accepted by the box in advance by repetition provided the clearance of 440 yards was available ahead of the home signal. When the regulation 5 acceptance was being used, however, the train was acknowledged with the 3-5-5 code which told Tunstead that the line was clear only as far as the Great Rocks home signal but that the train could proceed at caution.

The Tunstead signalman then had to transmit this information to the train being accepted and this was done by exhibiting a green handsignal to the driver who would give his acknowledgement by blowing the engine's whistle. Once this response had been given the Tunstead signalman was able to clear his signals and send the train on its way. (If the he was unable to show the driver a green handsignal - in the case, for example, of a train that had been allowed to trickle down the section whilst being offered on to Great Rocks Junction, the train had to be brought to a momentary stand at the starting signal, the enforced stop being the cue to the driver that the line was clear only as far as the next home signal).

(Overleaf) : The Jubilee 4-6-0's reigned pretty well unchallenged on the Manchester service for more than a quarter of a century and even now when the Midland line is mentioned, the image of a 5XP is often the first to come to mind. In the upper view 5570 'New Zealand' stands ready for the off with blower hard on and valves lifting, the driver looking back for the right away. In spite of Staniers' Swindon upbringing, the Great Western belief that engines should, like children, be seen and not heard did not permeate to the LMS where a considerable amount of noise, especially from safety valves, was de rigeur for any engine prior to moving a wheel. The view of 5570 was taken from platform 4 in 1939 whilst, lower, fifteen years later all that has changed is some resignalling and a change of livery; all express passenger engines being painted in Brunswick green from the early 1950's.

5570
L M S

45575

For a short time after the grouping the Hughes-Fowler 'Crab' 2-6-0's came close to becoming the standard LMS mixed traffic locomotive and was mooted as a running mate for the Compound 4-4-0 which almost became the standard express passenger engine. Events altered this intention considerable but 245 Crabs were eventually built from 1926 onwards, surviving until the end of steam. Although widely distributed over the LMS, they tended to be concentrated in Scotland and the L&Y areas with the result that they were uncommon on passenger services other than at times of peak demand when they could be regularly seen working excursion trains. 42772 therefore presented an interesting change from the normal run of 4-6-0's when it called at Millers Dale on an unidentified southbound excursion in 1951. To add to the novelty the 2-6-0 came from Longsight whose engines were only rarely seen working passenger services on the Midland.

Although Derby had a small allocation (three engines) of Crab 2-6-0's, it was rare to see them on passenger work although 2799 - which was subsequently transferred to Burton for working the beer trains to St Pancras - was used on a Manchester - Derby slow on an unrecorded day in 1937 where it seen being overtaken by Black 5 4-6-0 5262 of Sheffield (Millhouses) at the head of a Manchester - St Pancras express.

Class J mineral trains - the most common type of train on BR - had to be banked for the fourteen mile climb between Rowsley and Peak Forest and provided the unusual sight of trains running over long distances with an engine at both ends. In most cases power was provided by 0-6-0's as in this case, where Heaton Mersey 4F 43945 on the 14.45 Rowsley - Gowhole in 1954 takes a breather on the short 1/100 dip over the twin viaducts at the south end of Millers Dale. The banking engine, 44084 of Rowsley, also slackens off and the fireman uses the lull to do a spot of firing. The 20-ton brakevan was obligatory for trains on this route and were generally referred to as 'Queen Mary' brakes. As well as their braking power - which was considerable - they were useful in that the uncoupling of the banker at Peak Forest could be carried out by the guard who performed the operation by hanging over the edge of the veranda.

In the case of operations such as those above the 3-5-5 acceptance could only be used where specially authorised - each signalbox had a list of local regulations which supplemented the general block regulations - but there were a few instances where the warning arrangement could be used without specific authority. The most widely used of the general applications was when visibility fell to less than 200 yards during fog and falling snow with no fogsignalman was on duty and a signalman wished to divert a passenger train from, for example, the fast line to the slow line or some other unscheduled movement which called for a reduction in speed. In this case he would accept the train not by repetition (4 or 3-1 bells, depending on whether it was an express or a local) but by 3-5-5 which would ensure that it approached under caution and at slow speed.

Curiously the one part of the Millers Dale district where the regulation 5 (or warning arrangement as it was generally known) acceptance did not apply was at the triangular junction layout bounded by Peak Forest Junction, Buxton Junction and Millers Dale Junction, which was somewhat surprising given that there were no facilities for shunting trains and anything sent forward from Millers Dale had to run as far as Great Rocks before it could be recessed for a passenger train. This, therefore, imposed a heavy responsibility for sound judgement by the signalman at Peak Forest Junction who, when offered a train from the Buxton direction, had first of all to make sure that he had a suitable break in mainline traffic before accepting it - a class J could sometimes take an eternity to come off the Buxton branch and even longer to get up the hill to Great Rocks - and secondly to ensure that the block section was clear to Tunstead since all unfitted services coming from the Buxton direction had to be given a clear run from Buxton Junction in order to have a good start on the bank. Trains coming from Buxton were not banked and an enforced stand at Peak Forest Junction could, with a heavily laden 3F 0-6-0 struggling for breath, come close to stopping the job for some time.

Junction boxes such as Peak Forest Junction were instructive places for young railwaymen who needed to acquire - in addition to some experience in signalling rules and regulations - that most essential of railway skills: a sense of timing which was useful in handling aspects of work such as the following piece of history.

A Class J from the Buxton branch was be offered on and a mental calculation would be done to estimate the time it would pass and the time it would clear the section ahead. These estimates would be compared with the calculated approach of the next train due on the main line and a decision would be made. The timetable, incidentally, was of no use where unfitted goods trains were concerned. Passenger and express freight trains could be relied upon to run pretty well on time, give or take a few minutes, but unfitted trains could run anything up to an hour either side of their booked time. The passing times of A,B and C services would be exhibited on the noticeboard and, in most cases, memorised by the signalman. Other trains were dealt with as they came and regulated by a combination of judgement and experience. Communication was also necessary and a phone call to Millers Dale to confirm the state of the down line is made.

"The passenger will leave here at twenty five and I'm holding a Gowhole to follow."

A quick call to Tunstead.

"If I run the down Buxton ahead of the express, can you deal with it? It's a bit tight."

The sound of the Tunstead conferring with Great Rocks can be heard in the background.

"Right-ho, mate, let 'em come."

So the Buxton mineral is accepted from Buxton Junction and offered on to Tunstead, bells ring, levers crash and one hopes one's calculations will stand the test of reality. The minute hand of the clock moves faster than one can remember it doing before and one wonders if the risks connected with narrow margins are worth the trouble to the nervous system. If the Buxton goods stops the passenger there is going to be some written explaining to be done. The 2-1 (train on line) bell crashes the silence and is acknowledged. Shortly afterwards the sound of a 4F making a noise like a stick being

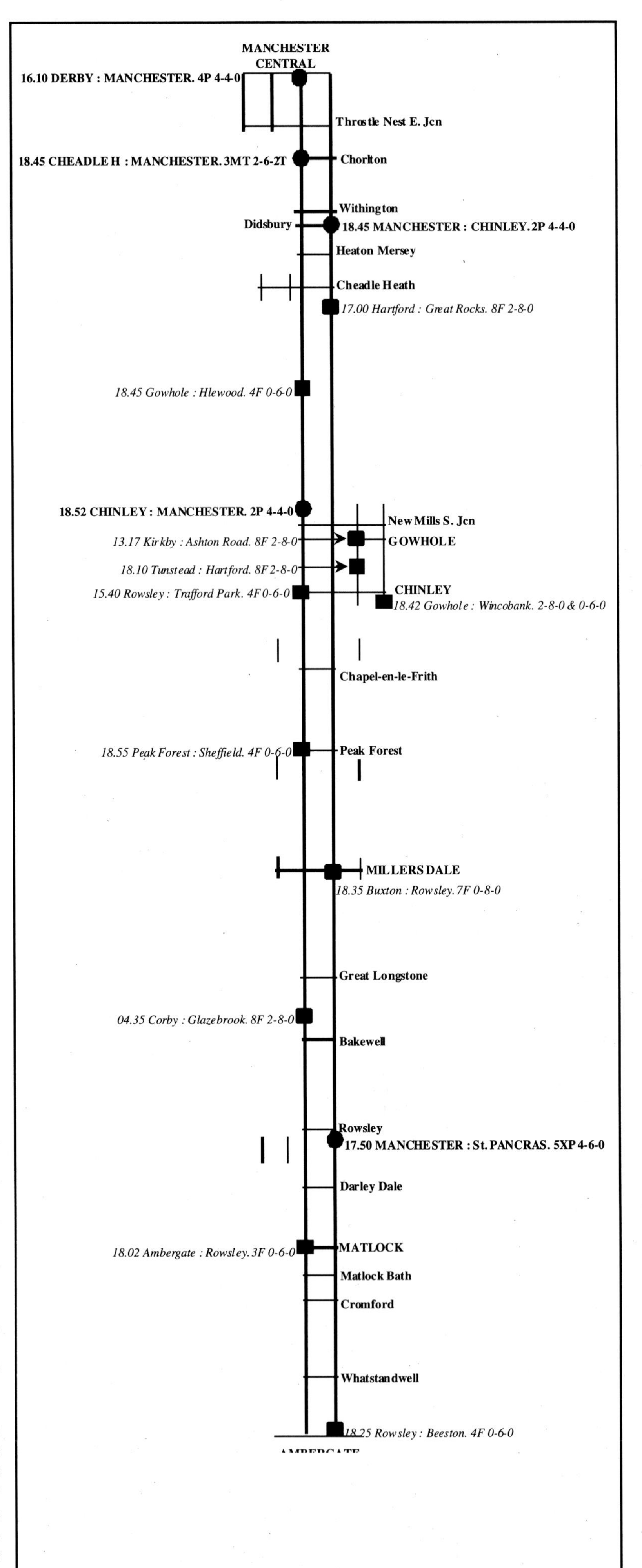

19.00 was a relatively quiet time on the line since it was the period when the line was turning attention from slow freight services to the night fast goods workings which were being prepared in the yards.

bashed against a wall assails the ears, the whistle adding to the racket as it pounds passed the box and disappears into the short tunnel beyond the junction. A train of wagon-wheels beat a slow staccato on the joints and eventually the brake bangs by, the guard leaning over the veranda.

"Gowhole!" he shouts putting his pipe back into his mouth. At least it might have been Gowhole, it could have been something obscene that sounded similar at speed and distance. Given the benefit of the doubt at least he knew where he was going - some guards seem to believe it necessary to remind every signalbox they passed of their destination.

"Hello control. Buxton goods off the branch at 17."

"Right"

A concerto of bells crashes out, a passenger on the up is heralded, accepted, offered on. Levers crash and a 5XP canters out of the tunnel with nine red and crimson corridors in tow, most with coach boards, yellow on red, proclaiming MANCHESTER (CENTRAL) - DERBY - LEICESTER - LONDON (ST PANCRAS) which is a nice touch reminding us that there is life beyond Rowsley after all. The Buxton goods has still not yet cleared and if it doesn't get a move on there will be questions raised in the house. Call attention from Millers Dale - acknowledged - and a peal of four beats rings out. This bit of line is clear so the train is accepted but unless that 0-6-0 picks up its skirts the home signal is about as far as it will get for some time. Train on line rings out load and clear but there is nothing that can be done until the Buxton gets clear at Tunstead. Fingers tap the window ledge in impatience - pace up and down the floor in case it helps - silence from Tunstead but not from the approaching passenger which can be seen from the corner of your eye; the whistle hooting away as some sort of raucous protest at being stopped on the worst part of the bank. A tall plume of steam burst skywards, echoing from the steeps sides of the rock cutting when - glory be - train out of section is received for the Buxton. No radio officer on a sinking ship sent out morse quite as urgently as the bells for the passenger are sent to Tunstead and acceptance is immediate. Has it come to a stand? Not quite. Home, distant and starter come off in the prescribed sequence and the compound opens up noisily. The fireman waves amiably but the driver - an old boy long enough in the service to remember the days when passenger trains only stopped when it told them to in the timetable - glowers ahead, as the train whuffles up to the heights and, but for a phone call later on, is forgotten.

"Derby control. How was that down passenger doing by you?"

"Er...all right, Why?

"Small engine. Lost a few minutes going up to Peak"

"Well...it was making a bit of a meal of the job going up the hill."

"They shouldn't put these museum pieces on the main line. Loco can explain this one."

"Give us the tools and we'll do the job, control."

The scarcity of industry in the area did not mean that the line lost any of its interest and in many respects Millers Dale was as fascinating a spot to watch trains as any on the line although one wondered why such a remote spot - where a stop by a passenger train, other than the Buxton shuttle, was almost an event - had been blessed with no less than five platforms, especially as there was no local population to speak of. No less impressive was the pleasing geometry of the trackwork and the particular way the four lines curved through the platforms in the most nicely formed angles imaginable. To add to the effect the track from the south entered the station over two long and impressive steel viaducts.

A curiosity of the layout was that the fast lines were situated on the outside, the two inner tracks forming the up and down slow lines; an arrangement that permitted non-stopping trains to pass through without having to diminish their speed appreciably.

Why the station - which was doubled in size between 1905-6 - should have been built to such generous proportions is difficult to see, whether the Midland Railway were anticipating an extraordinary growth in Peak District tourism or whether it was simply regarded as operationally convenient to have a commodious station roughly half way between Derby and Manchester are matters of conjecture but certainly there was no density of traffic in pre-1914 days that could not have been accommodated at a much smaller station. In its memorandum of the 1903 act, which included several other schemes, the company simply referred to the enlargement of the station and the new viaduct as the Millers Dale loop which suggests that the alterations were operationally rather than commercially based. Indeed it is quite probable that had the Midland been able to reach Manchester via Buxton and the LNWR then Millers Dale station would never have been built, or at the most would have been a very much smaller affair than the five platform structure that eventually came into being.

The principal role of the station was to act as a point of connection between the main line and the Buxton branch and for this purpose a Buxton-based motor train operated over the five and a half mile connection, running in connection with each main line working, all of which in the 1950's made a stop. The railway would have preferred to have given a town of Buxton's size and popularity something better than a connectional arrangement but operating considerations dictated otherwise. The Midland had from its earliest days opted for short trains at close intervals, as opposed to the infrequent and gargantuan affairs of the LNWR, and it was this policy which brought about its small engine policy stemmed. Trains leaving Derby and having to toil up to Peak Forest already had sections for Liverpool and Blackburn and the incorporation of a Buxton section would have been the straw that might have broken the compounds back, thus in most cases a change at Millers Dale was necessary. Buxton, therefore, was rather poorly treated in the question of through services to London and even in the heady pre-1914 days of the Midland Railway there were no more than two daily in each direction.

All through coaches on the expresses ceased with the last war and although the Liverpool and Blackburn portions were never reinstated, it took until 1957 for the Buxton facility to be restored; a brake-composite being attached to the 08.55 ex Manchester and returned on the 14.25 from St Pancras. Although this was only half the service the town had enjoyed in palmier days, it was of considerable interest to the enthusiast since the up coach was entrusted to a 3F 0-6-0 (usually 43329) which, after the express had departed for St Pancras, ran light to Rowsley and banked the 12.40 Longsight goods back to Buxton. The down coach, in the afternoon, was worked by a Fowler 2-6-4 tank which came out light from Buxton for the purpose.

The push & pull service was no less interesting since it was, by the mid-1950's, probably only train of its type on the LM which had not been handed over to an Ivatt 2MT 2-6-2T. It is difficult to criticise the small Ivatt tanks which were well-liked by their crews, light on fuel, easy to maintain and - as the SR discovered in the summer season around the Brighton area - could handle loads significantly more demanding than those normally associated with a class 2 engine yet, from the spectators point of view, there were so many of them that the grey hand of standardisation seemed to have the motor train in its grip. The LM liked push and pull trains and had a lot of them but so many were worked by the Ivatt tanks that sometimes one began to suspect there were rather more 2MT's than the 130 that were shown in the book.

The Buxton service was the exception and remained faithful to the 0-4-4T until dieselisation, which came relatively early. For many years Midand 1P 0-4-4T 58042 had been one of the regular engines - two locomotives a day were used - but it was replaced in 1950, not by one of the 2-6-2T's that were flooding the system but by a set of venerables which were steamed in random rotation: 46616, an LNWR 2-4-2 tank., 58083, a Midland class-mate of 58042 and 41905. The last-mentioned of the trio was something of an anachronism and its 0-4-4 wheel arrangement disguised the fact it dated only to 1932.

Although the shuttle was kept busy between Buxton and Millers Dale for much of the day, one of the sets was given an airing on the main line each afternoon by working the 16.25 stopping train to New Mills Central, returning with the 17.24 back to Buxton; the service running direct between Buxton Junction and Peak Forest Junction.

With its four-coupled engines the Buxton push and pull lasted as a reminder of pre-Ivatt days until as late as October 1957 when the branch train was one of the first on the LM to be taken over by a multiple-unit.

There was an irony in that the Buxton service, which had been overlooked for years and so retained its older motive power, overnight became the most modern on the system. Cynics on the inside suggested that the London Midland, who had had to have its arm twisted to take some diesel railcars, operated them where they would be least likely to be noticed. The rest of us would probably have preferred an Ivatt.....

THE RACING STRETCH

Monsal Dale was an early casualty and closed to traffic in August 1959, some four years before the Beeching axe made station closures an everyday event. Interestingly closure in those days did not mean demolition - Chiltern Green, for example, on the mainline near Luton, closed in 1952 yet was still in situ several years later - a fact which demonstrates the gulf which existed between the civil engineers and operating departments who, more often than not, were only just aware that the other existed. The closure of the station came as no surprise, least of all to the local population, most of whom lived in the village of Cressbrook which can be seen (just) on top of the hill in the background. Those who used the railway found it just as convenient to use Millers Dale. The train is an up goods from Heaton Mersey to Rowsley hauled by Stanier 8F 2-8-0 No. 48161.

The section to the south of Millers Dale was, for up services, the racing stretch where any time lost on the climb to Peak Forest stood a chance of being regained. It was also a stretch of line which required careful regulation since the scope for shunting freight trains was limited with no goods loops on the up line north of Rowsley other than Hassop which had no facing connection since its facilities were intended for visits by trip workings. To shunt a mainline train meant a reversal into the siding and in the majority of cases it was less troublesome to keep a train going until it got to Rowsley.

The three stations in the section - Bakewell, Great Longstone and Monsal Dale - between them serviced a population of less than 4,000, three-quarters of whom lived in or near Bakewell, and it is therefore not surprising that the passenger service was limited to little more than the handful of Manchester - Derby stopping trains although Bakewell was conceded a stop by the Nottingham - Liverpool express in each direction.

Bakewell also had the dignity of a starting train, which left at 07.35 each morning for Derby, Rowsley shed sending a Compound 4-4-0 light each morning for the duty. The engine remained at Derby throughout the day and returned to Bakewell in the evening with the reverse working, the 17.05 from Derby; the stock of which berthed overnight at Bakewell.

Local goods traffic was catered for by two services, the first of which was 71 target which, in the charge of a 3F 0-6-0, left Rowsley at 07.20 to serve Bakewell (07.45 to 08.57) and Hassop where it was due at 09.05. It returned to Rowsley

07.55 ST PANCRAS : MANCHESTER (1959)
5XP 45616 'Malta GC'. 8:273/290 tons

m.ch	Station	Grade	WTT	m.secs	mph	dbhp	pc
0.00	DERBY		0.00	0.00	-	-	-
0.61	Nottingham Rd	321		2.20	36.0	846	2
3.11	Little Eaton Jcn	1227		5.49	53.0	707	3
5.20	Duffield	2552		8.02	56.0	511	3
7.67	Belper	478		10.42	58.0	740	4
10.30	AMBERGATE	494	13.00	13.37	30.0	-	-
12.25	Whatstandwell	527		16.05	54.0	1418	7
15.22	Cromford	541		19.04	60.0	888	5
16.05	Matlock Bath	174		19.50	56.0	599	4
17.12	MATLOCK	359	22.00	21.24	-	-	-
					p.w.c.		
2.14	Darley Dale	19140		3.58	28.0	611	2
4.36	ROWSLEY	360	6.00	7.10	46.0	991	4
7.64	Bakewell	170		11.30	49.0	974	4
10.13	Great Longstone	200		14.33	47.0	740	3
14.21	MILLERS DALE	116	20.00	19.42	-	-	-
1.64	PeakForest Jcn	98		4.05	37.0	1271	3
4.45	PEAK FOREST	90	8.00	8.02	45.0	1539	6

Stranger in the Dales. Fowler 4F 0-6-0's were common currency all over the Midland and rarely warranted a second glance. 44220, however, would have raised some lineside interest as it worked north over Monsal Dale viaduct on 12th June 1948 since it was a Goole engine and therefore not usually seen so far south. The visit may have been occasioned by a visit to Derby works, the railways had only been nationalised for six months yet the 0-6-0 already had its new number and BRITISH RAILWAYS in full on the tender.

at 11.14, recessing at Bakewell for thirteen minutes - which meant reversing over to the down side - to detach any northbound traffic which was immediately picked up by the 11.33 Rowsley to Peak Forest which called from 11.51 until 14.15. When traffic demanded 71 trip was extended from Hassop to Monsal Dale where the sidings were worked from 10.20 until 10.45.

Bakewell was served by a second train, the 11.33 Rowsley to Peak Forest which worked the sidings from 11.51 until 14.15. Because of the need to make stops en route, neither the trip or the Peak Forest train was banked from Rowsley.

Much of the interest derived from the section - apart from the pleasure of sitting at places such as Longstone and watching the succession of train engines and bankers beating their way up the bank - was to exprience the effort produced by locomotives on express duties and how they matched, or occasionally bettered, the timings which generally allowed twenty-two minutes for the seventeen miles between Derby and Matlock and twenty minutes for the fourteen miles on to Millers Dale. The line from Derby to Peak Forest was an excellent test-piece for locomotives with a mixture of conventional high speed track as far as Ambergate after which it became a matter of rapid acceleration from speed restrictions such as those at Ambergate and Rowsley and, after the latter, a climb to the summit. The skills involved in running an unfitted mineral train have already been extolled; on this stretch on line, especially going north, similar qualities were demanded of express engines and their crews.

The standard engine for the line was, until 1958, the 5XP Jubilee 4-6-0 and it was unusual to find anything else working a Manchester - St Pancras train although the Stanier 5MT 4-6-0's deputised on special trains and at times of shortfall. It is popularly reckoned that, output for output, there was little to chose between the two classes although this is something of a fallacy since with the faster trains, especially those south of Derby and those on the London - Nottingham route, it was not difficult to predict from the reports in the control rooms which trains had Jubilee's and which had Black 5's; the latter usually managing to drop a couple of minutes on the longer and faster sections of line. The Jubilee's had that little bit extra that made all the difference on a fast schedule.

The first tabulated run shows a Jubilee (45616) at its best, running the down morning Palatine as far as Peak Forest but only just managing to keep time in spite of making a Herculean effort at times. The run was made after the 1957 accelerations ands the engine was having to maintain timings that at the time were usually worked by Britannia Pacifics although in this case the load had been reduced to eight vehicles. Had the earlier load of nine vehicles been taken it is doubtful whether the 4-6-0 could have kept time on its own although, under the 1957 'rules', the driver would have been entitled to ask for a pilot. (In 1957 when the accelerations were brought into being, the single engine load for a 5XP was set at 300 tons, a figure just inside the normal nine coach trains. As a result most of the surviving 2P 4-4-0's found themselves back on the main line as pilots to the Jubilee's until the arrival of Britannia's and Royal Scots).

On the 1/375 from Whatstandwell to Matlock Bath the 4-6-0 sustained 834 dbhp - the equivalent of 1000dbhp at 50 mph - whilst

By the early 1960's steam was starting to look rather jaded and this impression is exemplified by the begrimed condition of the 7P 4-6-0 which headed the up Palatine through Hassop on 4th June 1960. Few engines fell from grace quite as thoroughly as the Royal Scots: only a few months before the photograph was taken they were the most familiar type of engine on the LNW yet within a couple of years they had been ousted by diesels from most LMS workings, the survivors eking out a miserable existence on what remained of the Great Central.

on the recovery from the Rowsley slack an output of just under 1000 horsepower was achieved.

As a comparison, a record of a run on the 10.15 St Pancras - Manchester by a Black 5 4-6-0 a few years previous is illustrated and the figures suggest that although the maximum outputs of the two types of 4-6-0 were similar, the smaller engine was unable to sustain them for as long as the 5XP nor was it able to produce a high output at the same speeds as the Jubilee. (The pc figures in the logs are a weighting factor which makes an adjustment for the relationship between speed and horsepower. A pc of 4 is the equivalent of 1000 dbhp at 40 mph whilst a pc of 5 equates to 1000dbhp at 50 mph).

Because of the proximity of Derby the line was something of a proving ground for experimental locomotives - the most notable of which was probably a Clan 4-6-0 from the Highland Railway - especially after nationalisation when BR dabbled cautiously in the field of diesel traction. Most of the early types worked for short periods of time between Manchester and London whilst the Fell 2000hp diesel-mechanical 2-8-2 was allocated to the service for a number of years from 1951, its withdrawal coming after a destructive fire in Manchester Central. The difference between this locomotive and the other diesels was that it had a direct drive from the diesel engine to the axles, thereby making unnecessary the expensive and heavy electrical equipment of the others.

Until 1954 the Fell locomotive, 10100, was the most powerful of the diesels owned by BR and its output was approximately 25% higher than the 5XP 4-6-0's it was working with and the log of a run on the 16.15 St Pancras - Manchester shows the engine slogging its way up the bank from Rowsley to Monsal Dale outputting more than 1200 horsepower at the drawbar.

There were very few places where LMS and SR engines could be seen together - the two railways were rather far apart both geographically and operationally - yet when the motive power crisis on the late 1950's arose there were serious suggestions that the SR should part with some its light Pacifics to allow the Midland line to upgrade its services to 7P haulage. The proposal, with some help from the Southern, was vetoed by the Railways Executive and nothing came of the matter although, ironically, when the Southern, some years later, wanted replacements for their Merchant Navy Pacifics they cast their eyes - in vain as it happened - at the Stanier Coronation Pacifics.

Thus the only instance in which a Bulleid Pacific was seen on the Peak Forest line was in 1948 when 34005 'Barnstaple' worked the 10.15 ex St Pancras for a couple of weeks, becoming the first Pacific locomotive to work over the line. Details of the engines' performance is given in an accompanying table but one is bound to say that it was something of a disappointment, time was only just kept whilst power output was in the main no greater than might have been expected from a smaller locomotive and the output of just over 1000 dbhp in the climb to Monsal Dale was very little more than the Jubilee produced in its run.

An LNER B1 4-6-0 was also used on the 10.15 express at the same time and having looked at the output of a Stanier Black 5, the opportunity to compare the rival locomotive is irresistible. Although designed with much the same sort of work in mind on their respective systems, the amount of class 1 running achieved by the LNER 4-6-0's was but a mere fraction done by the Stanier locomotives; the reason being that the East Coast was so well stocked

DERBY : PEAK FOREST (1948)															
				LNER B1 4-6-0 61251 310/325 tons				SR 7P 4-6-2 34005 310/325 tons				LMS 5MT 4-6-0 45253 312/330 tons			
M.ch	Point	Grade	WTT	Actual	MPH	dbhp	pc	Actual	MPH	dbhp	pc	m.secs	mph	dbhp	pc
0.00	DERBY		0.00	0.00	-	-	-	0.00	-	-	-	0.00	-	-	
3.11	Lt Eaton Jcn	716		6.01	48.5	801	2	6.10	39.0	681	2	7.24	15.0	300	1
7.67	Belper	781		11.10	56.0	705	4	11.20	635.0	1130	6	15.31	50.0	595	2
10.30	AMBERGATE	494	15.00	14.12	32.0	-	-	14.48	22.0			18.54	27.0		
13.35	High Peak Jcn	789		18.28	55.0	895	4	19.21	49.0	902	4	23.21	53.0	888	4
					24.0								24.0		
16.05	Matlock Bath	268		22.18	34.0			22.34	46.0	672	3	26.25	45.0	517	3
17.12	MATLOCK	359	24.00	24.29	-	-	-	24.30	-	-		28.18	-	-	-
2.14	Darley Dale	19140		4.20	51.0	910	3	4.13	54.0	1040	3	4.32	50.0	831	2
					26.0				17.0	-			24.0		
4.36	Rowsley	360	7.00	7.29	32.0			7.34	32.5	-		7.54	31.5	-	
6.33	Haddon	117		11.30	26.5	690	2	11.40	30.0	745	2	11.50	38.0	920	3
7.64	Bakewell	170		14.02	35.0	895	3	14.04	36.5	927	3	14.13	36.5	656	2
8.65	Hassop	112		15.50	32.0	818	3	15.38	39.5	1307	5	15.49	38.0	1171	4
11.46	Monsal Dale	147		20.45	44.0	935	3	19.24	53.0	1416	6	20.00	45.0	1066	4
13.00	MP.158	106		23.06	29.5	574	2	21.12	42.0	826	4	22.09	32.0	659	3
14.21	MILLERS DALE	210	23.00	25.44	-	-	-	23.09	-	-		24.34	-	-	-
1.23	M. Dale Jcn	110		3.43	29.0	932	2	3.37	29.5	1008	2	4.22	26.5	732	1
4.45	Peak Forest	91	10.00	11.02	26.5	864	2	9.47	32.5	1131	4	12.03	25.5	844	2
	ROWSLEY : MP 158					796	3			1035	4			916	3

A passenger steps forward to board the 16.10 Derby to Manchester only to find that the train running into Great Longstone platform is the 13.17 Kirkby - Ashton Road on the barest of margins ahead of the passenger. The driver studiously contemplates the passing platform whilst 48144 of Canklow and a 4F 0-6-0 on the rear go flat-out for Peak Forest in 1954.

Great Longstone station looking north four years later in 1958 as the up Palatine, 14.25 Manchester to St Pancras sweeps through behind Jubilee 4-6-0 No. 45579 'Punjab'. Traffic may have been rather thin on the ground - the station closed in September 1962 - but that has not prevented the staff from enhancing the appearance of the station. It would take an extremely fastidious station-master to find anything amiss.

Compound 41173 of Trafford Park pulls away from Bakewell with the 16.10 Derby - Manchester (Central) in 1954. It is curious that these 4-4-0's spent their final days in the front line; some working over the stiffest stretch of the Midland whilst others bore the brunt of the Bedford - St Pancras suburban workings, neither a sinecure.

Only the East Coast seemed to take train reporting numbers seriously although, for once, they have been positioned correctly for the Palatine, 14.25 Manchester - St Pancras (1C73), which is seen arriving in Bakewell on 9th May 1964 behind one of the Sulzer 2500hp diesel-electric locomotives, two years after the class had displaced steam from express passenger workings out of St Pancras.

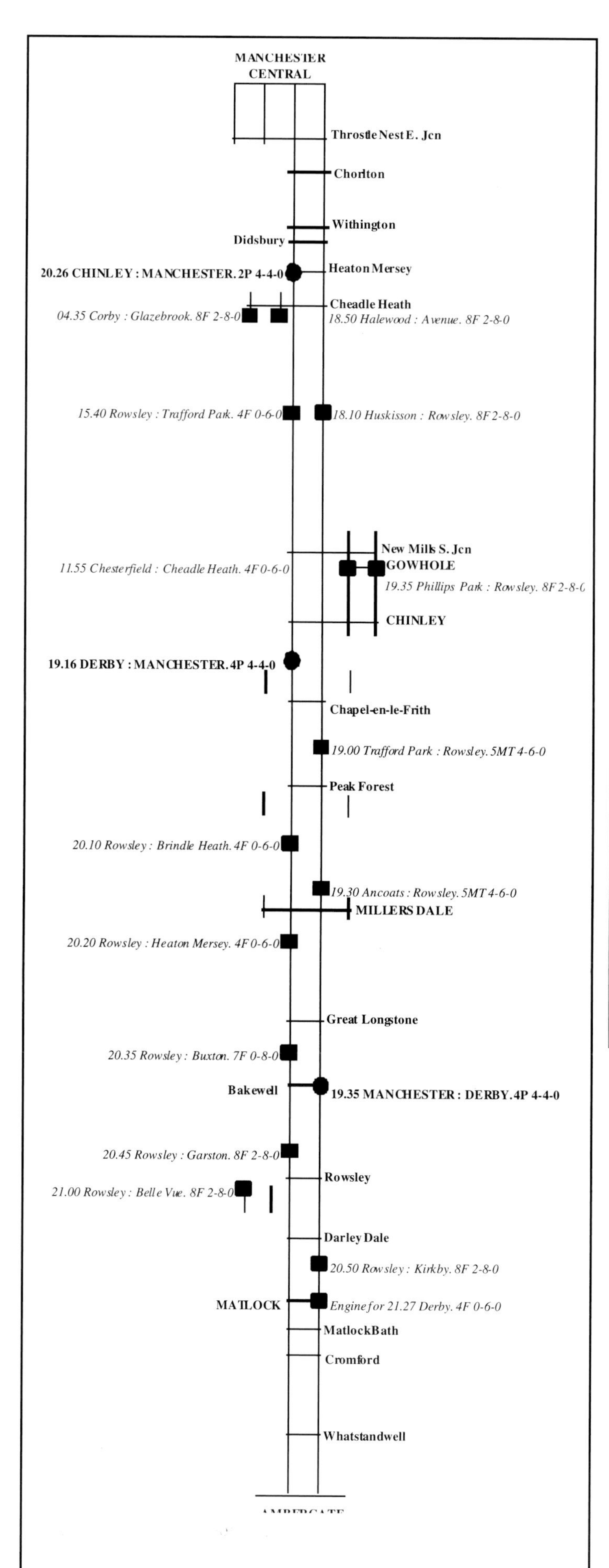

By 21.00 the night trains are starting to occupy the route, especially on the down side where the passage of the 19.10 ex Derby clears the line for the eight o' clock series of departures from Rowsley. On the up side a train of empties from Rowsley to Kirkby scuttles toward Ambergate, keeping clear of the 19.35 ex Manchester which, being the last passenger train of the day, opens the floodgates for a procession of southbound goods trains from the Manchester area.

16.15 ST PANCRAS : MANCHESTER (1952)
2000 hp Diesel-Mechanical 10100. 8:290/305

m.ch	Station	Gradient	W.T.T.	m.secs	mph	dbhp	pc
0.00	DERBY		0.00	0.00	-		
3.11	Little Eaton Jcn	716		5.12	61.0	1174	4
5.20	Duffield	2552		7.05	66.0	874	6
7.67	Belper	478		9.24	68.0	963	6
				Signal stop			
10.30	AMBERGATE	494	15.00	16.13	20.0		
13.35	High Peak Jcn	789		20.51	56.0	951	4
15.22	Cromford	349		23.00	49.0	298	1
17.12	MATLOCK		24.00	25.41			
2.14	Darley Dale	19140		3.57	61.0	1210	4
4.36	ROWSLEY	360	7.00	6.25	45.0		
7.64	Bakewell	170		10.43	48.5	1011	5
10.13	Great Longstone	200		13.44	47.5	789	4
11.46	Monsal Dale	357		15.25	55.0	1102	5
14.21	MILLERS DALE	116	26.00	19.03	-		
1.64	Peak Forest Jcn	98		4.43	35.5	1028	2
4.45	PEAK FOREST	90	10.00	8.54	42.5	1429	6

with Class 7 and 8 locomotives that very little of an express nature was left for the smaller machines. In fact the only regular high speed work that they were ever called upon to fulfil for any length of time were the two daily workings between Cleethorpes and Kings Cross. On the Great Eastern their thunder had been stolen by the Britannia's whilst their work on the Great Central was as second fiddle to the A3 pacifics. Whether the engine gave a representative performance on its visit to the LM in 1948 is a matter for study elsewhere but there is no doubt that on the run recorded its performance, measured in drawbar horsepower, was disappointing and markedly below that of the Stanier 5MT.

07.55 ST PANCRAS : MANCHESTER (1959)
7MT 4-6-2. 70004 'William Shakespeare'. 8:303/325 tons.

m.ch	Station	Gradient	W.T.T.	m.secs	mph	dbhp	pc
0.00	DERBY		0.00	0.00	-	-	-
0.61	Nottingham Road	321		2.18	43.0	1100	2
3.11	Little Eaton Jcn	1227		5.12	67.0	1387	7
5.20	Duffield	2552		7.00	65.0	413	3
7.67	Belper	478		9.12	70.0	1355	10
10.30	AMBERGATE	494	13.00	12.20	27.0	-	-
12.25	Whatstandwell	527		15.03	54.0	1425	6
15.22	Cromford	541		17.55	64.0	1254	8
16.05	Matlock Bath	174		18.43	60.0	647	4
17.12	MATLOCK	359	22.00	20.23	-	-	-
				sigs	39.0		
4.36	ROWSLEY	360	6.00	7.05	47.0	899	3
7.64	Bakewell	170		11.06	53.0	1273	6
10.13	Great Longstone	200		13.43	55.0	1178	6
11.46	Monsal Dale	357		15.13	60.0	1235	7
14.21	MILLERS DALE	116	20.00	18.37	-	-	-
1.64	PeakForest Jcn	98		4.20	39.0	1315	3
4.45	PEAK FOREST	90	8.00	8.02	49.0	1898	8

As a yardstick, to work a 300 ton train at an average speed of 60 mph on the 1/135 between Rowsley to Monsal Dale an output of about 1800 dbhp was called for; a feat that was just about within the capability of the 2500 bhp diesel-electric locomotives that worked the route in its final years. To find a steam engine to match the requirement would have meant looking at a class 8P which of course did not work over the route although the Britannia pacific in its performance came very close by averaging all but 1600 dbhp from Rowsley to MP 158. One cannot help wondering how much would have been saved in piloting costs - not to mention the accelerations that would have been possible - had this type of engine been allocated to the route when first introduced.

POWER COMPARISON
ROWSLEY : MONSAL DALE

Class	dbhp	pc	index
Britannia	1590	8	100
10100 (Diesel)	1245	6	78
W. Country	1035	4	65
5XP	998	4	63
5MT	916	3	58
B1	796	3	50

ROWSLEY

The common denominator during the ageing of Derbyshire seems to have been the 0-6-0 standard goods engine. A spectator a generation earlier or a generation later would still have seen the same sight - a goods train being worked by a Midland 0-6-0. 4019 trickles an up train through Rowsley station in 1935 as it waits for a road into the up yard. The locomotive dated from 1911 and still had thirty years of work ahead of it.

The Peak District, Settle & Carlisle and the Lickey Incline excepted the Midland was generally a fairly level railway with little worse than a few undulations in Bedfordshire and Leicestershire and as a result it was able to run full length goods trains for much of its length. The line to Manchester over Peak Forest was the principal exception and the severity of the gradients imposed an operational obstruction requiring a different method of working over the Peaks than that of the rest of the system.

The problem was that neither locomotives or wagon couplings could tackle the gradients up to Peak Forest with anything like a full load and therefore mineral trains had to be halved in weight for the journey the summit and this restriction called either for the lengthy diversion of traffic via Chesterfield and Hathersage, the construction of special engines or the siting of a marshalling yard at a point south of the severe inclines which started about twelve miles north of Ambergate where the Manchester route diverged from the rest of the Midland system.

Although some traffic was routed via Hathersage, the Hope Valley was not free from restrictions whilst it imposed additional mileage. Neither did the diversion address the problem of traffic passing between the south and Buxton where a heavy volume of traffic was exchanged with the London & North Western.

The design of engines specific to the Peak Valley could have become a possibility except that the governing factor in train weights on gradients of the kind encountered in North Derbyshire had rather less to do with tractive effort than with the strength of wagon couplings and indeed this factor was of such importance that the provision of banking engines for northbound trains was an much to prevent the effects of broken couplings as it was to provide additional traction.

The third option - the construction of a marshalling yard for traffic heading towards the Manchester, Buxton and Merseyside districts - was the one eventually adopted and culminated with the opening of the yard at Rowsley in March 1877. As a matter of history it should be stressed that the opening of the yard was as much a matter of evolution as a planned strategy since Rowsley had been the northern terminus of the line from 1849 until 1862.

Located to the west of the main running lines to the south of the passenger station, the yards at Rowsley

ROWSLEY DOWN YARD (NIGHTS) : 1954

Train	Arr	Class	Dep	Destination
20.25 Shobnall	22.18	E		
		J*	22.40	Ash Bridge via Buxton
20.30 Kirkby	*22.57*	*J**	*23.02*	*Ashton Road*
21.30 Chaddesden (MWF)	*23.10*	*F*	*23.20*	*Peak Forest*
21.10 Leicester	23.48	E		
21.30 Water Orton	23.58	E		
		J*	23.59	Longsight via Buxton
		J*	00.25	Buxton
22.18 Nottingham (Beeston)	*00.45*	*J*		
22.20 Birmingham (Lawley St)	00.58	E		
22.35 Nottingham	00.30	H	01.10	Brunswick
		E	01.35	Ancoats
20.55 Peterborough East	01.36	E		
23.55 Codnor Park	01.53	J		
00.01 Kirkby	02.12	J		
		E	02.32	Brewery
		H	03.00	Heaton Mersey
01.50 Stantongate (Toton)	03.25	H		
		F	03.40	Ancoats
		J	03.50	Buxton
		F	04.05	Brindle Heath
		E	04.15	Walton
01.40 Kirkby	*03.38*	*J**	*04.28*	*Gowhole*
00.50 Leicester (Humberstone Rd)	*04.35*	*F*		
03.43 St Mary's Jcn (Derby)	05.03	J		
03.10 Little Eaton Jcn	04.24	J*	05.04	Gowhole
03.18 Staveley	05.13	J		
02.35 Washwood Heath	*05.24*	*F*	*05.30*	*Brunswick*
		J*	05.35	Buxton
03.20 Kirkby	05.35	J		

** : Banked in rear from Rowsley to Peak Forest or Buxton.*
Through trains shown in italics

The original terminus of the line from Ambergate was superseded as a passenger station when the extension to Peak Forest and New Mills was opened. It did not however fall into disuse but was retained as a goods depot and was used extensively by the Express Dairies who brought in large quantities of milk from local farms for onward movement by rail. The view was taken on 8th August 1953.

were extensive and consisted of two separate yards for up and down traffic, the former comprising twelve through sidings with a capacity of 707 wagons whilst the down sidings were made up of twenty-two dead-end roads providing accommodation for 838 vehicles. The two yards were separated by a pair of running roads - the up and down goods - whilst a third (coal line) line bisected the down yard and gave direct access to the down sidings. In general terminating trains were routed by the last mentioned line - which was also known as the 'second down goods' - whilst through trains which called briefly for crew relief and the services of a banker were normally signalled via the down goods. Up trains which terminated at Rowsley ran on the up goods road and reversed into one of the four reception lines. The through arrangement of the up sidings did not allow trains to run straight in since there was no direct access to the sidings from the north, the northern end of the sidings converging into a shunting neck used for the remarshalling of traffic.

Given the mountainous nature of the line north of Rowsley, one might have expected the motive power depot to have been one of the first to receive the largest engines the system could offer. In fact the opposite applied and

ROWSLEY DOWN YARD (EARLY) : 1954

Train	Arr	Class	Dep	Destination
02.55 Kirkby	*05.56*	*J**	*06.08*	*Gowhole*
		J*	06.15	Buxton
18.00 Glendon (Kettering)	*06.32*	*J**	*06.40*	*Glazebrook*
22.40 ST PANCRAS	06.35	F		
		J*	07.05	Gowhole
		K	07.20	Hassop (Target 71)
05.35 Toton	07.20	H		
06.15 Swanwick	08.00	J		
		J*	08.45	Edgeley via Buxton
05.55 Tibshelf	09.08	J		
		E	*09.20*	*Ancoats*
07.25 Kirkby	09.25	J*	09.31	Gowhole
09.14 Little Eaton Jcn	*10.09*	*J*		
00.57 BRENT		F	10/27	BRUNSWICK
		J*	10.28	Longsight via Buxton
07.40 Staveley	11.09	J		
		J*	11.15	Buxton
10.45 Ambergate	11.28	J		
		K	11.33	Peak Forest (pick-up)
11.21 Matlock	11.35	J		
08.48 Water Orton (B'ham)	11.51	H		
		H	*12.02*	*Walton*
10.23 Codnor Park	*12.15*	*J**	*12.20*	*Agecroft*
10.30 Kirkby	12.29	J*	12.34	Ashton Road
		J*	12.40	Longsight via Buxton
11.40 Chaddesden (Derby)	12.48	J		
10.40 Avenue	12.57			
		J*	13.24	Garston

** : Banked in rear from Rowsley to Peak Forest or Buxton*
Through trains shown in italics

the Midland Railway's apparent love of 0-6-0 tender engines was nowhere as marked as it was at Rowsley which, as late in its history as 1950, was blessed with nothing larger than a fleet of 4F 0-6-0's for ordinary traffic together with an allocation of five 'Crab' 2-6-0's which were used on the fast goods services to the south.

The expense of working mineral traffic over Peak Forest was high and it is surprising that no effort appears to have been made to reduce the costs of operations. An 8F-hauled train from the Derby direction could bring in a maximum of 70 wagons which then had to be broken up at Rowsley into - assuming 4F 0-6-0 haulage northwards - three trains; the 4F limit being 26 vehicles. In the event of an 8F working north from Rowsley then the maximum could be increased to 37 wagons provided a banking engine was used as far as Peak Forest.

As at all major yards the loading instructions for making up train loads at Rowsley were complex and called for experience in their application. The subject was complicated by the fact that in making up a train for Gowhole the loading for the sections of line either side of Peak Forest had to be consulted and the lower of the two loadings applied. This ensured that neither engine(s) or cou-

Although the forty Stanier 5MT 2-6-0's lasted until the final days of steam - usually on engineering trains in connection with the LNWR electrification - they were too thinly scattered over the LM to make much of an impression and in any case were completely put into the shade by the Black 5 4-6-0's when they appeared, a year after the moguls, in 1934. On Friday 29th May 1964 42977 of Springs Branch, Wigan, appeared at Rowsley on the 06.21 goods from Buxton and was sent back with the 08.45 to Stockport (Adswood) and was caught by the camera topping up the tender as the banker coupled up to the rear of the train at Rowsley. The crew worked as far as Davenport Junction, Stockport, where they changed footplates with the 14.00 Longsight to Buxton.

plings were overloaded on the uphill section whilst braking power was taken into account on the descent north of the summit. There were some pitfalls to avoid such as the fact that Garratt 2-6-6-2's, LNWR 7F's and Austerity 2-8-0's could not take more than a 4F 0-6-0 load on the downhill stretch which meant that the Garratt was permitted to take a greater load from Rowsley to Peak Forest (48 loaded mineral wagons) than it was from Peak Forest to Gowhole (45). Beyer-Garratts were not often used over Peak Forest although one was tried on a service train during the war. No problems appear to have been caused going uphill but on the run downhill matters could have got out of control - presumably the train had a clear run through Dove Holes and Chinley - since, on inspection at Heaton Mersey it was discov-

The 11.30 Rowsley - Kirkby pulls out of the up yard with a train load of mineral empties behind Stanier 2-8-0 48225 on 1st July 1950.

Although useful to the operating department, there can scarcely have been a class of engine so heartily detested by locomen as the Austerity 2-8-0's which could conjure up freezing draughts in the cab on the warmest of days and rode in such a way as to loosen teeth. The sight of 90343 heading south from Rowsley on 27th June 1957 would have pleased local enthusiasts if not the train crew since the engine was allocated to Aintree (L&Y) and has clearly been misappropriated after having worked a special up to the Midland. It is interesting to note how the modern 16-ton mineral wagons had replaced the older wooden-sided 13-tonners by this date.

ered that every brake-block on the engine had melted and after this - and perhaps because of it - episode Garretts were rarely, if ever, used north of Rowsley although they were regular visitors from the south on trains from Toton.

The heaviest train possible was that permitted for a 9F 2-10-0 which was authorised to haul forty-one 13-ton loaded minerals over the Peak. These engines, which did not appear until 1954, were not regularly seen on the route until rather late in the day and for the most part 4F 0-6-0's and 8F 2-8-0's ruled unchallenged except on the LNWR workings to Buxton and Stockport which tended to be worked by G2a 0-8-0 locomotives.

Two especial headaches nursed by the yard Inspectors were the problems of maintaining a supply of suitable brakevans and banking engines. Because of the incline up to Peak Forest and the fear of unfitted trains dividing en route, all workings over Peak Forest had to be equipped with a 20-ton brakevan since they (in theory) had the capability of holding a loose train on the worst of the bank and preventing it from running back down the hill. Their capacity was set at twenty-six loaded mineral wagons - the maximum loading for a class 4F 0-6-0 - and any train that exceeded this limit had to have a banking engine in the rear as far as Peak Forest.

Brake vans were not controlled individually as locomotives were but, since they were

ROWSLEY DOWN YARD (LATE) : 1954

Train	Arr	Class	Dep	Destination
14.00 Darley Dale	14.13	K		
		H	14.30	Trafford Park
11.10 Santongate (Toton)	14.30	J		
		J*	14.45	Gowhole
03.25 Glendon (Kettering)	*14.59*	*J**	*15.07*	*Glazebrook*
13.17 Kirkby	*15.25*	*J**	*15.31*	*Ashton Road*
		J	15.40	Trafford Park
		J*	16.20	Edgeley via Buxton
14.45 Codnor Park	16.30	J		
15.00 Kirkby	16.55	J		
		H*	17.20	Garston via Buxton
04.35 Corby	18.10	J*	18.24	Glazebrook
18.13 Matlock	18.33	J		
15.45 Tibshelf	18.40	J		
18.02 Ambergate	19.20	H		
18.35 Chaddesden (Derby)	20.04	J		
		J*	20.10	Brindle Heath
		J	20.20	Heaton Mersey
		J*	20.35	Edgeley via Buxton
		H*	20.45	Garston
		J*	21.00	Belle Vue
		J*	21.58	Garston via Buxton

** : Banked in rear from Rowsley to Peak Forest or Buxton*
Through trains shown in italics

4F 0-6-0 44271 departs from Rowsley up yard with a special for Chaddesden, Derby, on 29th May 1964. This engine was destined to become the last 4F to be allocated to Buxton and was not withdrawn until January 1966.

In addition to the conventional remarshalling of traffic, Rowsley was also used to store large numbers of mineral wagons when not required by collieries. Typically the winter would see every available wagon pressed into service whilst the summer would have staff scratching their heads, wondering where they were going to find room for spare wagons. On 27th July 1957 Kirkby colliery was evidently in short supply as 8F 2-8-0 48383 has been detailed to work a special Rowsley - Kirkby and is seen approaching Rowsley South with its train of empty coal hoppers.

an essential part of a train, a careful watch had to be kept on their numbers and especially those of the 20-ton type which were needed for services over Peak Forest. As a general rule other types of van which arrived from the south were sent across to the up side to be worked out on trains heading for the Ambergate direction whilst any 20-ton brakes which materialised where concentrated on the down side where, without them, trains would have to be cancelled. It was the practice of Yard Inspectors when taking duty to assess the number of types of brakes that would be working in to the yard during their spell of duty, adding the result of their calculations to those which were already on hand to determine whether or not sufficient brake van were going to be available. If he position looked as though it was going to be tight arrangement had to be made with the district control - of which there was one at Rowsley until nationalisation - to get some additional vans worked into the area. This was usually done by getting an adjacent district to add whatever vans they could spare to a convenient train or - if the situation was dire - to organise a special 'engine and vans' to keep Rowsley moving. The district controls usually attempted to pre-empt shortage of brakevans by keeping a record of the numbers which entered and left the district (normally on the basis that one train equalled one brakevan) and were in a position to calculate whether the district was making or losing vans. The calculation referred to the district rather than individual yards and the Deputy Chief Controller - the man in charge of the district control - when he held his start of shift 'confab' with the Assistant Yard Manager to decide which trains were being run would include the topic of brakevans and whether or not action was needed to increase the number. (Conversely, when a foreign yard called out for help with brakevans, Yard Inspectors - usually aided and abetted by the controller - would swear blind that they couldn't possibly help and that they hadn't got a brake with which to scratch their backsides, etc.).

In addition to keeping a tally of twenty-ton brakevans, the Inspectors duties included keeping an eye on the banking engines of which ten were supplied by Rowsley MPD together five which came from Buxton and one each from Saltley, Kirkby and Longsight; a total of eighteen locomotives. Although their workings were strictly programmed it could never be assumed that they would arrive back punctually from Peak Forest or Buxton and a con-

Although predating the Stanier era, the 'Crab' 5MT 2-6-0's were well-liked by crews and did a great deal of valuable work on fast freight services that did not warrant a Black 5. Rowsley had an allocation of five of these 2-6-0's for the fitted goods to Birmingham and Somers Town, working in conjunction with engines of the same class from Saltley depot, one of which, 42890, arrives at Rowsley with the 08.48 class H from Water Orton, Birmingham. You had to watch your feet on these engines: the cab was significantly wider than the tender and a careless pace backwards could spell trouble.

Rowsley had two passenger turns for which three 4-4-0's were allocated. Two of them were 2P 4-4-0's whilst the third was a compound which generally worked the 07.35 Bakewell - Derby each morning, returning at 17.05 after spending the intervening hours on empty carriage duties at Derby. On 27th June 1957 compound 41185 backs onto the shed after running light from Bakewell after completion of the diagram. Later in the year the 4-4-0's were replaced by a trio of LMS 2-6-4 tanks.

tinuous watch had to be kept on the engines in order to ensure that there was always one available when needed. Although it was only 14 miles to both Buxton and Peak Forest, the time it took a banking engine to complete its work and return light was excessive and the norm for a single trip was about four hours. (Of the ten Rowsley turns, only one permitted a set of men to work two banking trips to Peak Forest within the compass of an

ROWSLEY UP YARD (NIGHTS) : 1954

Train	Arr	Class	Dep	Destination
		E	22.05	Brent
18.10 Huskisson	22.23	F		
		F	22.30	Little Eaton Jcn
19.35 Philips Park	22.48	H		
		H	22.55	Staveley
20.25 Moston	23.01	F		
21.20 Ancoats	23.37	E		
22.00 ANCOATS		*C*	*23/58*	*ST PANCRAS*
		H	00.10	Lawley St (B'ham)
21.40 Trafford Park	00.15	F		
		F	00.20	Kirkby
22.35 Heaton Mersey	00.42	F		
		H	01.30	Burton on Trent
		F	01.50	Leicester
21.05 Huskisson	01.50	E		
22.40 Ancoats	02.04	H		
18.50 Latchford via Buxton	02.20	F		
		F	02.30	St Pancras
22.14 Heaton Norris via Buxton	02.52	H		
21.00 Dundas Sdgs	03.05	H		
21.16 Garston	03.14	F		
		F	03.25	Nottingham
		F	03.35	St Mary's Jcn (Derby)
23.55 Brunswick	03.40	H	03.45	Spondon
21.25 Garston via Buxton	03.55			
		E	04.00	Washwood Heath (B'ham)
03.15 Buxton	04.15	H		
23.38 Moston	04.28	H		
		F	04.38	Kirkby
		H	04.50	Ilkeston Jcn
		F	05.10	Kirkby
00.05 Garston via Buxton	05.15	F		
01.30 Garston	05.30	H		

Through trains shown in italics

ROWSLEY UP YARD (EARLY) : 1954

Train	Arr	Class	Dep	Destination
		F	06.00	Leicester
03.25 Ashton Road	06.00	F		
		K	06.20	Matlock Bath
1.50 Ellesmere Port	06.30	F		
		H	06.47	Kirkby
05.40 Gowhole	06.51	F		
		J	07.05	Chaddesden (Derby)
06.40 Buxton	07.15	J		
		H	07.30	Kirkby
02.15 Garston via Buxton	07.34	F		
		J	07.50	Crich Jcn
03.29 Hooton	*07.58*	*H*	*08.04*	*Kirkby*
		H	08.30	Langley Mill
05.00 Widnes	09.35	F		
		F	10.22	Brands Sdgs
		F	10.35	Blackwell Sdgs
		H	10.42	Leicester (Wigston)
08.02 Belle Vue	*10.42*	*H*	*10.49*	*Kirkby*
09.00 Heaton Mersey	11.25	H		
		F	11.30	Kirkby
11.14 Hassop	11.56	K		
		J	12.13	Matlock
		K	12.23	Darley Dale
		K	12.35	Chaddesden (Derby)
11.35 Buxton	12.36	H		
10.50 Gowhole	12.40	H		
08.00 Garston via Buxton	13.15	J		
12.55 Buxton	13.55	H		

Through trains shown in italics

Diesel shunting locomotives never became established at Rowsley and although a pair arrived in the summer of 1959, within two months they had been sent away, leaving the LMS 3F 0-6-0T's to carry on with the work. 47460 poses at the shed on 27th June 1957 with 4F 0-6-0 44163 in the background. For reasons unknown the 0-6-0 tanks (and shunting engines generally) were known as 'Jinties' south of Leicester and 'Jocko's' to the north.

eight hour shift and the other turns either called for overtime or a change of footplatemen after the first trip).

Whether anyone ever sat down and attempted to put a cost to the working of trains from Rowsley to Gowhole is doubtful - ten economists would probably have come up with ten different conclusions - since one had to weigh on the one hand the cost of a single 4F 0-6-0 with 26 wagons as opposed to an 8F 2-8-0 with 37 but the latter having the additional cost of a banker which, unless you were very fortunate, would only manage one trip to Peak Forest within an eight hour shift. Lord Stamp, the President of the LMS, was a renown economist and his influence effected everything on the company from drawing pins to locomotives yet operations at Rowsley continued, apparently unquestioned. Perhaps his subordinates felt that the subject might be one challenge too many and that he should be kept well away from the area. Who knows?

Northbound express goods trains from Rowsley did not amount to much - the bulk of traffic was moved in class J mineral trains - and there were only five such departures a day (four class E and one class F), running in the morning with goods traffic for the Manchester and Liverpool area's. Generally no special arrangements were necessary for them provided they ran with a class 4F 0-6-0 load (45 wagons for a class E and 48 for an F) which was normally sufficient for the traffic on each. If loads did exceed this limit a larger engine (or a pilot) and a banker had to be provided although any sort of brakevan, other than a 10-tonner, could be used. The five trains were booked to be worked by Rowsley 4F 0-6-0's and no bankers were in fact allocated to them. (The presence of a forty-sixth vehicle could be guaranteed to throw the place into difficulties. Class 5 engines, and higher, were thin on the ground and those that worked into the yard had return workings and therefore could not normally be taken for a diversion over Peak Forest. Rowsley's small allocation of 2-6-0's was only just sufficient for the workings to the south whilst the provision of an additional banker meant the loss of an 0-6-0 and its crew for several hours. In most cases additional traffic waited for the next booked working or, if there was a respectable volume of stranded traffic, the control would arrange for a special train using a 4F and a set of spare men).

Through trains, especially special workings, provided problems for Rowsley because of the differing conditions which pertained north and south of the yard. For example Ancoats might start screaming out for additional vans - the provision of empty vans for goods yards was a topic in its own right - and a special might be arranged by the control at Derby with a full load for a 5MT 4-6-0. Running as a Class H the Black 5 would tear down the line with 63

ROWSLEY UP YARD (LATE) : 1954

Train	Arr	Class	Dep	Destination
		H	14.05	Staveley
13.08 Gowhole	14.30	H		
09.15 Walton	14.42	H		
		J	15.00	Avenue
		H	15.15	Washwood Heath (B'ham)
13.20 Philips Park	*15.54*	*F*	*15.59*	*Kirkby*
		G	16.05	Derby MPD (light)
11.05 Garston	16.08	F		
09.25 Dundas Sdgs	16.30	J		
13.50 Philips Park	16.38	H		
		G	16.40	Toton (Engine & Brake)
12.30 Walton	17.30	J	17.35	Kirkby
17.00 Peak Forest	17.45	J		
		H	18.25	Beeston (Nottingham)
		F	19.05	Langley Mill
		F	19.42	Blackwell
18.35 Buxton	19.51	J		
		J	20.15	Chaddesden (Derby)
		G	20.37	Matlock (light)
		J	20.50	Kirkby
19.30 Ancoats	21.28	E		
19.00 Trafford Park	21.50	H		

Through trains shown in italics

The Rowsley MPD coaling plant and associated buildings in 1957

vans in tow which, under the rules that governed any other part of the system, would get to Ancoast within a couple of hours of leaving Derby. On the Peak Forest route, however, the train would have to go into the down yard at Rowsley to reduce its load; the train either continuing forward behind the 4-6-0 with ten wagons less and a banker to Peak Forest or with only 48 vehicles which was a 4F load and the maximum allowed without an engine in rear. Alternatively the special could leave Derby with no more than 48 wagons and run through which rather under-utilised a large engine and still denied Ancoats all the wagons they wanted. Even if the train was routed via the Hope Valley the maximum permitted was only 53 wagons although the services of a banker could be dispensed with. (This option would probably die stillborn since the majority of Derby crews would not know the road via Hathersage and would need to be conducted from Chesterfield).

TIMING CALCULATIONS		
Class J. Rowsley - Gowhole and return		
Section	Mins	Total
Engine preparation	45	45
MPD to Yard	10	55
Rowsley start	3	58
Rowsley - Millers Dale	38	96
Millers Dale - P. Forest Jcn	6	102
P. F. Jcn - Peak Forest	14	116
Peak Forest - Chinley	19	135
Chinley - Gowhole	7	142
Gowhole arrive	2	144
Turn-round time	90	234
Gowhole depart	3	237
Gowhole - Chinley	10	247
Chinley - Dove Holes	13	260
Dove Holes - Peak Forest	11	271
P. Forest - P. F. Jcn	7	278
P.F. Jcn - Millers Dale	5	283
Millers Dale - Rowsley	26	309
Rowsley arrive	2	311
Yard to MPD	10	321
Engine disposal	45	366
Basic shift		480
Time available		114

There were a number of through trains at Rowsley which called principally to take water and a banker but also, if it was necessary, to reduce their loads although most of these workings ran with 8F 2-8-0's from Kirkby and arrived from the south with 37 wagons which they could work forward to destination provided Rowsley gave them a banker as far as Peak Forest. This was a heavy flow of traffic - it was the most regular of all the through services via Rowsley - and its purpose was to move coal from the Erewash Valley and Kirkby districts to the Manchester area with as little fuss as possible. It was, however, necessary to keep a close watch on their running - the control took an unusually keen interest in them - since a severely delayed working could throw the carefully planned banking arrangements to the wind and if a Kirkby train turned up out of the blue with no banker available, something either had to be conjured out of thin air pretty quickly or the train had to be quickly shunted clear of the running line before it stopped the job and reduced to 26 wagons, which meant blocking the yard and arguing with the Kirkby train crew who were already clocking up overtime. The controller who let a Kirkby train arrive unsuspected was not likely to be the most popular soul in the district for some time especially.

The hour by hour working of the yard was managed by the Yard Inspectors who planned their respective shifts with the aid of departure sheets not dissimilar to the departure lists depicted on these pages. Each siding in the yard would be dedicated to a destination and a continuous record was kept of the number and type of each wagon in each road. Upon taking duty each Inspector would read over to the controller a summary of his yard position and between them they would decide which trains were going to run for the coming eight hours and what each service was to take. Priority was, of course, given to goods - as opposed to mineral traffic - and anything of significance that had been left behind by the fast freights had to be sent forward as a matter of urgency even if it meant cancelling a mineral train in order to find an engine and crew for a special working.

Arranging loads between the District control and the yard also involved quite distant parts of the railway since agreement had to be obtained from the receiving districts. For example each of the Kirkby trains would be discussed with the Nottingham district who would not only advise on the destination of traffic that each train was going to bring but would have to 'agree' the number of empty wagons that each service would return with. Each colliery

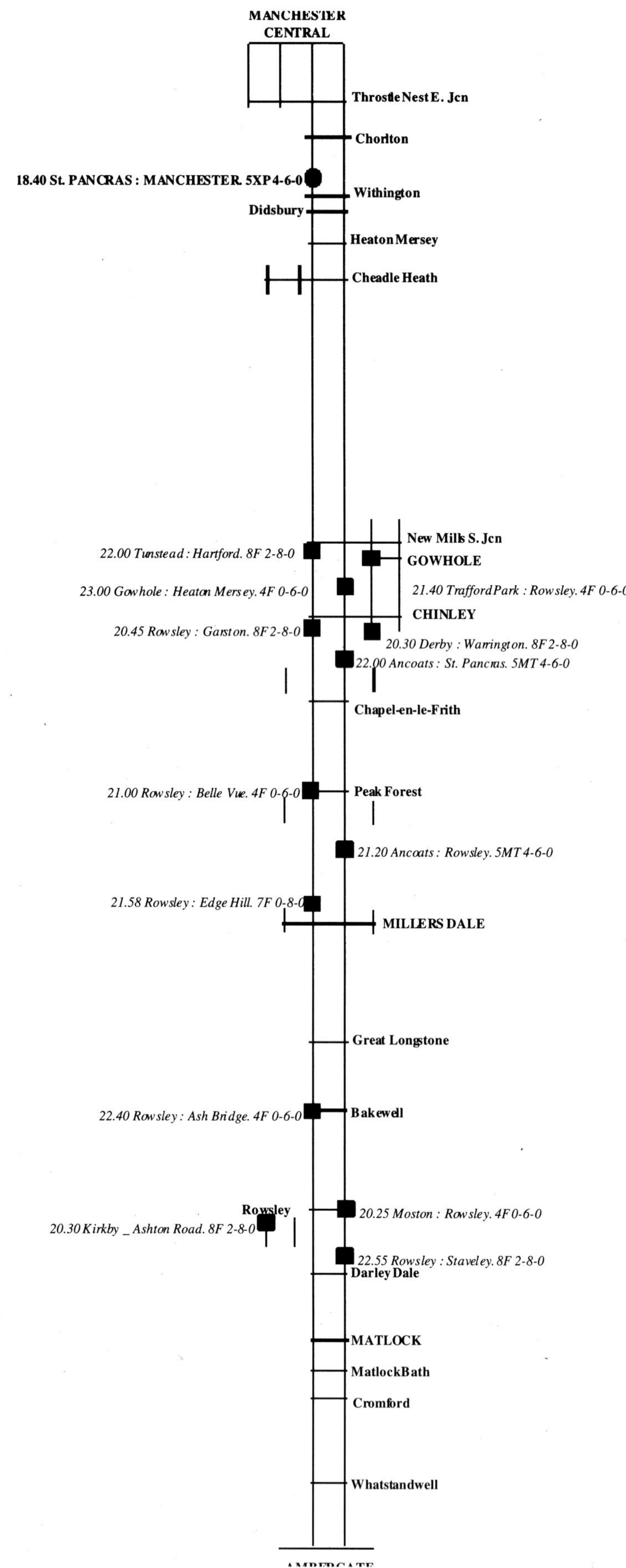

At 23.00 the evening express from London approaches journey's end and clears the way for a deluge of northbound trains from Rowsley, all of which get a clear run over the fast line as opposed to the usual dodging from loop to loop. The line south of Rowsley is kept clear for the spate of fast freights which cross the border at Ambergate between 23.00 and midnight. One down train, the 19.35 Chaddesden to Warrington, makes quite a detour and runs from Derby to Chinley via Clay Cross and Chesterfield; a diversion which not only saves a path over Peak Forest but spares Rowsley from having to find a banker. In the southbound direction a trio of express goods trains take advantage of the lull in passenger traffic by running main line through the Chinley area.

district made up a quota of wagons which it would need in the coming twenty-four hours and once this figure had been computed it was up to the control to scour the adjacent districts for empties and arrange for them to be returned

At quiet times - the summer - the demand for empties would be low whilst colliery output would be quiet and on some days not all coal trains would be required. Rowsley control would then cancel these trains and keep the engines and crew 'up his sleeve' in case there was a surplus of traffic in another direction for which special trains would be needed. On the other hand in the winter when the collieries were working flat out the booked service would probably be insufficient for the empties required by Nottingham and either Rowsley would be instructed to find engines and men for additional trains or Nottingham would be told to send an engine and brake across for them. A request - at the drop of a hat - for five hundred mineral empties ('pools' in everyday jargon) to Kirkby was quite commonplace and Rowsley would be expected to find engines and men for them as a matter of routine. No schedule - other than an estimated time of departure - would be drawn up and the trains would be regulated by the signalmen in between other trains of a higher priority.

The regard given to point to point timings varied from one type of train to another. The higher classification services had very strict timings which were not only mandatory but had to be adhered to and a careful watch was kept on these workings - in exactly the same way as was done for passenger trains - with any delay forming the basis of an inquest. Initially the controller would attempt to establish the cause but if further enquiries were needed, the matter would be passed upwards for more detailed enquiries to be made. Lower class trains - H and J services in particular - were more difficult to monitor since they usually crept from one block post to the next, in and out of every goods loop, and since the working book assumed - rather optimistically - a clear path it was usually rather difficult to determine whether loss of time was due to a tardy piece of driving or caution in approaching junction signals. Where 'off the cuff' special trains were concerned, timings were dispensed with altogether. The train would be given a notional departure time based on the time the engine and men were available and it would take its turn in the queue according to its classification. The controller would be vaguely aware that the time for a class J to run from Rowsley to Gowhole and back was 'about four and a half hours', the actual running time being about an hour and a half in each direction plus any delays for regulation purposes.

If however a special train was arranged by the timing department - in cases where several weeks notice of operation was given - or a new train was to be included in the timetable, then the timings would be calculated on a strict basis and would include allowances for starting and stopping. Assuming a clear run throughout and after allowing for engine preparation/disposal times and one or two other allowances, a set of Rowsley men could work to Gowhole and back with just over two hours to spare. The timing clerk however would have to plot a path for the train on a graph and he would know that if the total delays in shunting for other services came to more than one hundred and twenty-nine minutes (see the table attached) he would either have to find an alternative path or arrange for another set of men to prepare or dispose of the engine. If, at the end of the day, all efforts to find a path became exhausted the more unscrupulous elements in the timing office would circumvent the problem by sending a notice to the control with the terse message:

Mondays, Wednesday, Fridays 1 March to 4 April 1955.

Additional train 07.30 Rowsley - Gowhole Class J

Additional train 10.00 Gowhole - Rowsley Class J

Control to arrange

Having decided in his discussion with the district control which trains were going to run and what they were to take, the Yard Inspector would pass the information on to his Foreman shunter who would then take over the minutiae of the actual working. This would involve conferring as necessary with his shunting staff who would get down to the task of breaking up arriving trains, making up loads in the departure sidings and keeping the Inspector informed as to progress. The Inspector, for his part, would spend much of his time in trying to anticipate problems and updating the traffic position as approaching trains came close to the yard. Condensed details of all trains terminating at Rowsley would be telephoned to the Inspector by the controller as they came into the district together with an estimated time of arrival. The Inspector would make a mental assessment of how the traffic was to be worked forward and pass the information forward to his Foreman. More detailed information concerning the make-up of each train was 'wired' by the telegraph office to the Inspectors' clerk who would draw attention to anything in each train that appeared to be unusual or urgent.

On the statistical side a considerable amount of information had to be collated by the Inspector, partly to indicate to the Yard Master how effectively the yard was working - wagons per hour or per shift was the usual basis of reckoning - and partly to enable any 'lost' consignments to be traced.

Typically a clerk from the headquarters would telephone several times a day in an attempt to try and trace wagons that had not reached their destination and this usually involved him in speaking to every yard that may have dealt with the vehicles and finding out when they arrived and left each point along the route. Nine times out of ten it turned out that most of the wagons in question had run hot somewhere on the route and had been removed for carriage and wagon attention who lines of contact with the operating department were not always as streamlined as they might have been.

The trouble-shooting element of the Inspectors duties revolved around the business of assuring that everything was in its place for each departure. Where the engine, men and guard on their way? Was there a brakevan of the correct sort - was the supply of brakes adequate for the rest of the shift? Was the banking engine ready and had the trains' load been calculated correctly? This last point was especially important, not simply for the obvious safety reasons, but because trains were assessed on the basis of standard wagons and in making up a train those concerned had to equate each vehicle with the basic standard unit. It was a point which supported - indeed invited - contention and there was always some foreign guard who thought he knew better and would insist that his train had been overloaded. It was a fruitful source of delay, discussion and overtime.

The problems involving the banking engines have already been alluded to and one of the things that made it an ulcerous business - especially for the yard inspector -

was that there was no single individual who had very much influence over what the bankers did once they had left Rowsley whilst in the majority of cases it was impossible to do more than a single trip to Peak Forest without getting the crew to work overtime.

The banking engines actually appeared in the timetable and were given paths to return to Rowsley from either Peak Forest or Buxton but these slots in the timetable were theoretical and, given that a light engine did not usually warrant much of a priority in regulating terms, took no account of the state of play at the time an engine arrived at Peak Forest. Typically an engine would start to bank a train from Rowsley after the crew had been on duty for about an hour - they usually prepared their own engine - and the trip to the summit took the best part of an hour and a half. They would then sit at Peak Forest, often for quite a long time, until a path in the timetable occurred when they would be allowed to drift back downhill to Rowsley - an hours trip even for a light engine - by which time there was no possibility of their doing a second trip within the orbit of an eight hour shift. In fact of the twenty booked banking turns provided by Rowsley shed, only one was able to do a double turn to Peak Forest although this was partially due to the fact that the incidence of trains to be banked did not always fit nicely into a workable pattern for the bankers. (The one working that was booked for a double trip banked the 02.35 and 07.25 Kirkby - Gowhole trains which depended on good timekeeping by both trains south of Rowsley. It is probable that the scheduled banking arrangements did not work three days out of four with a substitute having to be found for the second Kirkby train).

The engines that banked over the main line were all allocated to Rowsley but those that assisted the Buxton trains came from a variety of sheds and included the Saltley engine off the 22.10 Lawley Street goods (05.35 to Buxton) and the Kirkby 4F which arrived in the district with the 03.10 Derby - Gowhole and then ran light to Rowsley to bank the 11.15 Buxton goods. A considerable number of the Buxton route services were worked as well as banked by Buxton engines, some of which ran light to Rowsley before starting their days work. Naturally close communication had to be maintained with Buxton loco to ensure that these engines were able to get to Rowsley in time for their workings.

A point of interest - not generally known - concerning banking operations was the way in which trains were started. Normally, with single engined trains, the guard would give the driver details of the trains loading and the right away, the guard swinging into his brake as it went by. With the length of the train separating two engines when banking was being undertaken, a different procedure had to be adopted and the signal to start was given to the banking engine which would whistle but not move until it had had an answering crow from the train engine. On nights of filthy

ROWSLEY (17D)
ALLOCATION
1950

Class	Engine
2P 4-4-0	40499
	40520
4P 4-4-0	41049
1F 0-6-0T	41875
5MT 2-6-0	42760
	42768
	42873
	42874
	42902
3F 0-6-0	43273
	43290
	43342
	43370
4F 0-6-0	43881
	43918
	43925
	43929
	44017
	44018
	44024
	44046
	44050
	44134
	44163
	44168
	44172
	44174
	44209
	44246
	44262
	44327
	44429
	44540
	44564
	44588
3F 0-6-0T	47447
	47457
	47459
	47460
	47461
	47679
2F 0-6-0	58189
	58219
	58224
	58226
	58228
	58254
0-6-0T	58850
	58856
	58860
	58862

Fairburn 4MT 2-6-4T 42228 and 5MT 2-6-0 'Crab' 42754 wait for a road to cross from the up main to the sidings and thence to Rowsley MPD on 27th June 1957. The 2-6-4 was a recent transfer from Derby, its purpose being to relieve the 4-4-0's of their passenger work, they were also used as banking engines for goods services to Peak Forest and Buxton.

Apart from the unrebuilt Patriot 4-6-0's, only the 5MT Crab 2-6-0's recalled the early LMS parallel boiler days and with 245 examples surviving until the last days of steam, were a familiar sight at most Midland and LNWR locations until the mid-1960's. 42942 of Buxton rests on Rowsley MPD on 27th June 1957 having arrived with the 18.35 class J goods from Buxton. It later returned home with the 22.40 goods to Ash Bridge.

weather with engines whistling all over the place, the difficulties connected with getting trains and their bankers on the move without incident can be better imagined than described.

The Running Foreman's duties at Rowsley loco, as elsewhere, were split between the provision of engines and men although the latter occupied rather more of his time than the other. Engine arranging was, in one sense, a straightforward task whilst in another it required a close rapport with the operating department whose needs more often than not varied considerably from the planned working. Essentially the Foreman would be concerned only with the trains that the depots engines were booked to work and periodically throughout the day he would be advised by the district controller of any changes that were being made to the timetable. Several times in a shift trains would be cancelled, diverted or run as specials and his principal responsibility to the operating department was to ensure that these amendments were catered for without delay.

He also had to view these alterations from a motive power angle, for example the diversion of a train from its booked destination to another could raise axle-weight implications with a lighter engine having to be substituted for the one originally booked. In addition he would have to advise the district control of how far his crew could work a particular train. The crew of a Derby service which had been cancelled to provide a set of engine and men for a special to Glazebrook via Cheadle Heath, for example, might only know the road as far as New Mills South Junction and - unless he happened to have a set of men on hand who could be substituted - he would have to ensure that the district control were aware of the fact. This was done by telephoning the message '12.00 special Rowsley to Glazebrook, engine 44429 Eager and Alert New Mills South': the code word 'eager' indicating the limit of route knowledge for the driver and 'alert' for the guard. It was then up to the district control to arrange for a set of men from Heaton Mersey to travel up to Gowhole or Chinley to conduct the special forward to Glazebrook or, if there were no men available to do this, to terminate the service at either Gowhole or Heaton Mersey and work it forward as another special when the resources became available. Great care had to be exercised in arranging for workings such as when the originating crew did not know the route throughout. If, for example, a Northwich crew were sent to Gowhole to relieve the train, the Rowsley men - if they had had a slow pas-

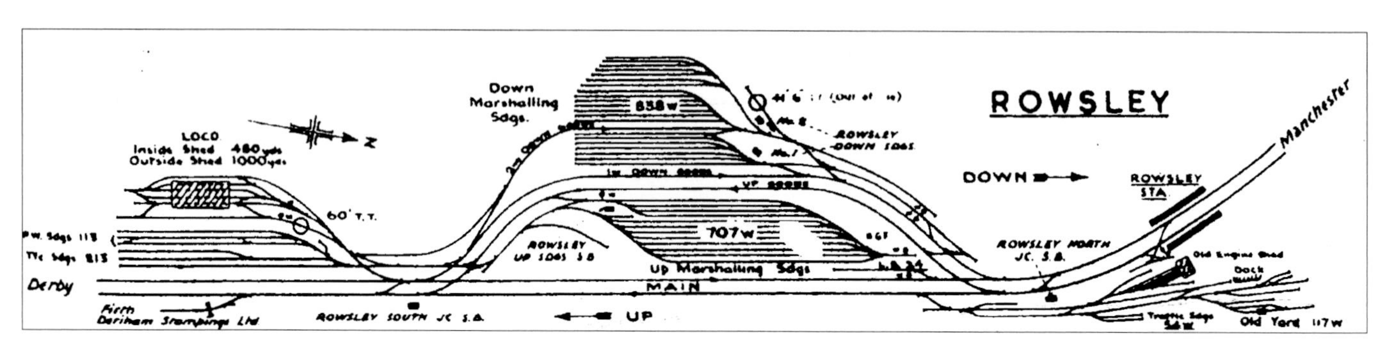

sage over Peak Forest - would bale out at Gowhole and return on the cushions whilst the engine would disappear to Glazebrook and Northwich, never to be seen again.

Bankers, as always, were a problem and when, for example, the control got its hands at short notice on an unbalanced 2-8-0 and decided to use it and its crew for a special to Agecroft, he would have to confirm with the yard that a banker was available or use his wits to find one. (When called upon to conjure an engine out of thin air - as Foremen were expected to do several times a day - the solution usually lay in redeploying the engines that were already at work rather than steaming one up specially. Apart from the fact that a cold engine required several hours - usually more - to raise steam, a little detective work over the telephone invariably 'made' an engine with a lot less trouble).

After being advised by the controller of what was running from the yard for the shift ahead, the foreman would consult his list of engines that were available and allocate them to trains, having consideration for workings that required anything over the basic class 4 loading which would mean providing a pilot engine and a banker. The allocation of engines would be made from the locomotives that were available on the shed since the arrival times of engines coming in off trains could neither be guaranteed or forecast because of the delays that were endemic with the sort of trains that Rowsley specialised in. It was a futile exercise to assume that because a Rowsley engine was due to arrive from Toton at, say, 18.00 it would be safe to allocate it in advance to a train due to leave the yard two hours later. Quite apart from issues concerning the mechanical state of the engine when it arrived back, it was quite possible - more than likely - that the engine would not arrive on shed until well after the departure time of the train it had been earmarked to work. Unlike passenger sheds whose engines came and went with more or less clockwork precision, it was rarely safe to estimate matters far in advance where goods traffic was concerned.

In spite of all the problems posed by bankers and late running, locomotives played only a minor part in the life of the running foreman and most of his energies went into organising train crew matters and dealing with the associated difficulties which were incessant. Anyone going into the Foreman's job and picturing it as some sort of paid hobby in which one painstakingly selected engines for trains as one (once) picked suitors for one's daughters was in for a disappointment of considerable magnitude. In a typical eight hour shift the foreman at Rowsley - and at any other shed - would spend about a quarter of an hour with engine matters, the rest of his time being preoccupied with crewing problems and queries from drivers and firemen most of whom had their own interpretations of their conditions of service.

It is doubtful if any profession has ever been surrounded with so much red-tape as that of engine driving and it was virtually impossible to transfer a driver or fireman from one job to another - as had to be done from time to time - without inviting contention. Almost every aspect of life was governed by national or local agreements which, when watered down with a good measure of local custom and practice, suggested that the best person to fill a running foreman's shoes was a lawyer as the following demonstrates:

Where it could be shown that a spare fireman would not be available and a relief driver had been deprived of a firemans turn by reason of a driver working his rest day, the relief driver should be given credit and payment for the firemans turn lost. In applying this arrangement, regard would be paid to the question of whether the senior relief fireman would have been available to work the turn in question. The senior relief fireman who was not working in the higher grade would be entitled to credit and payment for a higher grade turn provided he was available for the duty in question but was deprived of the turn.

And there were pages of such matter affecting every aspect of footplate life, all of which was grist to the mill for those who thought that they had been overlooked in some way and the foreman had no choice, if he was to succeed in his job, but to know the conditions - and the most practical way of interpreting them - back to front.

Strangely the railway gave absolutely no training (whatever) in this field and anybody entering the profession was expected to know, understand and implement the several hundreds of agreements as though they were common knowledge. The Trade Unions, on the other hand, were far more alert to the position and took considerable pains to ensure that the staff they represented had no grounds for ignorance.

About the only workings at Rowsley that could be described as routine were its passenger turns; two diagrams for which three 4-4-0 locomotives - a compound and two 2P's - were allocated. These left the shed at 05.40 and 06.20, the Compound often working the latter turn, running to Darley Dale and Bakewell respectively to work the 06.20 and 07.35 stopping trains to Derby. Both engines spent the day at Derby on ECS and station pilot duties and returned home with the 17.05 and 17.50 departures. Although - in the first half of the decade - 4-4-0's of both types were familiar enough on ordinary passenger work, by 1955 Standard 4-6-0's were beginning to thin their numbers but the enthusiast was able to take heart from the fact that such engines were still in daily use at Rowsley and at times it seemed as though they would carry on until displaced by diesels. Alas, it was not to be and by 1957 the new BR standard 4-6-0's and 2-6-0's had been built in such numbers that replacement was inevitable and in that same year Rowsley received a trio of 2-6-4 tanks which not only took over the passenger workings but - later in the day and after some stiff resistance from the footplatemens representatives who considered that they had too large a driving wheel for the job and insufficient water capacity - some of the banking duties.

It is an unfortunate fact that relatively few enthusiasts in the days of the steam status quo took the trouble to investigate and record the everyday workings of Rowsley and its shed and those that did make the pilgrimage did so, not because of the everyday business of working trains over the Peak, but to view the four North London 0-6-0 tanks which were based on the depot to work the Cromford & High Peak branch. Unfortunately this attraction could only be guaranteed at weekends - since the High Peak engines generally stabled out on the branch during the week - and thus the visits that were made occurred at a time when very little was happening on the main line.

If life at Rowsley could be difficult at times there was solace if not compensation to be gained from the rich variety of interest that coloured almost all jobs on the railway. It is true that income, relative to outside jobs, had declined but the railway provided most of its staff with a level of job satisfaction and prospects of advancement that would only otherwise have been found in the armed services during times of war. Whatever one did at Rowsley - motive power or operating - the problems that each shift posed were different, interesting and could be overcome by using a combination of wit and local knowledge. It was uncommon to go off duty without feeling some sort of sense of achievement and whilst few railwaymen were enthusiasts within the meaning of the act there were not many to whom the incessant ring of buffers and hissing steam was not music of a sort. To observe, at the end of an eight or twelve hour shift, a train pulling out of the yard and to know that some action of yours played a part in the running of that train bestowed a quiet satisfaction denied to those who followed more mundane, if better paid, careers.

Although the late 1960's proved to be a depressing period in the history of the Derby - Manchester line, not everyone has been content to leave the last word to the Beeching Axe and, thanks to the efforts of a number of especially dedicated enthusiasts, it is possible not only to travel over part of the abandoned route but to do so behind a steam engine.

The section that has reopened by the Peak Railway Society runs from their own station at Matlock - a short walk from the BR station - to Rowsley and is operated by a very respectable allocation of locomotives. Opening and operating the line as far as Rowsley has been a considerable achievement although it pales in contrast to the organisations' ambition to extend northwards through Millers Dale and on to Buxton. There is little doubt, however, that this project will be accomplished and the question is When rather than If.

For thirty years we have missed the main line over the Peak but thanks to the efforts of the PRS, it appears that the route is breathing again and it is possible, after so many years, to lie back in a corner seat and relax, eyes closed, to the sound of a steam engine ahead and remember......

MATLOCK

DARLEY DALE : AMBERGATE

The physical characteristics of the country, and as a result that of the line, mellowed considerably south of Rowsley and for the first time allowed trains of normal tonnages to be worked without assistance in either direction. A class J coal train from Derby to Rowsley was permitted to take up to 88 wagons with a Garratt whilst a 4F 0-6-0 could handle 48. In the up direction, because of the falling gradient, a class H train of empties could convey between 69 vehicles (4F 0-6-0) and 100 by a Garratt or 9F.

The southern section was also the oldest constituent of the Peak line, the line from Ambergate to Rowsley having opened in June 1848 as part of a patchwork of schemes which aimed at access to Manchester from the south. Originally it had been proposed to construct a line which more or less predicted the later Midland route to Buxton but continuing north to Stockport where it would connect with the LNWR. Several variations on the theme followed, all of which were killed either by opposition from the LNWR or the lack of confidence which followed the railway boom of the mid-1840's. Another abortive plan associated with the drive towards Manchester was a proposal to build a route from Ambergate to Boston via Nottingham and Grantham, the two ventures aiming at a trunk route connecting Lancashire and the east coast. In the event the only fruits of these ambitious plans were the lines from Nottingham to Grantham and the branch between Ambergate and Rowsley.

In spite of the grouping and nationalisation, Midland stations - and those of the other BR constituents - managed to preserve their pre-1923 individuality, a taste of which is given in this section of Matlock. The style of wood and metalwork had an unmistakable Midland flavour which could be sensed at St Pancras, Bedford and Manchester (Central) but not at Euston or Crewe which had a completely separate atmosphere.

Curiously the Midland did not own the branch between Ambergate and Rowsley but worked it on behalf of the Manchester, Buxton, Matlock & Midlands Junction Railway - which served none of the places in its name - in the hope that it could be used as a springboard to reaching Manchester, a prospect that seemed to recede when the owners of the Rowsley branch leased the line jointly to the Midland and the LNWR in 1852; both companies being major shareholders in the route.

At first the Midland hoped to come to an accommodation with the LNWR and suggested that their proposed extension from Rowsley to Buxton could be combined with running powers from Buxton to Manchester. The LNWR declined - one of their objects in retaining an interest in the Rowsley branch was to thwart any ambitions that the Midland had towards gaining access to Manchester - and the Midland was obliged to look for another ally with which to further its aims, the opportunity arising when the Great Central (then the Manchester, Sheffield & Lincoln) and the LNWR entered into a dispute over the question of access to the Peak Forest area.

Initially unhappy about concluding an alliance with the Midland - the MSLR was party to an agreement with the other companies operating in Manchester to obstruct plans by outsiders to infiltrate the area - but were persuaded when it became clear that the Midland was in earnest regarding its extension from Rowsley to the north and that they would reciprocate by granting running powers to the MSLR to Peak Forest.

The extension from Rowsley was opened in stages - including a connection at Ambergate to allow direct running between Rowsley and Derby - and through running from Ambergate to Buxton commenced in May 1863.

Although simultaneous construction of the Manchester line from Millers Dale Junction went ahead, the Midland remained conscious of the fact that their lease of the Ambergate - Rowsley section was jointly held with the LNWR and that outright purchase from the MBM&MJR by the enemy, when the lease expired in 1871, was a possibility that would severely hamper through running from London to Manchester by the Midland.

To guard against the possibility a pincer movement was organised by the Midland which involved the opening in 1867 of the Duffield - Wirksworth branch which, if it proved necessary, could be extended to Rowsley to connect up with the new route to Buxton and Manchester. Faced with the possibility of their line becoming a backwater the Directors of the Ambergate - Rowsley line had little choice but

WHATSTANDWELL STATION (NIGHTS) : 1954

Train	Down	Up	Destination
20.30 (J) Kirkby	*22/23*		*Ashton Road*
22.05 (E) Rowsley		*22/25*	*Brent*
22.30 (F) Rowsley		*22/53*	*Little Eaton Jcn*
22.55 (H) Rowsley		*23/20*	*Staveley*
21.10 (D) Leicester	*23/28*		*Rowsley*
21.30 (E) Birmingham	*23/37*		*Rowsley*
22.35 (H) Nottingham	*23/59*		*Brunswick*
22.18 (J) Beeston	*00/10*		*Rowsley*
22.00 (C) ANCOATS		*00/13*	*ST PANCRAS*
22.20 (E) Birmingham	*00/34*		*Rowsley*
00.10 (H) Rowsley		*00/35*	*Birmingham*
00.20 (F) Rowsley		*00/44*	*Kirkby*
20.55 (E) Peterborough (E)	*01/17*		*Rowsley*
00.00 MANCHESTER		**01/22**	**ST PANCRAS**
23.55 (J) Codnor Park	*01/26*		*Rowsley*
0.01 (J) Kirkby	*01/44*		*Rowsley*
01.30 (H) Rowsley		*01/52*	*Burton on Trent*
01.50 (F) Rowsley		*02/13*	*Leicester*
02.02 DERBY (PCLS)	02/20		MANCHESTER
02.30 (F) Rowsley		*02/52*	*St Pancras*
01.50 (H) Stantongate	*02/59*		*Rowsley*
01.40 (J) Kirkby	*03/07*		*Gowhole*
03.25 (F) Rowsley		*03/45*	*Nottingham*
03.10 (J) Little Eaton Jcn	*03/50*		*Gowhole*
03.35 (F) Rowsley		*03/55*	*Derby (St Mary's)*
23.55 (H) Brunswick		*04/07*	*Derby (Spondon)*
00.50 (F) Leicester	*04/09*		*Rowsley*
03.43 (J) St Mary's (Derby)	*04/17*		*Rowsley*
04.00 (E Rowsley		*04/18*	*Birmingham*
03.18 (J) Staveley	*04/39*		*Rowsley*
02.35 (F) Birmingham	*04/58*		*Brunswick*
04.38 (F) Rowsley		*04/59*	*Kirkby*
03.20 (J) Kirkby	*05/05*		*Rowsley*
02.55 (J) Kirkby	*05/19*		*Gowhole*
04.20 (H) Rowsley		*05/20*	*Ilkeston Jcn*
18.0 (J) Glendon (Kettering)	*05/30*		*Glazebrook*
05.10 (F) Rowsley		*05/42*	*Kirkby*
22.40 (F) ST PANCRAS	*05/43*		*ROWSLEY*

To compensate for the loss of the LNWR route between Manchester and Euston - it was in the throes of electrification from 1959 until 1966 - the Midland acquired a six-car first-class only Pullman multiple unit which ran from Manchester (Central) to St Pancras in three hours and fifteen minutes with an intermediate stop at Cheadle Heath. To maximise the set's utilisation it performed a return working to Nottingham - said to be the worlds most luxurious empty stock working - before leaving St Pancras in the evening on its return trip to Manchester. Plagued by rough riding bogies and declared redundant as soon as the LNW electrification was finished, it was given a trial by the GN between Kings Cross and Hull in a desperate attempt to find work for it but never again saw revenue-earning service.

WHATSTANDWELL STATION: 1954 (EARLY)

Train	Down	Up	Destination
06.00 ((F) Rowsley		06/21	Leicester
06.20 DARLEY DALE		**06.39**	**DERBY**
05.35 (H) Toton	06/54		Rowsley
01.30 (H) Garston		07/10	Kirkby
06.15 (J) Swanwick	07/27		Rowsley
07.05 (J) Rowsley		07/32	Chaddesden
07.10 DERBY	**07.36**		**MANCHESTER**
00.57 (F) Brent	07/46		Brunswick
07.30 (H) Rowsley		07/53	Kirkby
07.35 BAKEWELL		**08.04**	**DERBY**
07.50 (J) Rowsley		08/16	Ambergate
03.29 (H) Hooton		08/27	Kirkby
04.15 ST PANCRAS	**08/29**		**MANCHESTER**
05.55 (J) Tibshelf	08/39		Rowsley
07.15 MANCHESTER		**08/40**	**ST PANCRAS**
08.30 (H) Rowsley		08/56	Langley Mill
07.25 (J) Kirkby	08/58		Gowhole
07.24 MANCHESTER		**09.34**	**DERBY**
09.14 (H) Lt Eaton Jcn	09/42		Rowsley
09.06 NOTTINGHAM	**10/03**		**LIVERPOOL**
09.00 MANCHESTER		**10/29**	**ST PANCRAS**
07.46 (H) St Mary's	10.35		(Fwd at 11.03)
07.40 (J) Staveley	10/42		Rowsley
10.22 (F) Rowsley		10/42	Swanwick
10.24 DERBY	**10.50**		**CHINLEY**
10.35 (F) Rowsley		10/59	Blackwell
10.45 (J) Ambergate	11/00		Rowsley
10.42 (H) Rowsley		11/08	Leicester
10.23 (J) Codnor Park	11/14		Agecroft
08.02 (H) Belle Vue		11/25	Kirkby
08.48 (H) Birmingham	11/26		Rowsley
08.15 ST PANCRAS	**11/40**		**MANCHESTER**
11.30 (H) Rowsley		11/51	Kirkby
10.30 (J) Kirkby	11/56		Ashton Road
12.00 High Peak Jcn		12.08	Target 45
Target 45		12.18	Ambergate
11.40 (J) Chaddesden	12/22		Rowsley
10.40 (J) Avenue	12/30		Rowsley
10.15 ST PANCRAS	**13/05**		**MANCHESTER**
12.35 (K) Rowsley		13.15	(Fwd at 14.02)
11.35 MANCHESTER		**13.24**	**NOTTINGHAM**
13.05 DERBY	**13.32**		**MANCHESTER**
11.10 (J) Stantongate	13/58		Rowsley

/ : passing time

to conclude an agreement with the Midland giving them full control of the branch from 1871 and, as a result, security of the entire route up to the point of connection with the Great Central at New Mills South Junction on the outskirts of Manchester.

Services between London and Manchester started in February 1867 - delayed for two months by a landslide at Buxsworth - and by 1873 comprised five trains in each direction, the fastest of which covered the distance in five hours in spite of the circuitous routing over the last few miles, trains running via Woodley and Guide Bridge until the opening of the Ashburys - Belle View cut-off in August 1875. Liverpool coaches were included on the principal trains, marshalled on the rear from London to facilitate their removal at Woodley Junction, the best time from St Pancras being six hours and twenty minutes.

No dining facilities were available at that time and the Midland appears to have had its own views on digestive systems, the timetable announcing that the five minutes trains stopped in Derby was to be regarded as a refreshment call.

The final links in the chain were completed after the Midland had been admitted into the CLC agreement in 1866 and were spread over a considerable period of time, commencing with the opening of Manchester Central and the diversion of trains via Stockport in 1880 and finishing with the opening of the Disley cut-off in 1902.

Although poorly populated and served by an irregular service of passenger trains

WHATSTANDWELL STATION: 1954 (LATE)

Train	Down	Up	Destination
		14.02	Chaddesden
03.35 (J) Kettering	14/23		Glazebrook
14.05 (H) Rowsley		14/48	Staveley
13.17 (J) Kirkby	14/51		Ashton Road
13.45 MANCHESTER		**15/11**	**ST PANCRAS**
15.15 (H) Rowsley		15/40	Birmingham
15.00 (J) Rowsley		15/55	Avenue
14.45 (J) Codnor Park	15/58		Rowsley
13.20 (F) Philips Park		16/21	Kirkby
15.00 (J) Kirkby	16/27		Rowsley
16.05 (LE) Rowsley		16/33	Derby MPD
16.10 DERBY	**16.36**		**MANCHESTER**
16.40 (LE) Rowsley		17/06	Toton MPD
14.15 ST PANCRAS	**17/10**		**MANCHESTER**
16.00 MANCHESTER		**17/23**	**ST PANCRAS**
17.05 DERBY	**17.26**		**BAKEWELL**
04.35 (J) Corby	17/40		Glazebrook
14.50 MANCHESTER		**17.49**	**DERBY**
12.20 (J) Walton		17/58	Kirkby
15.45 (J) Tibshelf	18/04		Rowsley
15.30 LIVERPOOL		**18/21**	**NOTTINGHAM**
17.50 DERBY	**18.21**		**DARLEY DALE**
18.02 (J) Ambergate	18/33		Rowsley
17.46 BUXTON		**18.43**	**DERBY**
18.25 (H) Rowsley		18/50	Nottingham
16.15 ST PANCRAS	**19/20**		**MANCHESTER**
17.50 MANCHESTER		**19/22**	**ST PANCRAS**
19.05 (F) Rowsley		19/26	Langley Mill
18.35 (J) Chaddesden	19/37		Rowsley
19.16 DERBY	**19.44**		**MANCHESTER**
19.42 (F) Rowsley		20/05	Blackwell
20.15 (J) Rowsley		20/42	Chaddesden
09.35 (J) Dundas		21/17	Kirkby
19.35 MANCHESTER		**21.32**	**DERBY**
18.40 ST PANCRAS	**21/43**		**MANCHESTER**
21.27 (J) Matlock		21/44	Chaddesden
20.25 (E) Burton	21/58		Rowsley

/ : passing time

Toton-based 8F 2-8-0 48331 passes Whatstandwell goods station with the 18.25 Rowsley - Beeston (Nottingham) on 24th May 1952. Although the site had been the location of the original passenger station until November 1894, it is interesting to see that the down platform has been allowed to survive for a further fifty-six years. The replacement station was situated about a quarter of a mile to the south.

- Matlock with its population of about 7,000 was the most important station south of Rowsley - the wayside stations contributed quite handsomely to the goods revenue of the line and occupied no less than six engines and men (1954) in conveying general goods traffic and, more significantly, stone from the quarries at Matlock and Cromford together with exchange traffic for the Cromford and High Peak branch.

The Cromford and High Peak probably attracted far more attention from enthusiasts than the mainline ever did, being famed for its extreme gradients and unusual motive power that for many years consisted of four retired outside-cylinder North London 0-6-0's which survived until being superseded by a similar number of LNER J94 0-6-0T's in 1956.

The operators regarded it in a more sober vein, viewing the line as a means of gaining access to the several quarries and asphalt works that it serviced, running two trips per day - both were allocated target numbers which was something that bordered on the officious since there was little likelihood of them being confused with anything else - plus a third engine that transferred traffic from the Midland's High Peak Sidings to Cromford Wharf, about a mile distant, where they were taken over by the trip workings. (It should be pointed out that the table giving details of the movements at High Peak Junction has deliberately blurred the gap between High Peak and Cromford Wharf. In point of fact the C&HP trains started from the Wharf whilst those of the Midland did not stray onto the branch. The working between the two was not timetabled and ran as a continuous feeder between both points).

One of the trips, target 74, worked from half-past seven in the morning until two in the afternoon, running from Middleton to Hopton whilst the other, 75 target, ran a trip from Middleton to Friden and back before finishing its day with a run to Hopton. (Trains were not permitted to run on the Cromford & High Peak during the hours of darkness). Traffic was exchanged with the Midland at High Peak Junction, Cromford, and with the LNWR at Friden; a trip running daily from Buxton and back with one of the shed's 3F 0-6-0's.. From the Midland end of the line, the High Peak line was served by two trip workings, one from Derby and the other based at Rowsley, each bringing in traffic that had arrived in the area during the night together with any empties that had been called for. Loaded traffic was taken forward to Chaddesden yard, Derby, by the Rowsley working whilst the Derby-based train returned to Ambergate, spending the afternoon shunting the area before returning to Derby via Rowsley.

Of the other points between Rowsley and Ambergate, Matlock commanded the most attention and, unusually for a wayside station, its importance was sufficient to warrant a call by a pair of mainline good trains, the 03.38 from St Mary's bringing in traffic that had arrived in Derby during the night, followed an hour later by the night goods from London. The station also had its own trip working - target 70 - whose 3F 0-6-0 left Rowsley at 06.20 each morning to spending the greater part of the day in servicing both Matlock and Matlock Bath. In the evening any remaining traffic for the south was taken forward to Derby by an engine and brake which ran up from Rowsley.

HIGH PEAK SIDINGS (1954)

Train	Arr	Dep	Destination
		07.35	*Hopton*
08.15 Hopton	*8.40*		
		09.05	*Friden*
		11.15	*Hopton*
07.45 St Mary's	11.20		
		12.00	Ambergate
12.00 Hopton	*12.05*		
		12.30	*Hopton*
12.35 Rowsley	12.55	13.10	Chaddesden
13.35 Hopton	*13.58*		
11.55 Friden	*14.05*		
		14.30	*Hopton*
14.05 Rowsley	14.28	14.44	Staveley
14.40 Hopton	*14.45*		
15.00 Rowsley	15.30	15.50	Avenue

Cromford & High Peak services (in italics) started from Cromford Wharf, a mile from High Peak Junction and traffic was tripped to the Wharf as it arrived at High Peak Sidings by one of the NLR 0-6-0 tanks.

The stopping trains could produce a surprising variety of motive power - anything from a Compound to a 5XP - and on 24th May 1952 Black 5 4-6-0 44938 of Trafford Park prepares to stop at Whatstandwell as it makes for home with the 19.16 from Derby.

A second 3F 0-6-0 was used for target 71, a mid-day trip which served Darley Dale, whilst a third, based on Derby, served Whatstandwell in the late morning whilst shuttling between Ambergate and High Peak Junction. In retrospect it is amazing that half a dozen locations located in one of the most lonely parts of the country aggregated no less than twenty-two freight arrivals and departures and although it has become fashionable - more often than not by those who had no dealings with the subject - to deride the pick-up goods, the fact is they moved a prodigious amount of traffic with equipment that had paid for itself several times over. The 3F 0-6-0 may have had something of a superannuated appearance by the 1950's but there is an irony in the fact that the decline of the railways' finances coincided with their disappearance. It is also a fact that the local goods trains were awarded a high priority by the operating department since if for any reason one of them was cancelled, a considerable amount of traffic would be stranded for some time. In extreme cases of shortage a mineral train would be cancelled in order to provide an engine and men for a local trip.

FITTED GOODS SERVICE : ROWSLEY (1954)

Train	Arr	Dep	Destination
20.25 Burton	22.18	01.35	Ashton Road
21.10 Leicester	23.48	02.32	Brewery
21.30 Water Orton	23.58	03.00	Heaton Mersey
22.20 Lawley St	00.58	03.40	Ancoats
20.35 Peterborough E.	01.36	04.05	Brindle Heath
00.50 Leicester	04.31	04.15	Walton
22.40 St Pancras	06.35	09.20	Ancoats

Main line traffic was lighter in terms of trains than it was north of Rowsley because of the greater tonnage that could be conveyed in each train, but it was nevertheless impressive and there were few times in the day when the line was quiet for long. The greater part of the traffic came from the Kirkby area where an allocation of about forty Stanier 8F 2-8-0's spent the greater part of their lives running to and from Rowsley via Pye Bridge, the Butterley branch and the Ambergate north curve, hauling up to seventy mineral wagons on each train provided banking assistance was given from Ironville Junction up to Swanwick Sidings.

Although outside the scope of this book, it is worth recalling that Kirkby was one of the best places there was to study mineral train workings since it served a hinterland of some twenty collieries (many of which were also worked by the Great Central) and was a hive continuous activity. Everywhere one looked there were always 0-6-0's struggling up the hills, taking empties to the pits and bringing loaded wagons out to be marshalled at Kirkby into mainline trains, many of which ran to Rowsley and beyond to fuel the industrial fires and domestic hearths of Manchester and Liverpool. The marvel was that such a huge volume of coal was moved daily with so little fuss.

For the most part express goods traffic from the south ran only as far as Rowsley where it was broken up into sections for Manchester, Liverpool and Buxton to be worked forward over the Peaks. There were seven such trains all of which ran during the late evening or night and reached Rowsley between quarter past ten and half past six the next morning. The first wave consisted of two trains from Birmingham and one each from Peterborough (East), Leicester and Burton whose traffic was remarshalled and forwarded on the early morning departures for Ashton Road, Brewery, Heaton Mersey, Ancoats, Walton and Brindle Heath whilst the second wave comprised a train each from Leicester and St Pancras with traffic for the 09.20 Ancoats goods Ancoats and the local trips. An additional point of interest was the fact that in spite of thirty years of grouping and nationalisation the flows of traffic - fast and slow, passenger and goods - were all purely Midland. Through working from 'foreign' railways were non-existent.

To say that the fast freights were taken seriously would be an understatement and every minutes' delay had to be accounted for in exactly the same way as for passenger trains. Details of their running - usually minutes late on and off the district - had to be relayed to the headquarters office with plausible explanations given for any loss of time. On a bad night these

Showing the revolving bunker to advantage, Garratt 47976 runs south of Whatstandwell on its way light to Toton on May 24th 1952 after working to Rowsley with the 11.10 ex Stantongate (Toton). Although popular overseas, articulated engines had little success in the British Isles and only thirty-four examples were ever produced for main-line use. Generally detested - especially so by their traincrews - the LMS Garratts were withdrawn from service as the BR 9F 2-10-0 locomotives became generally available.

inquests could try the control clerk sorely but there were occasions when an element of humour crept in as on one particular night when a fitted goods had dropped two minutes which had initially been explained as 'difference of clocks'.

The headquarters clerk was in his first week of service and, a little embarrassed at having to interrogate 'real' railwaymen, accepted the excuse. His chief - who had long experience of the districts and their skill in inventing excuses - took a dim view of it and ordered him to go back to the control to get the real reason for the delay. With carefully controlled patience the trains clerk in the district control attempted a long explanation of how and why signalbox clocks sometimes varied by a minute or two, an excuse which was punctuated by the headquarters clerk who wanted to know why signalmen didn't check their clocks three times a shift and shouldn't the District Signalling Inspector be told about it, and so on.

Eventually the district controller noting that his clerk was pulling his hair out by the fistful listened in to the conversation.

"..for Gods sake," the district clerk bellowed down the telephone, "the first bobby reported the train when the engine was passing and the other when the brake went by. That and a minutes difference in clocks give you the two minutes you want."

The headquarters clerk didn't like it and said so politely but at length and eventually the controller, winking at his clerk, butted into the conversation.

" Excuse me for interrupting but I've spoken to the driver after he was relieved."

TRIP WORKING : ROWSLEY - AMBERGATE (UP) 1954

Train	70	45	70	71	-	-	-	-
Rowsley	06.20		12.13	12.23	12.35	14.05	15.00	
				12.33				
Darley Dale	06.35/09.35		12.28/14.05					
Matlock	09.42		14.13					21.27
Matlock Bath								
Cromford								
High Peak Jcn		12.00			12.55/13.10	14.28/14.44	15.30/15.50	
Whatstandwell		12.08/12.18			13.15/14.02			
Destination		Ambergate				Staveley	Avenue	Derby

Coals to Newcastle. Successors to the Garratts - and many other types of goods engine - the 'Spaceship' 9F 2-10-0's were the most widely used of all the BR standard classes and proved to be as capable on express work as they were on the heavy mineral traffic for which they had been designed. 92152 of Saltley, Birmingham, takes the Manchester road at the south end of Ambergate station on 27th August 1960 with a heavy train of limestone. The mystery of the piece is why such traffic should be heading towards a limestone producing region.

"Oh good. Does he say why he lost the time?"

"Absolutely. Japanese coal, engine steaming badly. Cost him two minutes."

"Thanks very much indeed. I am grateful."

"Don't mention it old boy......."

A week later the loco running superintendent received a memo requesting him to ensure that Japanese coal was not used on engines working fast freights.

"When I was at school," he observed throwing the letter into his fire, "we *exported* coal to Japan....."

Less amusing was the amount of work that had to be done in the yards as soon as the express freights had arrived. Any excuse for leaving traffic behind had to be a good one and the disciplined tradition of shunting the trains quickly and efficiently was something that rapidly communicated itself to newcomers. To most people Brewery was a place where beer was produced but to staff on nights at Rowsley the name was a pseudonym for a couple of hours of rapid shunting and train preparation, transferring wagons for the eastern part of the Lancashire & Yorkshire from the others that had come in from the south. To add to the woes of the shunting staff it was commonplace for the higher echelons of the yard to not only watch the shunting of the goods trains but to take a unusually close interest in what was being done. It did not pay to either delay the Brewery or to leave traffic off it and the same applied to the other express goods trains.

Compared to goods trains, passenger services were few and far between and consisted in the main of seven express workings in each direction together with five stopping trains, the latter running via Stockport and taking about three hours for the journey to Manchester. There was very little science involved in the timing of either, the London trains left St Pancras at fifteen minutes past the hours they operated (apart from the 12.15 which didn't exist and the evening express which left at 18.40) with the stopping trains being fitted in as best they could. Very few of the latter actually connected with the fast trains at Derby - only the 10.15 and 16.15 expresses had connections waiting for them - the favoured option being to start a local off from Derby and have it overtaken either at Chinley or on the Stockport loop.

The population living on the southern end of the line was not nearly dense enough to warrant much more than the most basic of services and there were times of the day when even Matlock - which was served by most of the expresses - was overlooked as was the case during the early afternoon in the gap between the 10.15 and 14.15 departures from St Pancras. The only option available for Matlock passengers was the 11.45 Bradford express, which required a change of trains at Trent Junction, and the 16.10 stopping train from Derby which reached Matlock at 16.52; five hours as opposed to the usual three. To compound matters the 14.15 ran non-stop from Derby to Millers Dale, the only train to do so, and any pas-

AMBERGATE : ROWSLEY TRIP WORKINGS (DOWN) : 1954							
Train	-	-	45	70	71	70	45
From	03.38 Derby	22.40 St Pancras	07.45 Derby				
Whatstandwell			10.35/11.03				
High Peak Jcn			11.20				
Cromford							
Matlock Bath				10.15		15.10	
Matlock	04.30/04.42	05.55/06.20		10.22/11.21		15.17/18.13	18.49/19.01
Darley Dale					14.00		
Rowsley	05.03	06.35		11.35	14.13	18.33	19.20

BR Caprotti 5MT 4-6-0 73139 eases an up express over the 15 mph restriction through Ambergate on 27th August 1960. The train is coming from the Manchester direction and is taking the Derby road. The route to Codnor Park - used mainly by the Rowsley - Kirkby services - diverges to the right of the train, the sixth coach being over the junction. The line from Derby to Sheffield lies to the rear of the photographer although non-stopping trains used an avoiding line a short distance to the south of the station. Whilst the train in the photograph cannot be identified, the use of a Rowsley-based engine suggests a summer special since suitable locomotives based at goods depots were often transferred at weekends to passenger sheds for excursion purposes.

sengers for Matlock had to change at Derby and go forward on the 17.05 local to Bakewell.

In the up direction all Manchester - London expresses called at Matlock although there was a long gap at one point in the day (10.21 until 15.03) because of the omission of a midday train from Manchester.

It might have been expected that the stations around Matlock would have been better served had the local train service operated between Buxton and Derby, the two largest towns in the area, rather than Manchester, but in fact Buxton was all but isolated from the south apart from the connections at Millers Dale and a solitary though train - in one direction only - which left Buxton at 17.46 for Derby. As a result the twenty miles separating Buxton and Matlock normally took three quarters of an hour whilst Ruskin's assessment of the time needed to get from Bakewell to Buxton was on the optimistic side.

The reason why the train service never improved - the timetable rarely changed from one issue to the next - lay in the relative importance given to freight traffic and the fact that passenger activities took a rather low priority. The value of the stopping trains came from their non-passenger activities - parcels receipts far outweighed the value of passenger tickets - whilst to alter their timings would have meant hundreds of man-hours being expended in revising the goods timetable in order to find a path. In addition to this for every one of the dozen or so goods trains affected, amended engine and crewing diagrams would have to be recalculated and reissued, an exercise which was likely to be far more costly than any additional income derived from altering the timing of a local train.

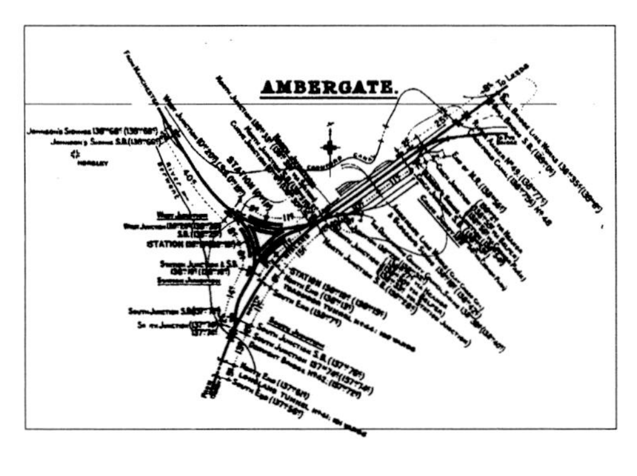

If a timetable worked it took a very powerful argument to get any changes made although it is true to say that by 1956 the Midland woke to the possibility that some amendments were long overdue and in the following year made a number of substantial alterations which included restoration of the midday service in each direction between London and Manchester.

Most of the stations south of Rowsley were of the conventional two platform design, lacking in any distinctive features of significance to the operating staff except for the last point on the line, Ambergate, which was one of only three triangular stations in the country - Queensbury and Earlestown being the others - with separate platforms for the Derby - Manchester, Derby - Sheffield and Sheffield - Manchester lines. Two of these saw regular use and were served by local trains to and from Derby and Manchester or Sheffield whilst the third, the north curve, had existed for a rather desultory service of local trains to Pye Bridge and Mansfield until their withdrawal in June 1947 after which it saw the occasional summer special and the frequent procession of mineral trains which ran between Kirkby and Rowsley. In spite of its unusual geometry Ambergate was no especial paradise for enthusiasts - a great deal of walking was required every time a signal came off - since the Derby - Sheffield lines were on a loop to the south of the station and the express traffic between the two points passed out of sight of the station.

During the 1950's there was not the slightest doubt about the future and security of the Derby - Manchester route. Goods and mineral traffic was heavy by any reckoning whilst the express passenger services were given a significant boost in 1957 by additional trains, faster schedules and the arrival of Britannia Pacifics and Royal Scot 4-6-0's. In 1959 it

4F 0-6-0 44299 of Staveley heads towards Derby with an up coal train on 25th September 1954. Passenger traffic was dense on this section of line and it was therefore most unusual to see a mineral train running on the fast line. 44299 was following in the wake of a Jubilee-hauled express and is making the most of its opportunity before being 'put in' on the goods road further towards Derby.

Journeys end for us but not for Jubilee 45616 'Malta GC' as it waits for the right-away from platform 6 at Derby with a Manchester (Central) - St Pancras express in 1953. The requirements of the Midland's Manchester route was astonishing considering that class 6P engines were the norm. Having spent an hour and three-quarters in battling its way over the Peak district, 45616 will now be expected to run hell-for-leather on a very fast route all the way to London. It is difficult to think of any other main line that used medium sized locomotives to such an extent.

A point of interest during the 1950's was the Fell diesel mechanical locomotive which was allocated to Derby and alternated between stopping trains to Manchester and the St Pancras - Manchester expresses. Quite apart from its shape, which was stark even by diesel standards, its appearance was further marked by coupling rods which were painted bright red. Originally the locomotive appeared as a 4-8-4 with the coupling rods connecting all eight driving wheels, a feature which was changed a short time after its introduction, altering the wheel arrangement to a 4-4-4-4.

was selected as one of the early ventures into dieselisation when the - not altogether successful - Metrovick CoBo type 2 locomotives started to be diagrammed in pairs for some of the Manchester - St Pancras expresses, a trend that was taken a stage further in 1960 when the Midland Pullman multiple unit arrived to inaugurate a new, first class only, business working between Manchester and London. In November of the same year the first of the Sulzer type 4 diesel-electrics started work on the line, a class of engine that enjoyed a longer reign on the Midland than did the Jubilee's which preceded them.

Three-quarters of the way through the diesel conquest matters changed quickly and dramatically, starting with the sudden evaporation of goods traffic in the early sixties followed by a growing preference by both industrial and domestic users for fuels other than coal.

High value goods traffic disappeared almost overnight to the motorways whilst, by 1965, the only major users of coal were the electricity generating stations whose needs could be served with a relatively small number of trains which, in turn, needed much less intermediate remarshalling. This change in methods brought into being, for the first time, an era when the very existence of railways was called into doubt and by the time the LNWR electrification had been completed between Manchester and Euston, the Railways Board itself was debating whether or not the Midland had any sort of a future between Derby and Manchester. Irrespective, however, of whatever crumbs the Midland might have been left after the LNW electrification, it was a time when the attention of railwaymen focused not on how the system might be expanded to meet the changed circumstances but upon how it could be dismembered, demoralised and disintegrated.

Where this instinct for self-destruction had its roots is a mystery but it is a matter of history that railway managers willingly - and often with enthusiasiasm - assisted in the decline of their own industry.

One recalls at a major junction not a million miles from the Manchester - Derby route how local railwaymen fell over themselves to reduce the facilities at a mainline junction for some months in order to allow the opposition to build a road over the track. Never can there have been an army that so wilfully handed victory to its opponents.

Background played its part: whatever railwaymen had had to do they generally did thoroughly and in many cases during - and after - the Beeching era, they used this talent for thoroughness against themselves without reflecting on the fact that it was certain to ensure the destruction of the system in a far more efficient way than simple market forced could have produced. In the 1960's the railways had very few friends outside the industry yet, inexplicably, the greatest blows were scored by those from the inside.

With external competition attacking from one front and its own Board on another, there could only be one end and there is no profit in dwelling upon it except to recall that the shock of learning in 1964 that Rowsley yard was to close, was very quickly overtaken - two years later - by the even greater shock that the entire line was to close.

In the autumn of 1966 all freight traffic other than that originating at Peak Forest was diverted to other routes - chiefly the Hope Valley - and in the following spring the stopping passenger service was withdrawn leaving only the remnants of the express workings, most of which operated between Manchester and Nottingham, handled for the most part by diesel multiple-units.

Few but the most optimistic suspected that matters would be allowed to continue and in July 1968 the entire route between Matlock and Peak Forest Junction was closed leaving only the Manchester - Chinley - Sheffield service at one end of the route and a railcar service between Derby and Matlock at the other.

The wisdom, or otherwise, of closing the route is a matter for conjecture but it is indisputable that to travel by train from Manchester to Derby or the East Midlands nowadays is not an undertaking to be made lightly. It is also a fact that, thirty years after its closure, the roads between Manchester and Buxton or Derby are no better than they were half a century ago and the traveller has lost the one option that guaranteed him a fast - and scenically pleasant - passage over the Peaks.